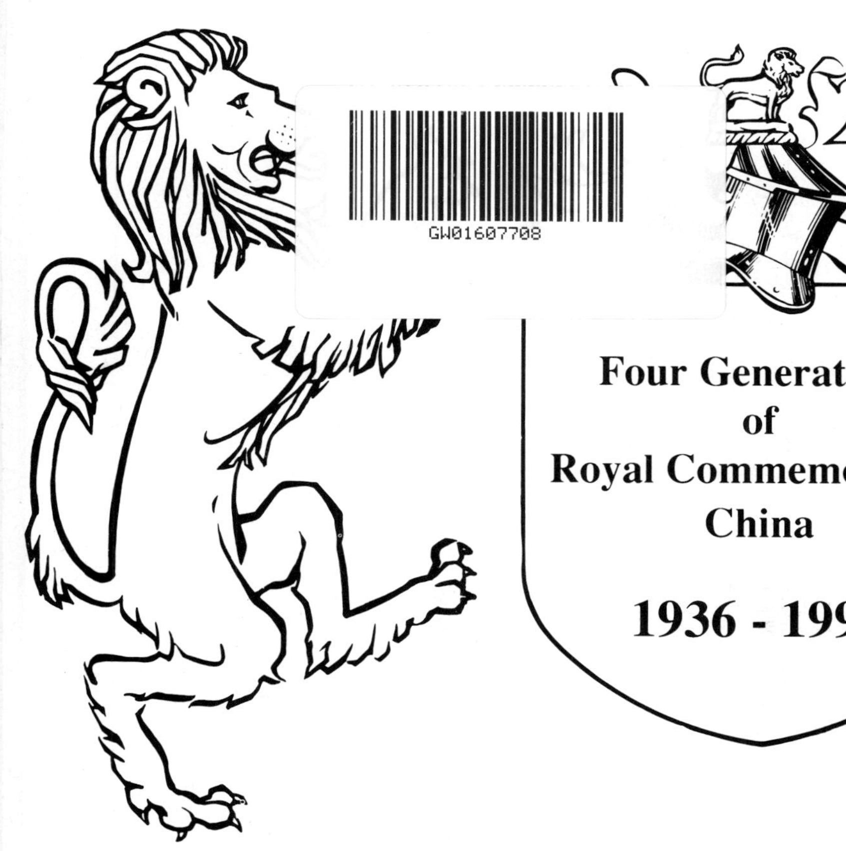

Four Generations of Royal Commemorative China

1936 - 1990

M. H. DAVEY & D. J. MANNION

Acknowledgements

The favourable response we received to our first venture "Fifty Years of Royal Commemorative China 1887-1937" encouraged us to document some of the remaining 50 years. Along the way we have been helped by many old friends as well as some new ones, all of whom have freely shared their considerable knowledge, supplied us with photographs and, in many cases, allowed us to photograph items from their collections. To all of these and, of course, to our long-suffering wives, we extend our grateful thanks.

Marigold and Maurice Ayres, Michael and Lynn Colbert, Dennis Colton, Ron Gough, Peter Gray, Terence and Jean Higgins, Steven Jackson, Margaret Kessel, Tony and Ann King, Michael and Heather Legg, Sheila and Ken Mardell, Chris and Sue Motley, Peter and Sue Rees, William and Janet Sayers, Christine Sbresni, John Shaw, Janet and Ron Smith, Steven Swaine, Nick and Jean Taylor, Ernest Titmuss, David Warburton, Paul Wyton.

Aynsley China Ltd; BBR Auctions, Elsecar; British Pottery Manufacturers' Federation; Burgess & Leigh Ltd; Coronet Pottery; The Heritage Collection, Newton Abbot; The Peter Jones Collection, Wakefield; Scotts China Shop, King's Lynn; Valerie Baynton, Curator, Sir Henry Doulton Gallery; Gay Blake-Roberts, Curator, Wedgwood Museum; Harry Frost, Curator, The Dyson Perrins Museum, Worcester; Joan Jones, Curator, Minton Museum; Margaret Sargeant, Curator, Royal Crown Derby Museum.

Colour photographs by Nick Taylor and Northern Counties Photographers. Photographs by courtesy of The Trustees, Dyson Perrins Museum, Worcester **(532, 598, 606)**; Royal Crown Derby **(501, 523A)**; Royal Doulton **(558)**; Burgess & Leigh **(597)**.

First published in Great Britain in 1991 by
Dayman Publications
28 Box Lane, Hemel Hempstead
Herts HP3 0DJ

ISBN 0 9513489 1 4

Printed by Hill and Garwood Printing Limited, Watford.

Contents

Colour Plates

Front cover: FC1 A family portrait of the Prince and Princess of Wales and the two Princes is shown on the plate from *Royal Albert*. FC2 *Aynsley* made this colourful plate for the coronation of Queen Elizabeth II in 1953, showing a popular portrait flanked by flags. FC3 For the Queen Mother's 80th birthday *Spode* produced this lavishly decorated loving cup in a limited edition of 500. FC4 This *Coalport* loving cup for the 1977 jubilee shows a profile of the Queen against a white ground. Limited to 1000. FC5 Three attractive pin trays made in 1936 and 1937 by *Royal Crown Derby* show sepia portraits of Edward VIII, George VI and Queen Elizabeth. FC6 Prince of Wales feathers dominate this outstanding covered vase made for the wedding of Prince Charles and Lady Diana Spencer by *Royal Crown Derby*. Limited to 200.

Introduction

This book, a companion volume to "50 Years of Royal Commemorative China 1887-1937", has been compiled on broadly similar lines, with the same main objective of providing a simple, illustrated guide to royal commemorative china produced between 1936 and 1990.

There is a slight overlap with "50 Years...", in that we have included items marking the 1937 Coronations of Edward VIII and George VI. In the main these are pieces which were not in the first book and we feel sure that this additional selection will be welcomed by collectors. However the major emphasis is on post-1937 events.

Once again, most pieces illustrated come from private collections and we hope, therefore, provide a fair representation of what today's collector has found to be of interest. We have tried to include a balanced selection of the "everyday", the scarce and the truly rare, with the emphasis on those pieces which the collector will still have the opportunity of finding.

Given the very large quantities of commemoratives that have been produced for some events after 1937, the decision as to which items to include and which not, has been particularly difficult. To some extent the choice is personal, but we have also tried to reflect the collections to which we have had access. If we have failed to include some of your most favoured pieces then we can only apologise.

Over the last few years the collecting of British royal commemoratives has grown into one of the major hobbies not only in Great Britain but in many countries overseas.There has been, therefore, a commensurate interest by manufacturers to meet this increasing demand and to produce large quantities of items for a whole range of events. Some perhaps a little "suspect" to the purist! Certainly one is very well aware of the increasing "commercialisation" of the commemorative "business" with the advent of advertising and marketing techniques more commonly associated with the selling of consumer packaged goods.

Nonetheless what we are seeing is an ever increasing diversity of commemoratives, both in quality and in imaginative style. The "big ears" mug of Prince Charles **(KK5)** is a good example of a really contemporary piece that could only have been produced in today's more liberal times. Similarly Carlton Ware created some interesting and amusing pieces for the 1981 Wedding **(608)** which will surely stand the test of time.

During the period covered by this book we also note the concentration of manufacturers into larger groupings. Royal Doulton, for example, currently has within its group such famous names as Minton, Royal Crown Derby, Paragon China and Royal Albert. All well known makers of royal commemoratives. Similarly Royal Worcester controls Copeland-Spode and Hammersley.

Sadly some of the most famous names associated with the production of royal commemorative china have disappeared; William Lowe (1930), C T Maling (1960), Shelley (1966), and the Lambeth factory of Royal Doulton closed in 1956. At the same time, however, a number of smaller companies such as Panorama Studios, Coronet, Caverswall and Sutherland entered the field and produced a range of items which have gained widespread approval by collectors.

Noteworthy too is the increasing trend towards the production of limited edition commemoratives. In the early part of the 20th Century Thos Goode and Co had pioneered the commissioning of limited edition items, especially from Copeland-Spode. Their pieces were generally of very high artistic and production quality. Whilst Goode continued to commission items in the Thirties their golden age came to an end with the Coronation of George VI, although a pottery tyg of their traditional type was made for the 1953 coronation **(492)**.

It was with the Silver Jubilee in 1977, that the large scale production of "limited" editions really got under way. Coalport, in particular, seems to have taken this new development most to heart. They produced limited edition ranges of goblets **(EE6)**, mugs, loving cups and plates to be sold under their own name and also as specially commissioned ranges for a variety of institutions **(JJ5)**. Wedgwood too began to capitalise on the increasing popularity of the mugs designed by Richard Guyatt by producing a Queensware version **(L8)**, sometimes more than one, and a black basalt version in a limited edition **(N5)**.

Others too, like Peter Jones of Wakefield, saw the value in creating special commemorative pieces for the "collector market" **(QQ6)**.

In general terms one can perhaps divide the period covered by this book into four distinct periods:

1937 to 1939.

These three years covering the Coronations of Edward VIII and George VI together with the 1939 State Visit to the USA and Canada are perhaps the end of an era of royal commemoratives. Those produced for these events seem to have evolved over the years from Victoria's Jubilees. The great names in potteries were still producing wares which were distinctly theirs. Doulton, Shelley, Hammersley, Aynsley and Copeland for example continued to issue pieces which bore their unmistakable, individual hallmarks, with shapes and decorative styles that had developed over the previous half century.

1940 to 1952.

During, and in the years immediately after, the Second World War no decorative china wares (and thus no commemoratives) were produced for the home market. As a result only two manufacturers are known to have marked the wedding of the Queen and Prince Philip in 1947, Minton (back cover) and Ewenny Pottery. And no commemoratives were issued for the birth of Prince Charles in 1948, or Princess Anne in 1950. Nor was the death of George VI commemorated. A few pieces were made to mark State visits in 1947 and 1949 but we had to await the Coronation of Queen Elizabeth to experience a revival of royal commemoratives in quantity and variety.

1953 to 1977.

The Coronation provided the first major opportunity for the potters and the country to break away from the restrictions imposed by the War. Everyone was looking for a chance to celebrate and the potters did the nation proud.

Many of the commemorative wares followed traditional lines but the use of hand enamelling was already more limited, and even the deluxe pieces had become more prosaic than heretofore. And following the Coronation relatively small amounts were issued to mark quite important events such as the Investiture of the Prince of Wales (1969), the silver wedding of the Queen and Prince Philip (1972) or the weddings of Princesses Margaret (1960) and Anne (1973). The floodgates were however re-opened for the 1977 Silver Jubilee. Vast amounts of wares were made, and for the first time we see extensive use of the limited edition for the mass market by such potters as Coalport and Wedgwood.

1978 to date.

The production of commemoratives has increased dramatically. Major and minor events are being covered by a bewildering array of wares. Births, visits, weddings and anniversaries of all the Royals seem to provide an endless source of inspiration to potteries and for "special commissions". Scarcely a year has passed in this period without the issue of a commemorative. Whilst some collectors find these "modern" commemoratives to be less interesting than those of earlier periods, there is no denying that we are witnessing a broadening of appeal, and perhaps with a little more time behind us it will be easier to sort the wheat from the chaff.

Meanwhile we sincerely hope that this small volume will again go some way to increase the enjoyment of this most interesting hobby.

As before, we have used the term porcelain to indicate a translucent body, all others being described as pottery or stoneware. Dimensions to the nearest half centimetre are given for the height of mugs, jugs, beakers, vases and tea ware and for the diameter of plates and bowls.

The numbers for the illustrations follow on from those in "50 Years of Royal Commemorative China 1887-1937" in order to make cross referencing as comprehensive and easy as possible.

The "proposed" Coronation of Edward VIII • 1937 •

Within a few months of his Silver Jubilee celebrations George V died at Sandringham on 20 January 1936. He was succeeded by his eldest son, the Prince of Wales, who took the title of Edward VIII. As Prince of Wales, Edward had travelled officially and privately to all corners of the globe. He had visited countless factories, mines, potteries, shipyards, commercial concerns and community projects of all kinds. He was immensely popular and was regarded as someone who had the common touch. Such was this adoration that even the "man about town" image was totally acceptable to a population experiencing economic depression and social deprivation.

As the Heir Apparent, he had unparalleled experience of all levels of society and as an officer in the Grenadier Guards he had seen at first hand the horrors of war in Europe. His preparation for succession had been more thorough and broadly based than any previous British monarch. Whilst George V had gained widespread love and admiration, it was with a very definite sense of hope for the future that everyone turned to his popular son Edward.

The Copeland mug **(262)** perhaps best exemplifies this feeling. He was clearly "new generation". His upbringing and attitudes had not been dominated by Victoria as had his father and grandfather. Alas the hopes of early 1936 were soon dashed, for by the end of the year the crisis over the question of whether Edward was to be allowed to marry Mrs Simpson, an American divorcee, had resulted in the King's Abdication on 10 December 1936. His younger brother, Albert, Duke of York succeeded him as George VI.

On the announcement of the abdication the pottery manufacturers were thrown into some confusion since large quantities of commemoratives had already been produced for the forthcoming coronation. It had been anticipated that some millions of pieces would be needed and, in fact, very few manufacturers had not expressed an intention to celebrate the event with their own wares. Paragon alone were advertising a range of 50 different items to a design which had taken some nine months to complete, with sales being carefully geared to the Christmas trade.

The Pottery Gazette review for January 1937 devoted a complete article to the effect of the abdication on manufacturers and retailers. It would seem that whilst costly lithographs would have to be destroyed, there still remained a brisk demand for items still in stock which the general public were regarding as having some historical significance. The Gazette suggested that items from stock might be given the superscription "Abdicated Dec 10th" and argued that this would give the pieces further historic character. How right they were, and we now know that many manufacturers took up this idea by adding an underglaze or overglaze inscription to an existing design. However, we know of very few manufacturers who were brave enough to produce a specially designed item recording the abdication **(AA1)**. But, having had their fingers slightly burned, who can blame them?

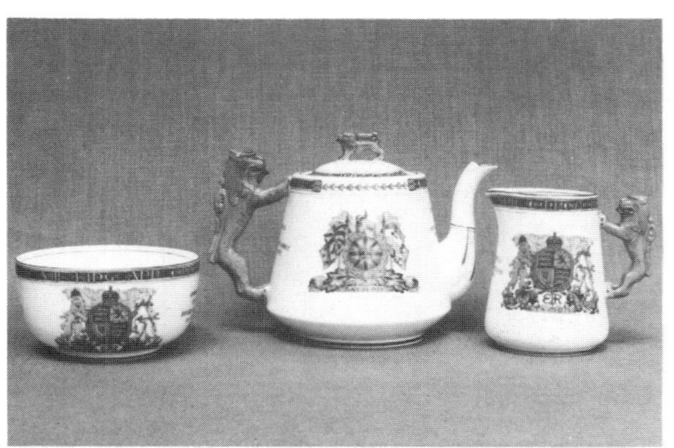

392

*392 Many collectors have wondered whether *Paragon* produced a teapot with the well-known lion handle. Here's the answer. A cone shaped teapot (14.5cm) with Royal Arms on the front, Empire flags on the reverse, inscriptions behind the spout and handle which is shaped as a well proportioned brown lion. The lid finial is also a lion. The milk jug (10.5cm) and sugar bowl (6cm) complete this most unusual and scarce trio.

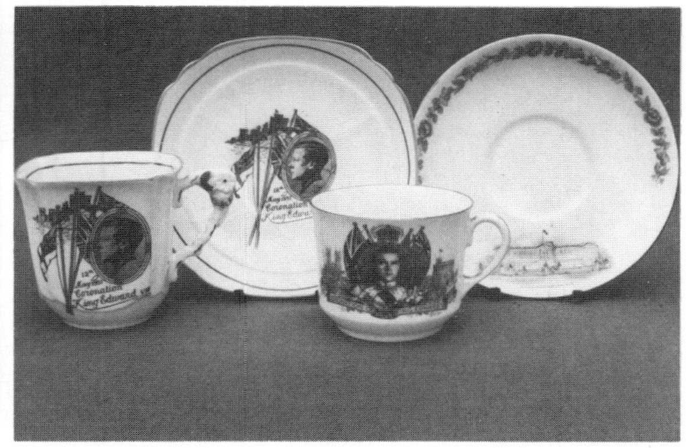

393 394

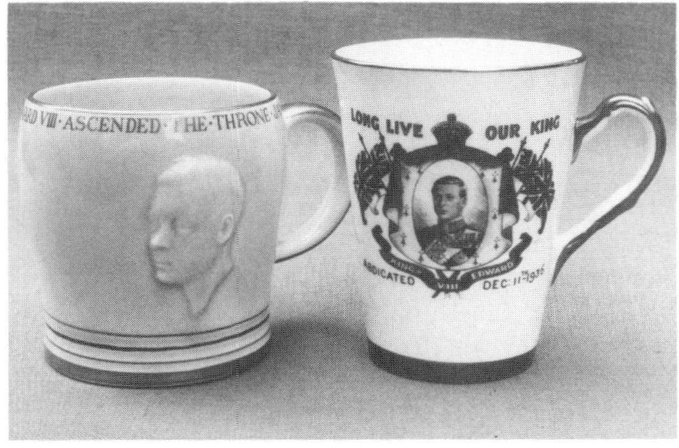

395 396

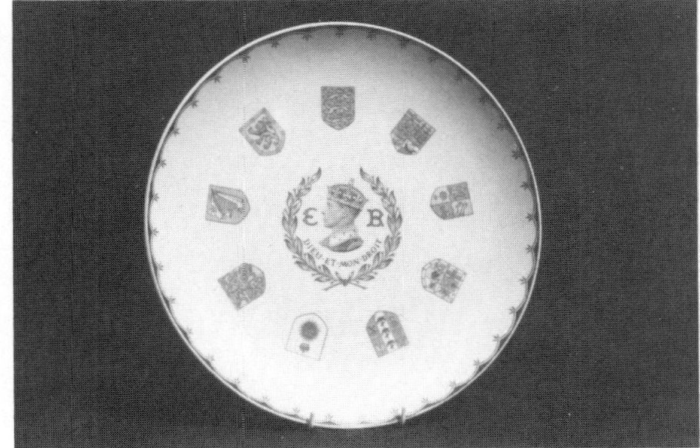

397

*393 This porcelain cup and saucer (7.5cm) from *Royal Stafford* has a "deco" feel. The portrait, view of Windsor Castle, and inscriptions are in light brown. The flags are coloured. The fluted cup has a four cornered shape with the handle modelled as flowers. All inscriptions are in a distinctive script. On the reverse "Long may he reign".

*394 A printed sepia portrait of Edward, framed by coloured flags, Windsor Castle and Westminster Abbey, are on the front of this slightly waisted porcelain cup and saucer (6cm) from *Aynsley*. On the reverse are the Arms of six Empire countries whilst the saucer shows Buckingham Palace.

*395 Two Abdication pieces in contrasting styles. The *Crown Devon* pottery mug (9cm) has a relief moulded head beneath an inscription "Ascended the Throne Jan 20 1936. Abdicated Dec 10 1936" printed in gold. On the reverse a crown in relief. Handle, rim and foot have gilt lines.

*396 This flared (10.5cm) porcelain mug has a sepia printed portrait of Edward within a cartouche of hand enamelled drapes and flags. "Long live our King" is gold – printed above the portrait with the Abdication date beneath in black. On the reverse a lion rampant and coronation date. Gilding to rim, handle and foot. *Bell China*.

*397 Keith Murray, whose facsimile signature is on the reverse, designed this large (31cm) slightly dished pottery plate for *Wedgwood*. The profile of a crowned Edward is framed by his cypher and laurel. Arms of the Home Countries and Empire form an outer circle. The design is all in blue on a cream body and has a most elegant look. This design also appears on mugs and bowls. Another Keith Murray treat-ment uses a relief portrait **(N3)**.

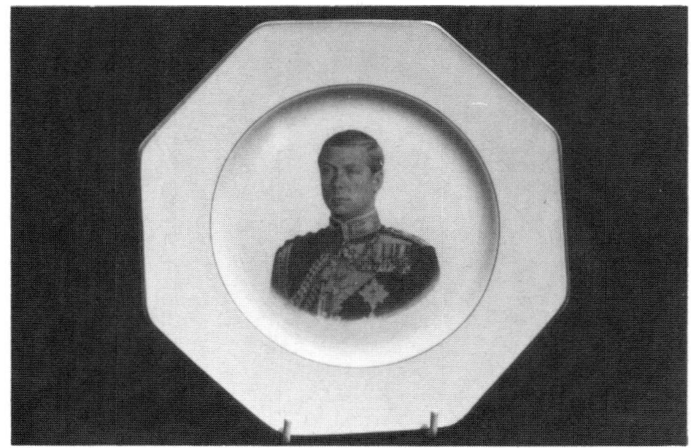

398

*398 A rather handsome but sombre sepia coloured portrait is the only decoration on the front of this octagonal, pottery plate (12cm) from *Wedgwood & Co* of Tunstall. But the really interesting information is on the reverse for it marks the Accession of Edward as King on Jan 20th. Such pieces are very scarce.

*399 Seen here a further example of a *William Moorcroft* commemorative **(AA7)** in the shape of a tobacco jar (16cm). National emblems, crown and inscription in low relief are against a mottled blue/green ground. Coronation date is shown on the reverse. A very collectable item.

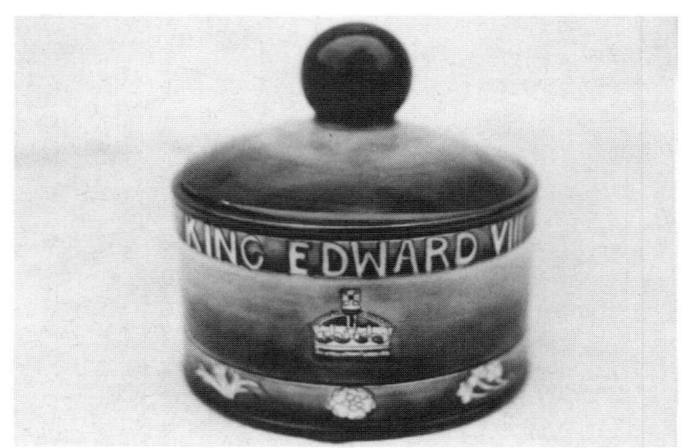

399

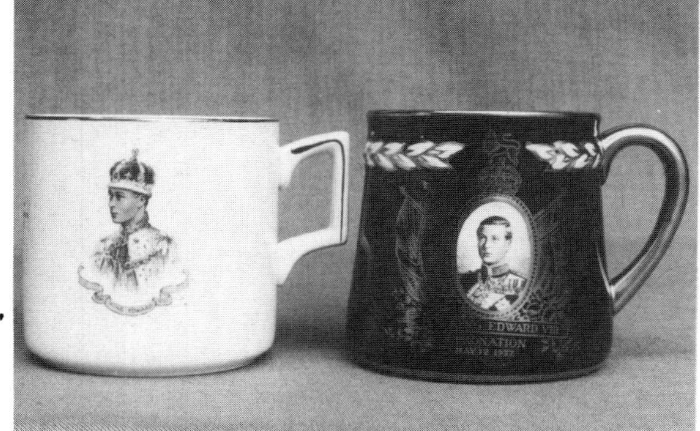

400 401

*400 A full colour crowned portrait of Edward in coronation robes decorates the front of this pottery mug (8cm) from *Alfred Meakin*. An inscription printed in brown and a crown and sceptres are on the side and reverse. Similar portrait at **(251)**.

*401 This very fine porcelain mug (8cm) by *Crown Staffordshire* has an elegant sepia portrait of the King within an oval frame and flags which are all printed in gold. On the reverse a crowned cypher. The laurel leaves around the rim are raised and painted white and gold. The body is deep cobalt blue and the handle is gilded. A truly luxurious mug.

*402 Shows the *Hammersley* mug (9.5cm) which was designed for the coronation of Edward VIII and later adapted, with a changed inscription and all gold handle, for the coronation of George VI (**129**). Crossed coloured enamel flags dominate the central design. Sceptres, orb and flora decorate the back. A most attractive item and very typical of the quality and attention to detail we have come to expect from this manufacturer.

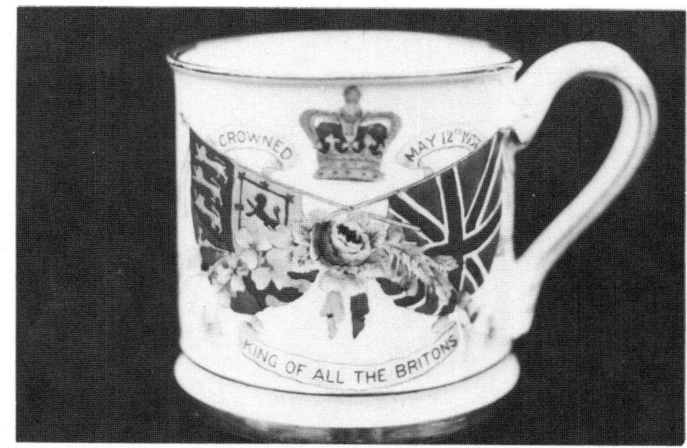

402

*403 This porcelain mug (8cm) made by *Hammersley* has the same basic design as that shown in **(G1)** for George VI except for the inscription referring to Edward VIII which reads "Acceded January 20th 1936; crowned May 12th 1937". Other potters' designs for Edward VIII were also modified for George VI.

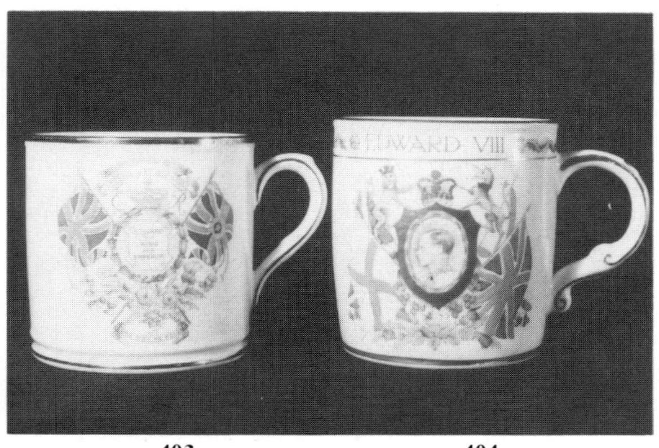

403 **404**

*404 A most pleasing piece (8.5cm) from the *Foley China Co.* which shows a black and white profile of Edward VIII within a gold shield, supported by coloured enamelled flags and royal beasts. On the reverse is a date and cypher. Gold lining decorates the top and bottom rims and handle.

*405 *406 *Minton* produced both these coronation pieces. The design of the beaker (10cm) is somewhat similar to **(cover BK1)** though the rim is not flared and the portrait is in sepia. The reverse shows a gold crown and date.The flared mug (9cm) shows Edward's portrait in black and white against a yellow shield. Red, white and blue bands decorate the inner rim and an inscription records the event on the reverse. Both pieces are, unusually for Minton, made of pottery.

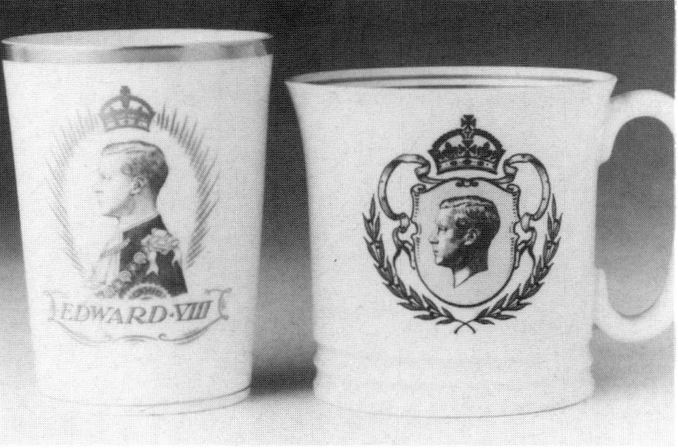

405 **406**

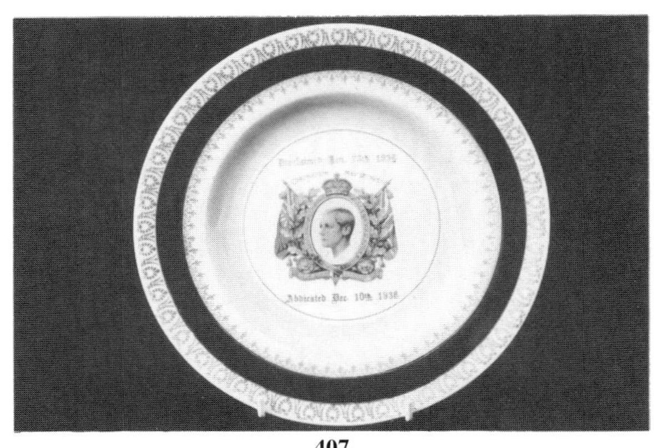

407

*407 The dates of the public Proclamation (Jan 23) and Abdication (Dec 10) of Edward VIII are recorded on this pottery plate (23cm). The transfer is the same as that seen on **(245)** where "proposed" has been later added to the coronation inscription for May 12th 1937. A plain blue band is contained within two gold printed patterned borders. No manufacturer's backstamp.

*408 This pottery mug (9cm) is from *Booths*. On its sand coloured body is a striking portrait printed in black. On the reverse the Coronation details are also in black. It matches a similar design for George VI **(308)** and is also made in white.

*409 When King Edward VIII abdicated, a number of items made for his coronation were suitably overprinted or inscribed to record the event. This pottery beaker (11cm) is the same as **(266)** but has been inscribed with a quotation by the Queen Mother which reads "Ever keep a grateful memory of my dear son in your hearts" dated 12.12.36. A most unusual piece and quite rare.

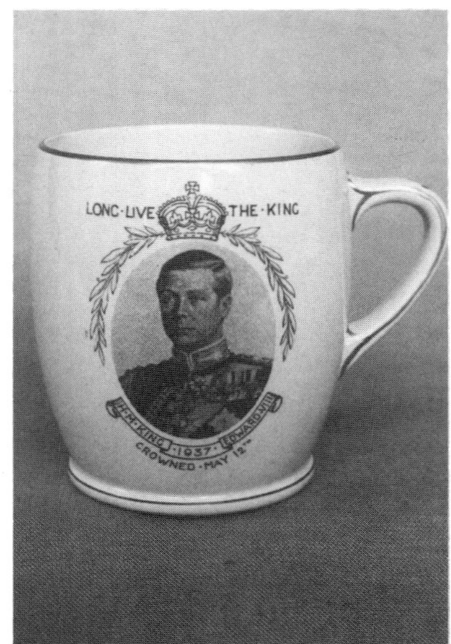

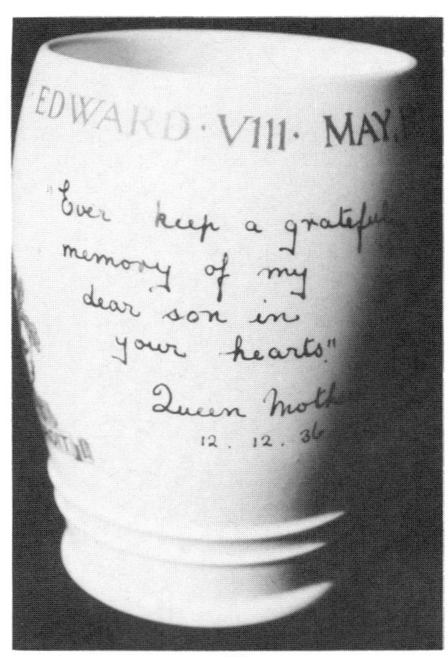

408

409

The Coronation of George VI • 1937 •

Albert Frederick Arthur George second son of the then Duke and Duchess of York (later George V and Queen Mary) was born on 14 December 1895 at York House in the grounds of Sandringham. Throughout his early years Prince Albert, essentially a shy person, had always played second fiddle to his elder brother Edward, although they shared many experiences as cadets and naval officers together. His natural shyness allied to a severe speech impediment conspired to make "Bertie" much happier away from the limelight.
He was created Duke of York (the traditional title for the monarch's second son) in 1920, and was married in 1923 to Elizabeth Bowes-Lyon, daughter of the Earl and Countess of Strathmore. They were a very popular couple and began taking a fuller role in royal activities culminating in the world tour of 1927 in which they opened the New Federal Parliament Building in Canberra. The tour was a huge success and marked the turning point for Albert's confidence as a royal representative.
The Abdication of his brother came as an immense shock to Bertie and at the time there was grave concern as to whether he was strong enough to take over as King. However, despite some political preference for his younger brother, the Duke of Kent, he did become King and, as is now well known, with the stout support of Queen Elizabeth, overcame his shyness to become a well liked and astute sovereign, seeing Britain through the traumas of the Second World War, and the immensely difficult years of post-war change.
Understandably, nothing seems to have been produced commemorating any specific royal occasion during the war, though Paragon made a series of cups and saucers with patriotic themes, one of which referred to the fact that the King and Queen remained in London.
The May 12 1937 date proposed for the coronation of Edward VIII was retained for that of George VI. Similarly most of the potters retained designs originally intended for Edward, and hastily carried out whatever adaptations were possible in the short time available. Some were very simple e.g. Hammersley **(295)** and Paragon **(BB4)**. But those based on portraits now had to accommodate a Queen consort as well as the King **(211)** vs **(417)**. The Copeland mug **(290)** commissioned by Thos Goode lacks the style of its Edward original **(262)** although the portrait of Elizabeth, taken by Vandyk in 1926, is delightful. The "aspirational feel" has gone together with title King-Emperor. The two princesses, Elizabeth and Margaret Rose, were included on many pieces **(529)** and the Marcus Adams photograph of the royal family appeared on a very large number of wares **(415)**. Certainly a great deal was done to promote the family image, something which had been impossible for Edward and now in the troublesome times after the Abdication seen to be vital in establishing George VI and Elizabeth.

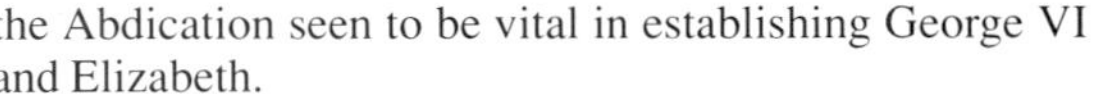

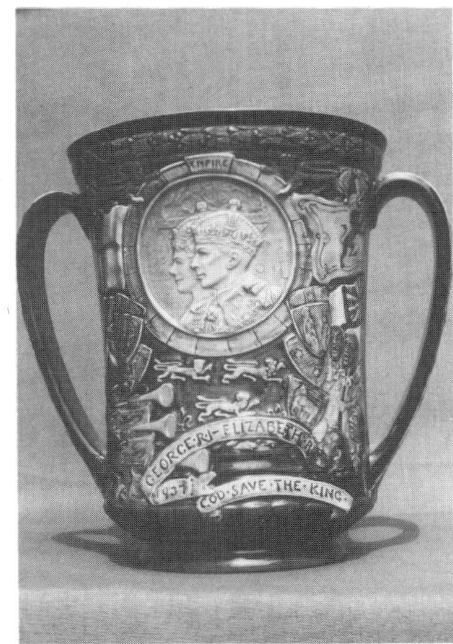

410

Although there was little that was really "new" for George VI's Coronation, at least one piece was original; the tyg which commemorated "1936 Year of the Three Kings" **(319)**. Despite the shortage of time Coalport produced an exquisite lidded vase **(EE5)**. And for the collector there is a very interesting selection of portraits, often of the couple as Duke and Duchess of York in the twenties and frequently from Court photographers Vandyk, Bassano and Marcus Adams.

*410 This large, pottery loving cup (26.5cm) from *Royal Doulton* has a most intricate design. On the front a medallion portrait of George and Elizabeth is surrounded by flags, shields, heralds and "George-Elizabeth 1937...God save the King". On the reverse a mounted herald is seen in front of Windsor Castle. The whole, very colourful design is in relief, making for a most striking commemorative. The base carries a comprehensive inscription, including "George VI and Elizabeth...loved and honoured by all their loyal people", together with the piece's individual number of a 2000 edition. Designed by C.J. Noke and produced by Burslem. See also **(FF6)**.

*411 *Adderley* made this quality porcelain beaker (11cm) which shows a raised enamelled cypher framed by gold foliage and coloured crown. The coronation date appears on the reverse with banded inscription, to upper and lower rims, all in gold.

*412 The base of this porcelain mug (l0cm) bears the retailer's mark for Thomas Goode & Co. who have been responsible for commissioning many fine commemoratives. Black and white portraits of the King and Queen are framed in narrow gold bands with accompanying coloured decoration and inscription. The reverse refers to the accession date (Jan 20) and Stuart descent from 1371 to 1936.

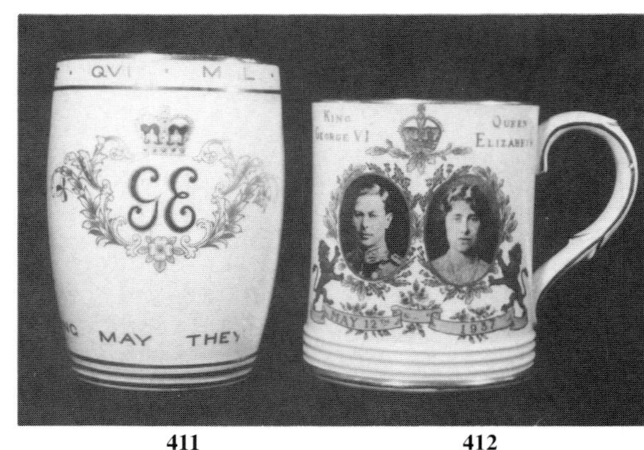

411 412

*413 A fine, porcelain mug (5cm) from *Royal Stafford* has portraits of Their Majesties, printed in black within oval frames on the front with a Royal cypher on the reverse. The flared shape, elegant handle and simple, single colour presentation of the portrait, make this a most attractive mug.

*414 Here we have a porcelain loving cup (7cm), yet another variation by *Aynsley* in the range of commemoratives produced by this major pottery. This example has a white body with full colour printing but also has elegantly moulded handles with touches of gilt. The reverse has shields of Empire countries. **(D6) (293) (300)**.

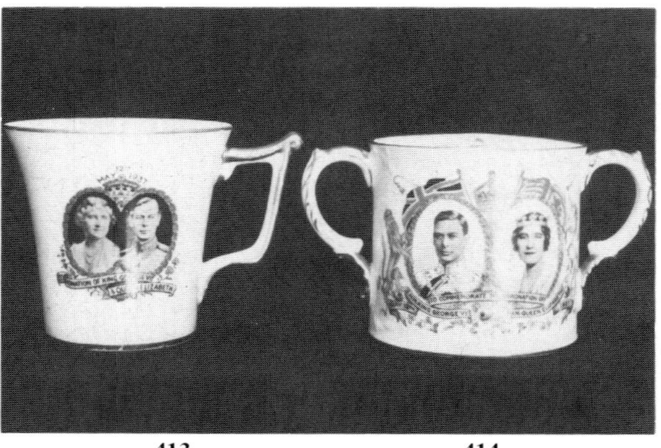

413 414

*415 The very popular family portrait group by Marcus Adams decorates the front of this porcelain loving cup (8cm) from *Thomas Kent*. The reverse lists the members of the Royal Family in a frame supported by lion and unicorn.

*416 Delicate sepia printed portraits of Their Majesties in separate cartouches of coloured national flowers with hand enamelled flags between, and resting on two recumbant lions form the decoration of this attractive porcelain mug (9cm) by *Grafton China*. On the reverse are entwined cyphers and Coronation date. See **(242)**.

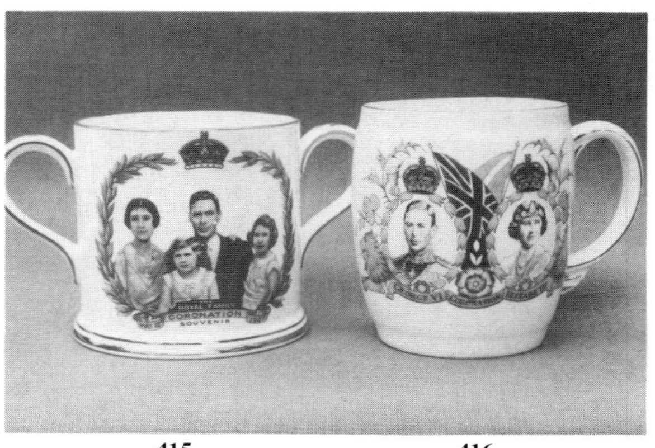

415 416

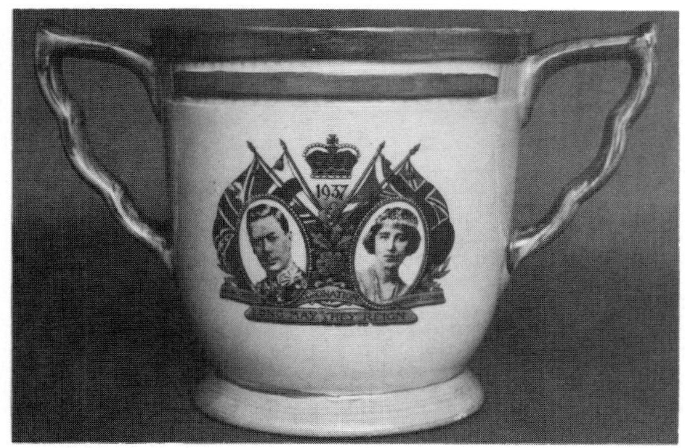

417

*417 An example of the way in which *Royal Doulton* would adapt existing blanks to new uses is this pottery loving-cup (12cm). First produced in 1935 for the death of George V **(371)** it was redecorated as a coronation piece for Edward VIII **(211)** and now here it is again for George VI. Crudely coloured blue handles rim and foot with a colour transfer print on front and reverse. Both 1937 pieces are very difficult to find.

*418 *Morley Fox & Co* produced this small (9.7cm) pottery can shaped mug. It shows the Proclamation being read at The Royal Exchange with the Lord Mayor leading the cheers. All the figures are in full colour and there is a herald on the reverse. A similar mug was issued for Edward VIII. See **(246)**.

*419 This sandy-coloured pottery flask (19cm) was made by *Crown Ducal* for the Emu Wine Company of Australia. On each side are the hemispheres on which the countries of the British Empire are coloured in red, and there is a commemorative inscription on the front of this unusual advertising piece.

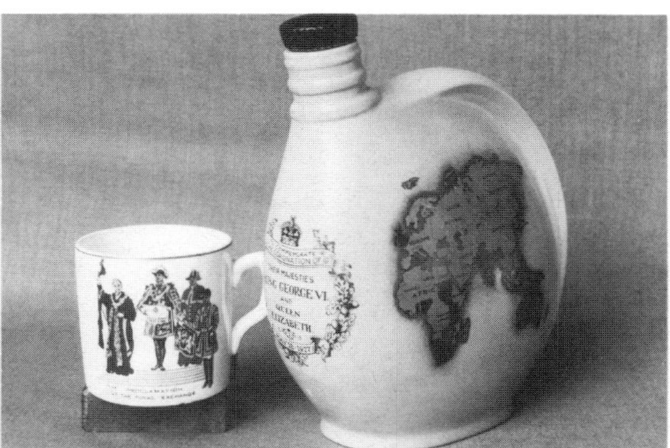

418 419

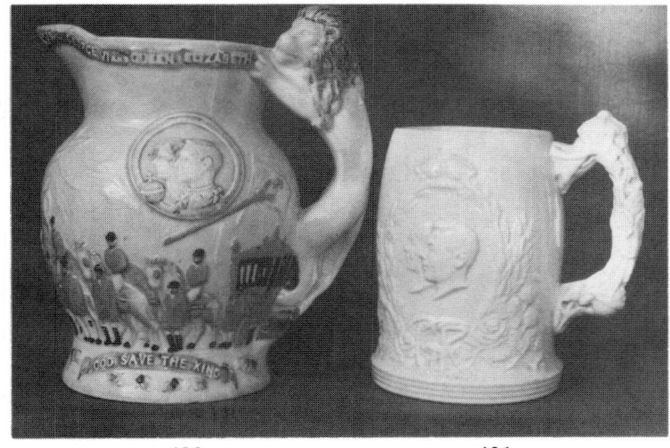

420 421

*420 This very large (19cm) pottery musical jug has no maker's mark. The body is ivory coloured with relief moulded medallion portraits of Their Majesties surmounting a continuous scene, in colour, of the Royal procession to the Abbey. Inscriptions are at the base and rim, and the whole, striking effect is completed by a beautifully moulded handle in the form of a lion.

*421 *Royal Winton* made this pottery musical tankard (14cm). The whole is cream coloured with moulded portraits within a frame of laurel on the front and the Royal Arms on the reverse. The intricately patterned handle has national flowers and a crown.

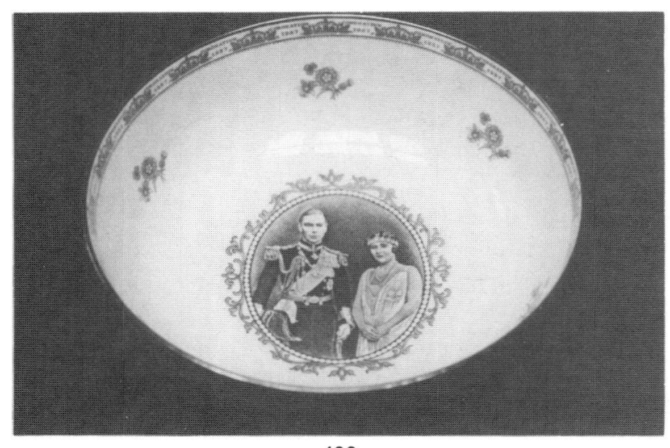

422

*422 *Copeland-Spode* were commissioned by the Clothmakers' Guild to produce this superb pottery bowl. It features a sepia portrait of Their Majesties set in the base of the bowl. National flowers encircle the inside, and crowns and 1937 are on the rim. This bowl matches the very fine tyg seen at **(R2)**.

*423 Another variation from *Tuscan China*. A flared, porcelain mug (11cm) with sepia portraits of Their Majesties in oval frames surrounded by hand enamelled flags."Long may they reign" is in a ribbon below. On the reverse a blue printed fleur-de-lis, national flowers and the Coronation date. See also **(10) (247)**.

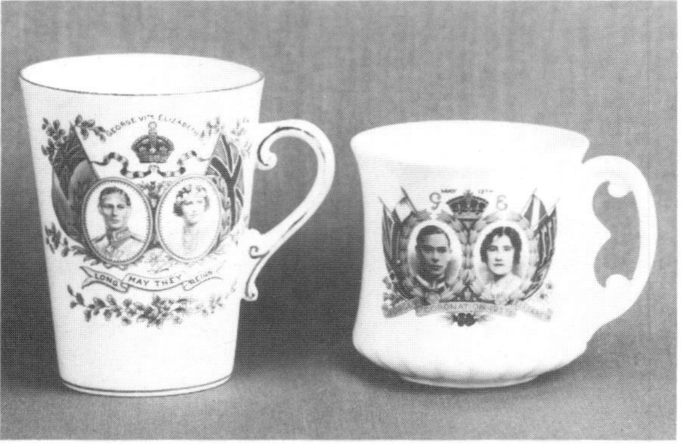

423 424

*424 Here is a very interesting porcelain mug (8.5cm) from *Royal Doulton*. Whilst the colour transfer on the front of the mug, the same as shown at **(280)**, is unusual in that it was not exclusive to Doulton, take good note of the moulded handle. Yes, someone produced a George Sixth piece on an "E" for Edward body! The mug lacks gilding so maybe was never intended for sale. See also **(FF1 & 5)**.

*425 This pottery mug (8cm) is made by *W.H. Goss*. The front has a sepia colour transfer of Their Majesties surrounded by laurel and flags. On the reverse is a sepia crowned GV1R cypher. The rim foot and handle have gold trim. See **(299)**.

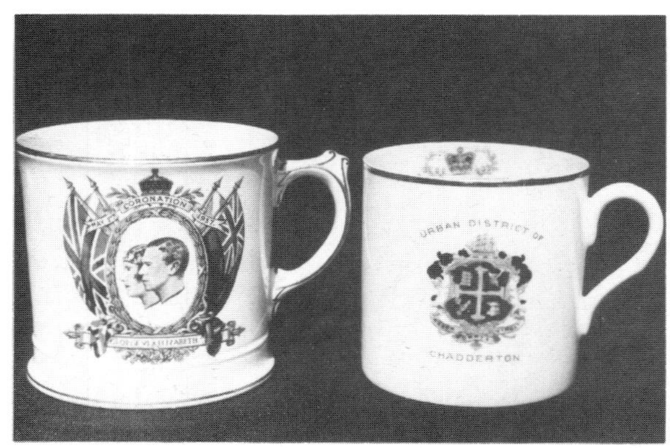

425 426

*426 The Urban District of Chadderton whose Arms decorate the front of this porcelain mug (7cm) from *Shelley* also commissioned a similar piece for the Silver Jubilee of George V **(207)**. The reverse carries "Long live King George VI & Queen Elizabeth" in a frame of laurel. Inside is a crowned trumpet and Coronation date. No doubt an Edward VIII mug was issued.

The Coronation of Elizabeth II • 1953 •

Princess Elizabeth was born on 21 April 1926, the first child of the Duke and Duchess of York. At the time it was considered most unlikely that she could ever be very high in the line of succession. Her uncle, the Prince of Wales, was still a comparatively young man and it was confidently expected that he would marry and produce an heir to the throne.

The York's chose to remain somewhat in the background of public affairs, pleased to fulfil their obligations when called upon, but leaving the limelight to the Prince of Wales. For the first 10 years of Elizabeth's childhood she led a life befitting that of a princess, but lacking the intensity of purpose one might expect for a future Queen of England.

Events leading to the abdication of Edward VIII are now well recorded, but at the time they came as a shock and bitter disappointment to the King's subjects at home and abroad. Thus Elizabeth was thrust into the public eye as a future Queen and her education took a new direction which would prepare her for the throne. These preparations continued through the difficult war years and, despite advice to the contrary, King George and Queen Elizabeth decided not to send their two children to the comparative safety of Canada.

In 1947 Princess Elizabeth was married to the Duke of Edinburgh and, in the next few years, there followed an intensified programme of royal duties involving both Princess Elizabeth and the Duke. It was in Africa, on the way to a projected tour of Australia and New Zealand **(706)**, that Princess Elizabeth was told of the death of her father George VI. Though the King had been in ill health for some time, his death was sudden and completely unexpected.

Coronation day was set for 2 June 1953. Recovering from the war years had been slow and times were still uncertain. Nevertheless, a year earlier the country had been treated to the spectacle of the Festival of Britain and had demonstrated its enthusiasm for pageant and festivities.

The potters had been curtailed in their production of decorated items for the home market (back cover) but, as export markets became satisfied, the restrictions were lifted with encouragement coming from the Design Centre for their best designs. Most of the established manufacturers were represented and, by and large, styles were similar to those of the pre-war era. Paragon continued their gold lion-handled loving cup **(490)** which had been so successful in 1936/37 and introduced attractive cups and saucers **(476)** which were later continued as coronation anniversary pieces. The Eric Ravilious pint sized mugs for 1937 were adapted by Wedgwood and, for the first time, the Richard Guyatt mugs **(442)** came on the market.

Prince Charles and Princess Anne featured on various pieces using a Marcus Adams portrait **(455)** and these proved to be very popular.

In spite of the austere times, quality items were produced, including the loving cups from Tuscan **(CCI)** and Hammersley **(435)**, plates from Aynsley **(CC3)** and, of course, the Minton orbs and beasts.

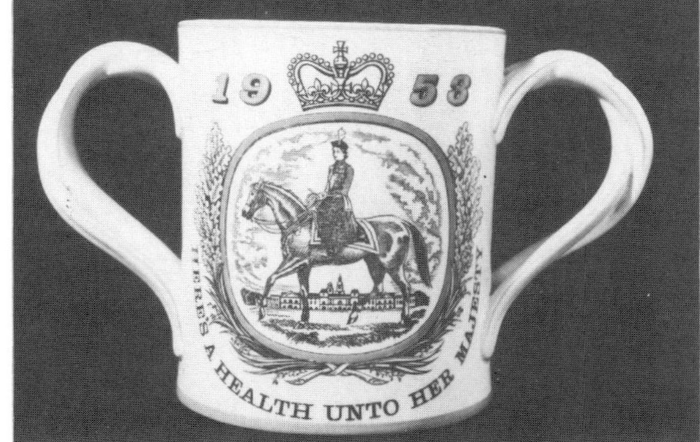

427

*427 This large, pottery loving-cup (14cm) was commissioned by Courage & Co., the brewers, from Royal Doulton. The front shows the Queen on horseback at the Trooping of the Colour ceremony. The designer, Milner Gray, has chosen to illustrate the scene in an "engraving" style, all in black with touches of pink on the rim, entwined rope handles, date and frame. The reverse carries a coat of arms surmounted by a crown, all black with the ER cypher in pink.

*428 The front of this pottery mug (11.5cm), by *Arthur Wood,* shows a young, informal portrait of the Queen, whilst the reverse has Westminster Abbey and cypher. The design is printed in brown with touches of colour on the Abbey, cypher and lion handle.

*429 This mug (8cm) marked *Kelsboro Ware,* has a colour transfer on the front with details of the Coronation date on the reverse.This lion is "crowned" and there is gilding on his crown and the rim.

*430 From *Prinknash Abbey* comes this brown, moulded pottery mug (13cm) with lion handle .The waisted body carries the Royal Arms and "Coronation June 2nd 1953 Elizabeth II Regina" in relief.

*431 This porcelain *Crown Staffordshire* mug (7cm) features a full colour transfer of the Royal Arms within a shield with "Coronation of Queen Elizabeth II June 2nd 1953" on a red ribbon below. On the reverse EIIR and crown in gilt.

*432 Another variation on the Arms is seen on this delightful, small porcelain (6cm) mug from *Arthur Bowker.* The Garter belt is used to frame the Arms. The design is colour printed. The elaborate lion handle is richly gilded. On the reverse an EIIR cypher and Coronation details.

Two pottery plates illustrate different interpretations of the same portrait of the Queen.

*433 *Royal Winton* (22cm) uses a full colour transfer showing head and shoulders of the Queen wearing blue Garter sash surrounded by laurel and flags.

*434 By contrast, this plate (22cm), predominantly in green, is completely covered with decoration. The broad border of oak leaves and acorns is interspersed with the royal standard, coat of arms, Union Flag and crown. Queen Elizabeth's portrait is shown in the centre. Similar to **(692)** produced for the 1939 visit of George VI to the USA. Made by *John Maddocks.*

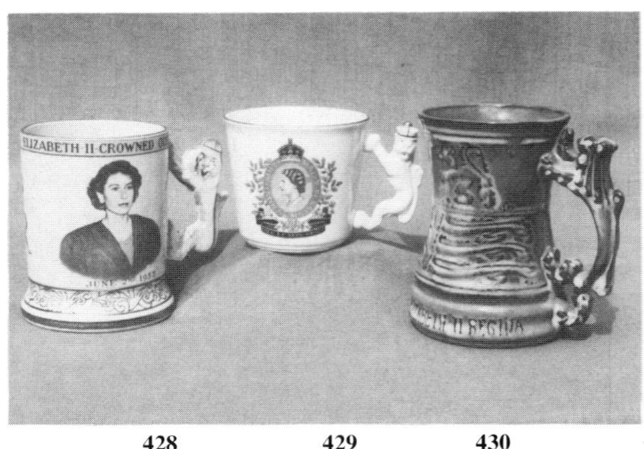

428 429 430

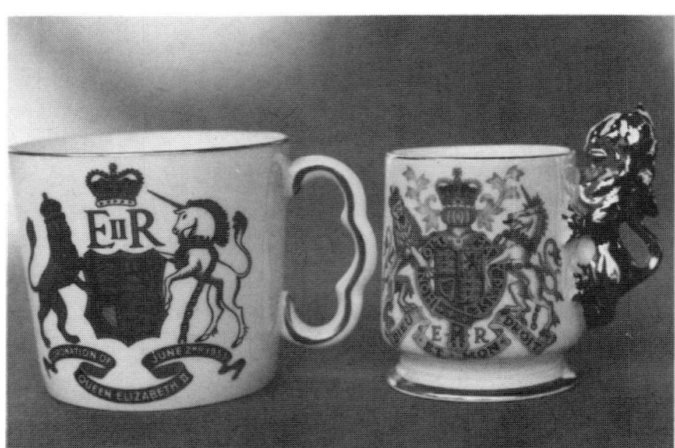

431 432

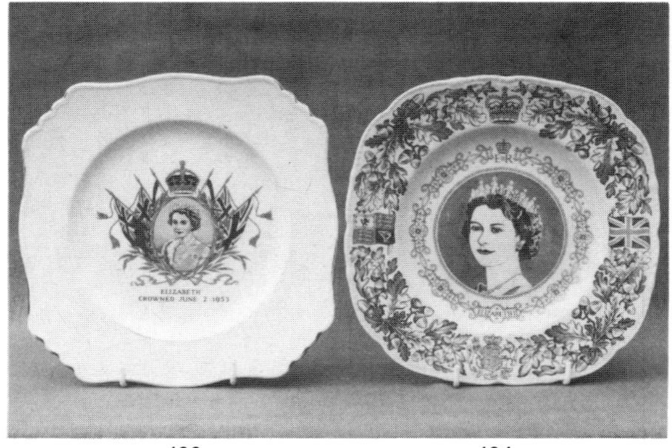

433 434

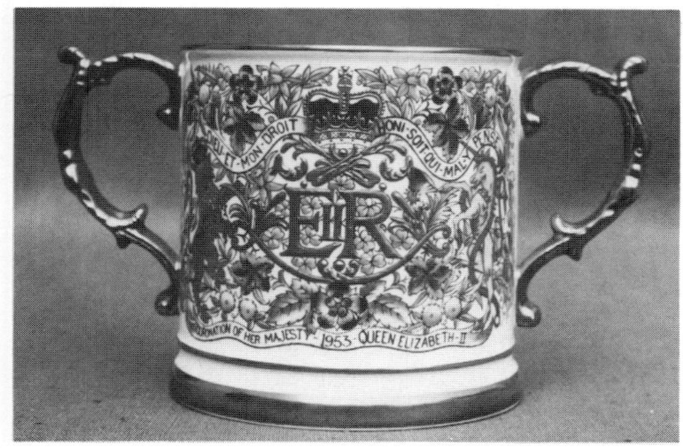

435

*435 Occasionally manufacturers will produce items in very limited editions or as special commissions. The porcelain loving cup (10cm) from *Hammersley* is one such piece and may, in fact, be unique. Lavish raised gold decoration has been used for the crown, cypher and royal beasts against a detailed background of coloured national emblems. Extensive gilding to rims and handles enhance the quality. The reverse design is based on the Archbishop's mitre, crook and cross, together with emblems and inscription. The backstamp reads "A perpetual coronation memento, special EIIR design by F.G. Clay for Hammersley".

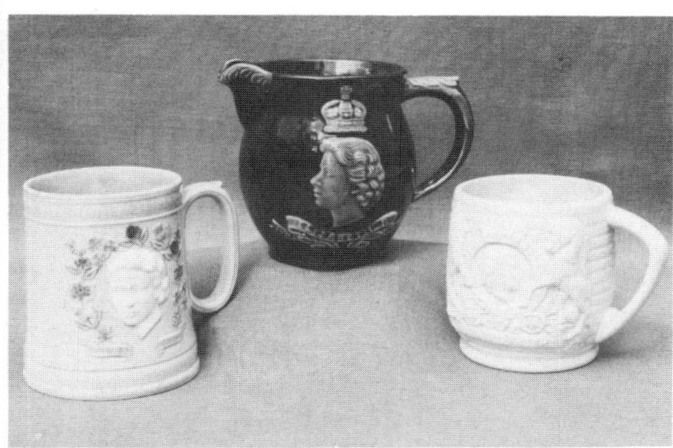

436 437 438

*436 On the front of this cone-shaped, *Melba Ware* pottery mug (9.5cm) the Queen's head in white is surrounded by coloured national flowers. The reverse has a cypher and laurel in the same colour as the body, in this case pink, though other colours were made.

*437 This elegant, small jug (10cm) comes from the *Dartmouth Pottery*. The body is in the more traditional highly glazed brown and black with the decoration in honey. The reverse has a moulded coat of arms. A very pretty piece.

*438 *Beswick* produced this mug (8.5cm) which has the Queen's head in profile within a Garter supported by the lion and unicorn. The reverse has a spray of floral emblems with "Elizabeth and Philip" entwined. This example is ivory but other colours were produced. Similar wares for the 1937 Coronations **(238)** were made by this "collectable" manufacturer.

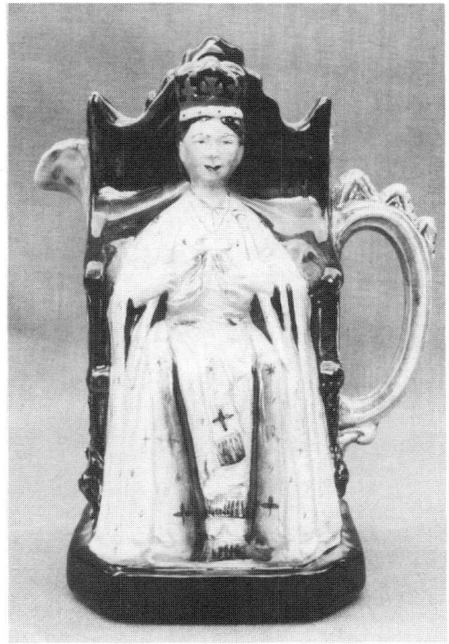

439

*439 Something "a bit different" is this decorative jug (18cm) from *Burgess & Leigh*. A full-length, painted sculpture of the Queen seated on St Edward's Throne forms the front. On the reverse is a cypher and crown. The piece is colourful and entertaining. On the base is a brief history of The Great Gothic Chair and The Stone of Destiny. This company is renowned for producing unusual, moulded commemoratives **(282) (288) (448) (597)**.

Illustrated here are two Devon ware mugs but with very different approaches.

*440 The mug (9.5cm) by *C.H. Brannam* of Barnstaple is all in one colour, deep blue, with the Coronation inscription incised in black. Typical work of this famous North Devon manufacturer - a simple yet elegant piece.

*441 The tankard-shaped mug (9.5cm) comes from the *Honiton Pottery* and has a very pretty applied piping cypher on the front. On the reverse "1953" surmounted by a crowned lion gardant. The delicate design is in a mixture of pink and blue on a white body.

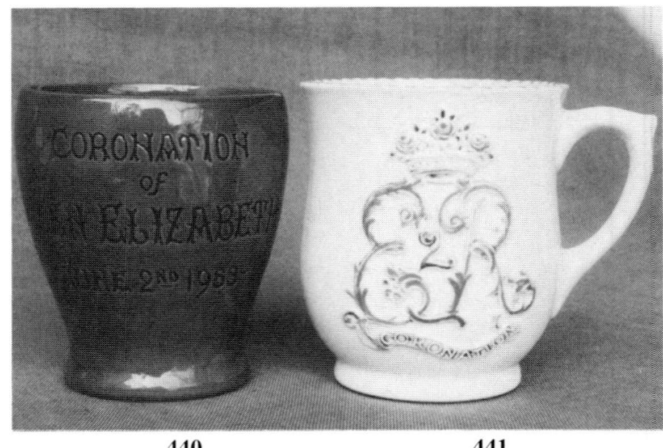

440 441

*442, 443 In 1936 *Wedgwood* commissioned Eric Ravilious, a young artist who had had some considerable success in glass and furniture design, to extend his talents to ceramics. One of his first tasks was to design pint size creamware mugs for Edward VIII's coronation **(301)**. Sadly, in 1942, he was killed whilst on active service. On the right is shown this Edward VIII mug with pink band and yellow fireworks adapted by Wedgwood for the 1953 coronation. The other, on the left, is one of the several designs in the same body by Richard Guyatt and shows crown and beasts in black outline with an inscription to the inside rim.

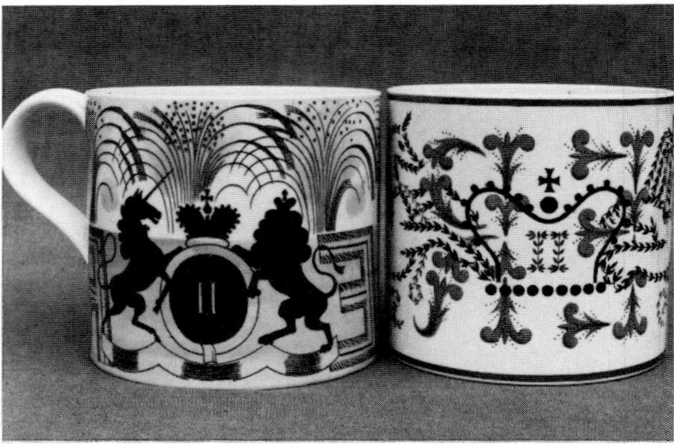

442 443

*444 This unusual, fine porcelain lidded pot (19cm) comes from *Adderley China*. The white body carries a black "engraved" Royal Arms on both front and rear, with "Queen Elizabeth...God Bless Her" on the lid. The crown finial and all the rims are gilt. Details on the base indicate that it was designed by Professor R.W. Baker and engraved by R. Austin R.A. of the Royal College of Art. The edition was limited to 200 individually numbered pieces. See **(478)**.

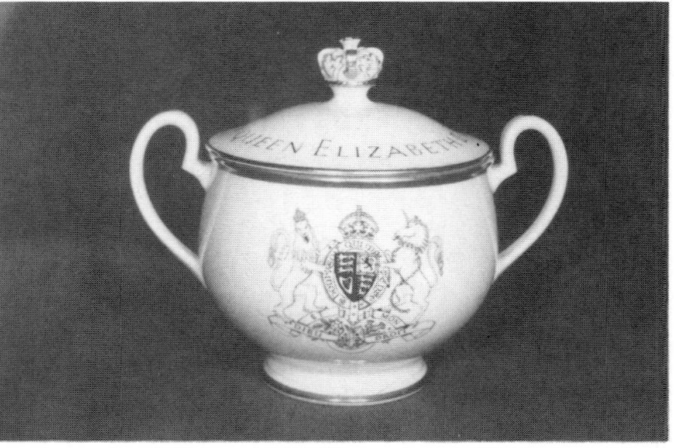

444

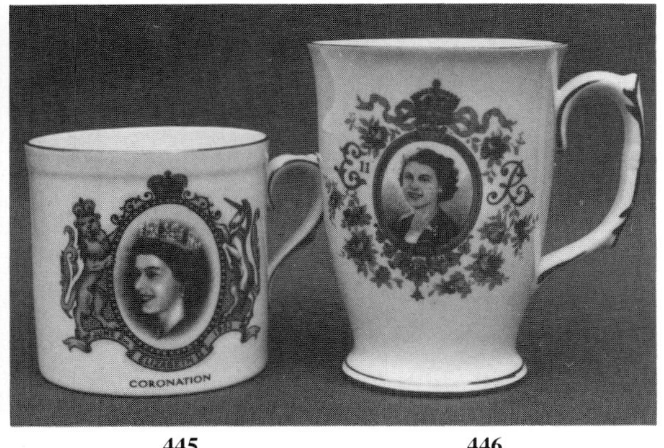

445 446

*445 A framed portrait against a pale yellow background, supported by gold coloured lion and unicorn is shown on this mug (7.5cm) made by *Royal Grafton*. The reverse is simply inscribed with a cypher and crown. Rim and handle are lined in gold.

*446 The taller mug (11cm) is made by *Royal Albert* shows an informal sepia portrait of Queen Elizabeth within a gold band. Surrounding floral decoration is in blues, pink and green. A coloured coat of arms and inscription is to be found on the reverse. Similarly the rim, handle and foot have been gold lined.

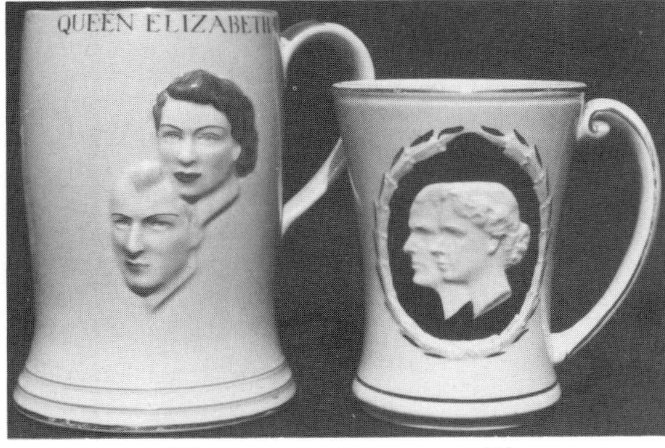

447 448

*447 The tall (13.5cm) ivory, pottery musical tankard is typical of the work of *Crown Devon*. The relief moulded heads are carefully coloured giving a simple but striking effect. On the reverse a printed cypher and flags together with an inscription around the rim.

*448 Another relief moulded treatment is seen in this waisted, pottery mug (11cm) from *Burleighware*. The medallion portraits are set against a deep maroon background. The reverse of this example states it was presented to commemorate the official opening of English Electric's Preston Works sports field on July 11th 1953 **(288) (439) (597)**.

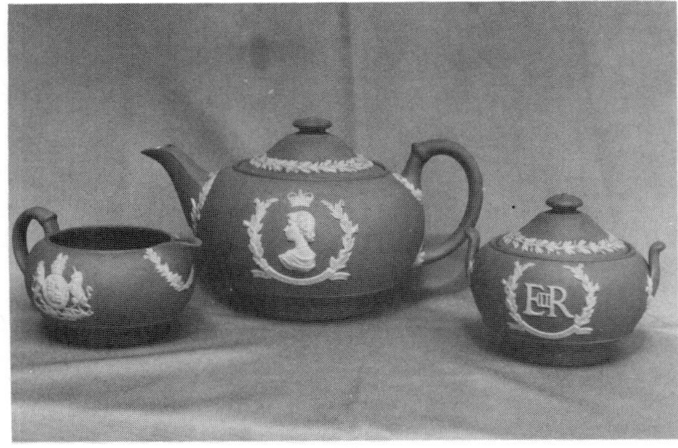

449

*449 Illustrated here are tea pot (12.5cm), lidded sugar (9.5cm) and cream jug (6cm) in the light blue jasper ware so typical of *Wedgwood*. The applied, white, relief decoration of Royal Arms and Cypher are on the two smaller pieces whilst portraits of the Queen and Duke of Edinburgh are on each side of the tea pot. Acanthus leaves decorate handles, lids and spouts. On the base "1953 Coronation. Wedgwood pale blue jasper. Made in England".

*450 Shown here are two porcelain mugs. Both are 9cm tall, and feature "E" handles. On the left, from *Stanley China*, is an example which has a fairly common transfer printed in colour but to which has been added a row of gilt crowns around the rim, and a rather ornate "E" handle.

*451 This shape was used by *Royal Doulton* for their earlier piece marking the proposed Coronation of Edward VIII see **(FFI)** and also for a mug which bore a portrait of Elizabeth as a young Princess at the time of her parents' Coronation in 1937 **(529)**. A similar piece with "G" handle see **(FF5)** is also to be found. We have not seen an "M" for Margaret version.

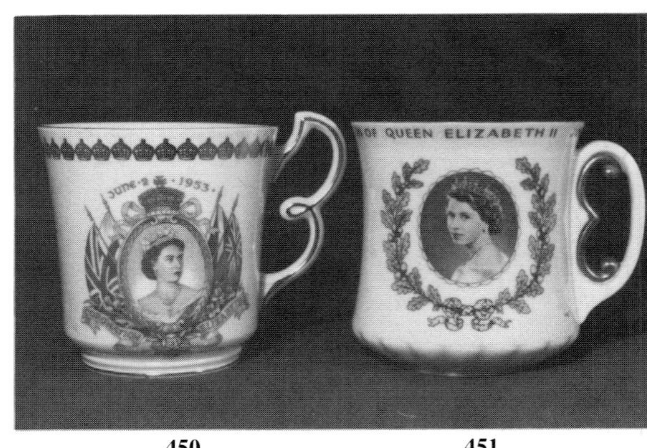

450 **451**

452 **453**

*452 Loving cups, particularly popular with manufacturers in 1937, remained firm favourites for the 1953 coronation **(456)**. A large coloured coat of arms dominates the front of this one (9cm) in porcelain by *Stanley China*. Upper and lower bands are in gold as are the two handles. Coronation date is on the reverse.

*453 By contrast, a formal sepia portrait of HM the Queen is shown on this fine porcelain mug (8.5cm). Extensive use is made of gold lining to the rims and handle. A simple inscription on the reverse reads "EIIR Long may she reign" but noticeably there is no reference to the coronation date. Made by *New Chelsea*.

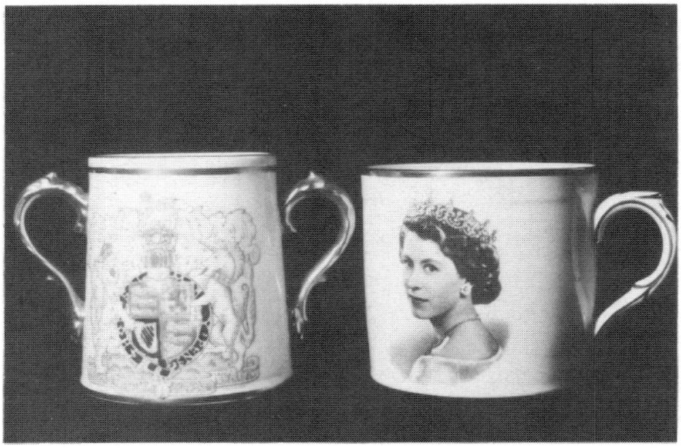

*454 *Salisbury China* produced this tall porcelain mug (9cm). A coat of arms, lion and unicorn in predominantly reds, blue and gold are shown with an inscription below. A feature of this mug is the broad gold foot and upper rim together with a gold lined handle. Crown and cypher also in gold are on the reverse.

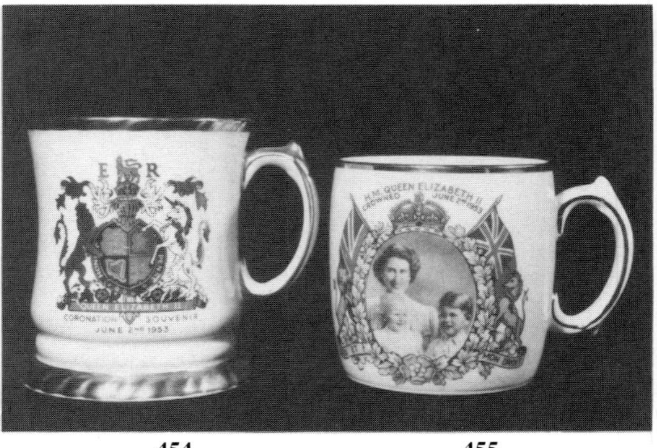

454 **455**

*455 Marcus Adams portraits of the royal family were used by numerous manufacturers to decorate their commemoratives **(317, 285, 275)** and this one (7.5cm) in porcelain also comes from *Salisbury China*. The portrait is in sepia supported by coloured flags and emblems with a simple cypher in blue on the back.

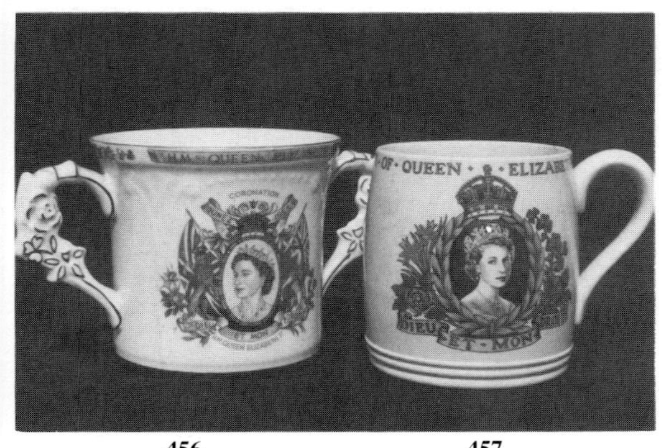

456 **457**

*456 This porcelain loving cup (8.5cm) has moulded handles bearing national flowers picked out in gilt. The sepia portrait is surrounded by flags and supporters. On the reverse a cypher in blue encircled by brown acanthus leaves. Around the flared rim "HM Queen Elizabeth II crowned 2nd June 1953". From *Cartwright & Edwards* whose crown and "Victoria" mark are on the base.

*457 A barrel-shaped, pottery mug (8.5cm) by *Copeland-Spode*. The sepia portrait is surrounded by full colour national flowers with the inscription beneath on a blue ribbon. An entwined EP in sepia surrounded by laurel is on the reverse. The rim carries the Coronation date in brown.

*458 Certainly one of the most striking and decorative commemoratives for the Coronation is this large porcelain loving cup from *Aynsley*. A full colour portrait framed by gilt laurel leaves on a body of deep maroon with large gilded handles on which is the date "June 1953" create a most luxurious feel to this piece. It is a limited edition but the number was unstated.

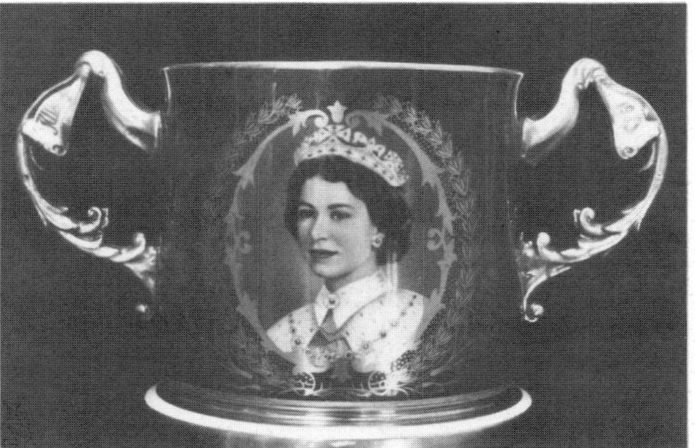

458

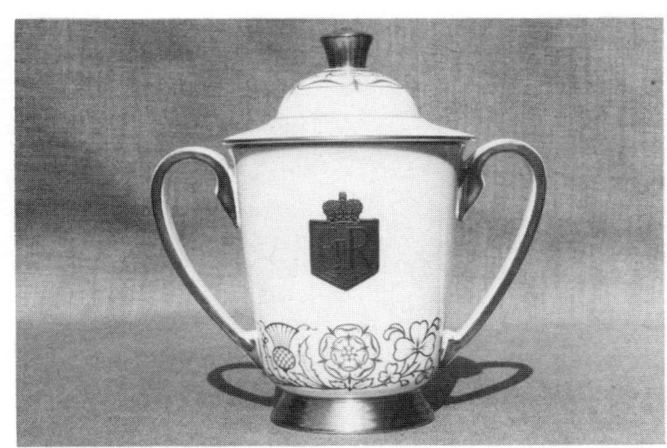

459

*459 From *Minton* comes this fine porcelain loving cup (14.5 cm). The front and reverse are decorated with the Royal Arms and a shield bearing EIIR. National flowers encircle the base. All decoration is in gold giving a typical Minton quality look. This example, unusually, has a lid. Designed by John Wadsworth. Some items from the range were produced in limited numbers in other colours **(plate GG)**.

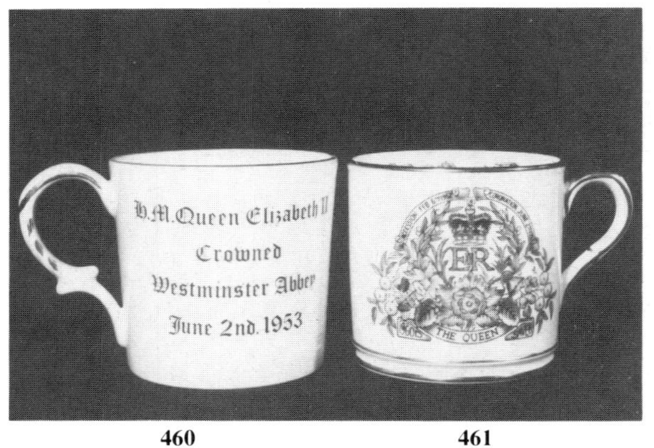

460 461

*460 Two quality porcelain items from *Aynsley* and *Hammersley*. That on the left (8cm) shows a simple inscription in blue recording the event. The reverse lists the Kings and Queens of England, a feature later seen on other commemorative pieces from this manufacturer **(564)**.

*461 A cypher and crown surrounded by a colourful emblem decoration dominate the front of the other mug (8cm) Similar motifs appear on the reverse and inside rim, with gold lining to base rim and handle.

*462 This elegant porcelain plate (26.5cm) is instantly recognisable as *Paragon*. The border is in pale turquoise with gilded rim and the surrounding inscription is printed in light purple. The Royal Arms in the centre are printed and hand enamelled. The designer's facsimile signature "P. Johnson" appears beneath the Garter belt. A de-luxe version with cobalt blue rope border was also issued.

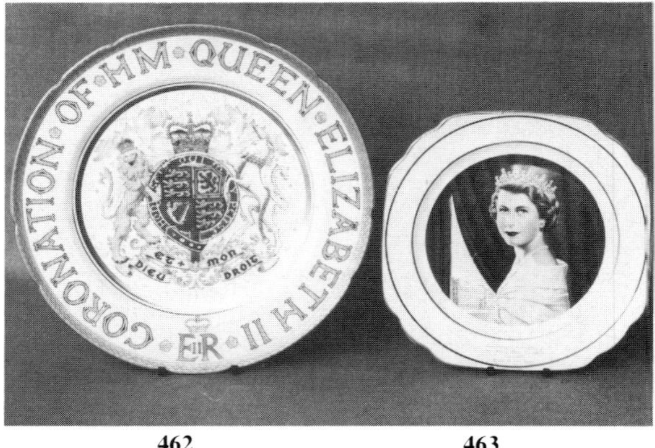

462 463

*463 The striking, full colour, portrait on this porcelain plate (20cm) was painted by Allen Hughes and was used on a number of commemoratives produced in the USA for Elizabeth's Coronation. The same portrait also appears at **(RR3)** on a plate celebrating The State Visit in 1957. Made by *Popegosser China USA*.

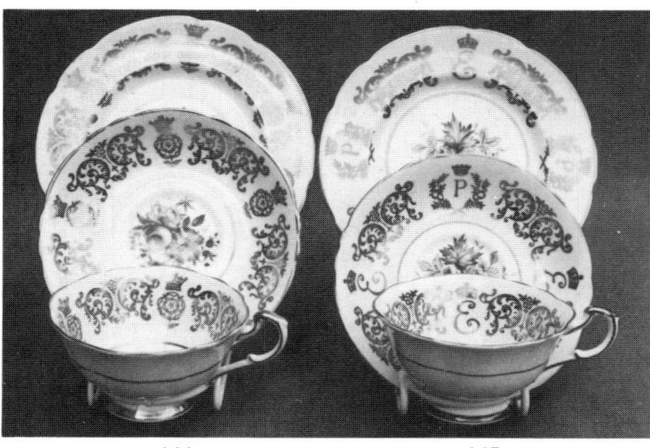

464 465

*464, *465 Two sets of cups (5.5cm) saucers and plates commemorate the 4th and 5th anniversaries of the coronation of Queen Elizabeth in 1957 and 1958 respectively and form part of a collection of seven such trios made by *Paragon* to commemorate the anniversaries from 1954 to 1960. Though the shapes are the same, the designs and flowers differ. The two shown have a duck egg blue background with gold decoration and a central floral theme. Not easy to acquire a complete set.

*466 This miniature "tea for two" set comes from *Brentleigh*. Made in pale ivory pottery (teapot 6cm, cups 4.5 cm) the colour transfer printed design consists of profile of the Queen, EIIR cypher, and crossed flags. The simple "deco" shape makes this a very elegant child's service.

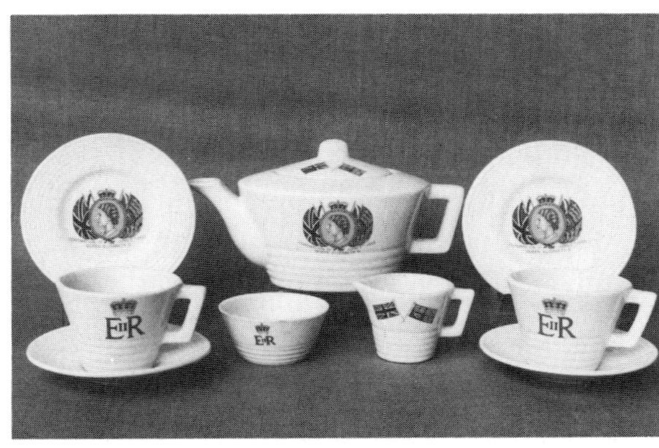

466

*467, *468 A most striking pair of plates (24cm) commemorating the accession of Queen Elizabeth II in 1952.

Deep red borders enclose portraits of the Duke of Edinburgh and Queen Elizabeth which are shown against softly coloured backgrounds. That on the left is appropriately a seascape with the faint outline of a warship in the background. The other shows the familiar outline of Windsor Castle. Painted by F. Wright and made by *Grosvenor China*.

Accession pieces for any monarch were generally made in small quantities and are difficult to find.

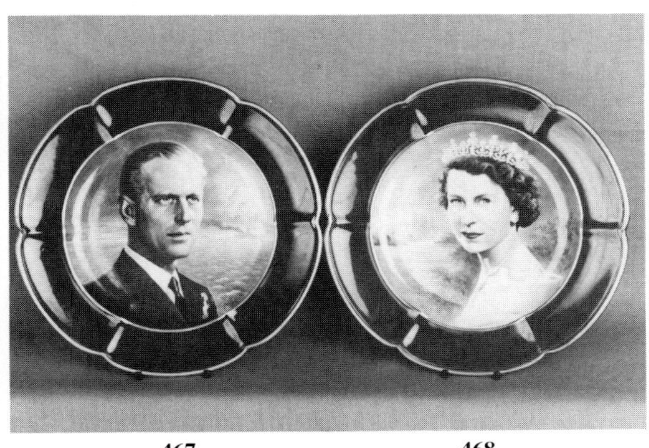

467 468

*469 This barrel-shaped pottery mug (9cm) in light blue comes from the well known Staffordshire company *Dudsons*. The applied relief decoration, an EIIR cypher on the front and a crown on the reverse, together with national flowers, is all in white.

*470 Bold moulded decoration painted in black and red on a green background make this cone shaped pottery mug (7cm) a striking example of studio pottery wares. On the reverse "QVR" in black. Made by *Tom Quec*.

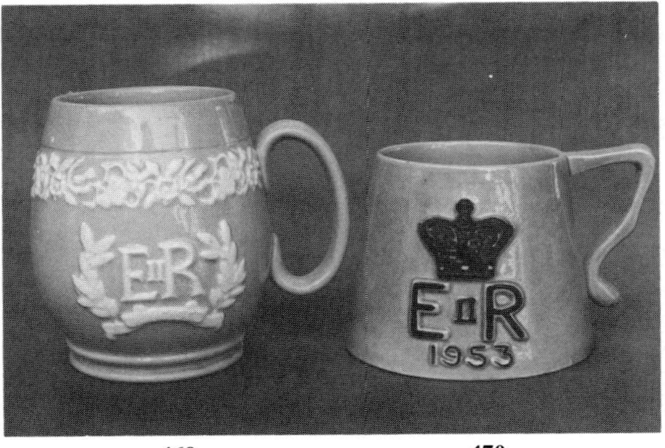

469 470

*471 Two studio pottery mugs made to very distinctive designs. That on the left (11.5cm) comes from *Holkham*, Norfolk **(511)** and shows a raised crown and cypher on a broad green band against a cream ground. A date in similar fashion is shown on the reverse.

*472 The other (9cm) shows a raised cypher and date in brown against a mustard ground with a broad brown band to the upper rim and handle. Made by *Cobham Pottery*. Studio and Art pottery **(148)** **(218)** have become increasingly popular with collectors in recent years with a corresponding interest in the commemorative wares.

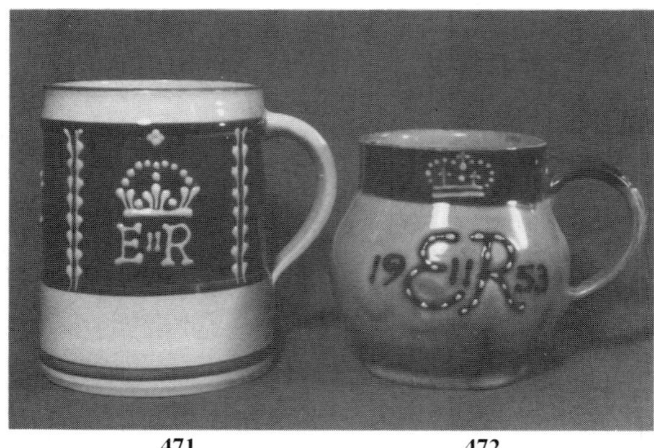

471 472

*473 Prince Charles appears on this dish made at the time of the coronation by *Paragon*. The portrait and inscription are in sepia with a narrow gold band to the rim see **(CC8)**.

*474 *Maling* produced a number of items for the coronation using this design. A sepia portrait is set within a pale blue frame and decorated with coloured emblems. The overall colour of the plate is pale green. Sadly, Maling closed some 10 years later and ended a long association with the production of commemorative items.

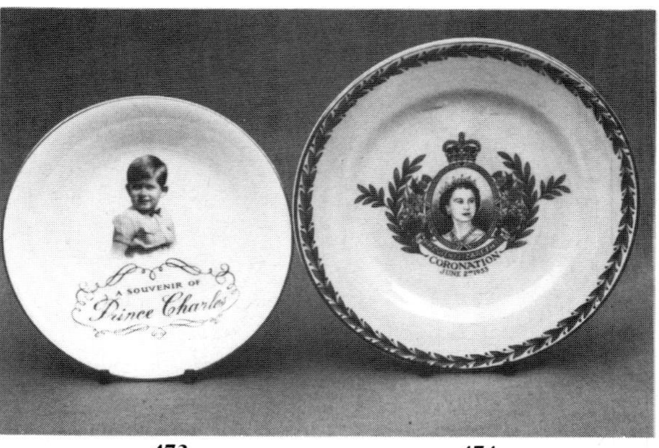

473 474

Paragon China produced a number of commemoratives for the Coronation including several teaware designs, of which two (both 7.5cm) are shown here. These designs were also used as the basis for a number of "Anniversary" cups and saucers issued between 1954 and 1960 **(464, 465)**.

*475 On the left the crowned EIIR cypher, printed in yellow, is surrounded by a border of national flowers printed in natural colours.

*476 This version has a coloured spray of flowers filling the centre whilst decorative scrolls in blue and cyphers in yellow are printed around the border. Backstamp and inscription in full are given on the saucers.

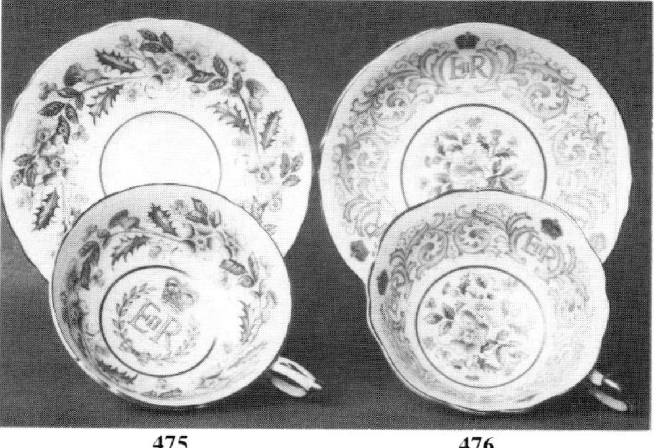

475 476

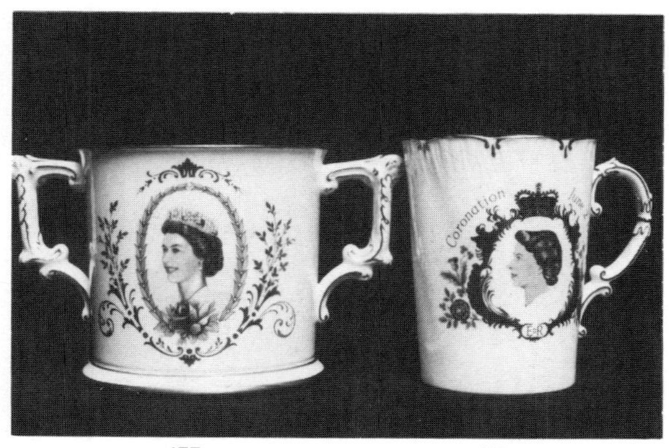

477 478

*477 This pale ivory porcelain loving cup (10cm) comes from *Royal Crown Derby*. On the front is a full colour portrait of the Queen within a frame of green laurel and gilt floral sprays whilst the reverse has a delicate gilt "trellis" motif and coronation date. The handles, foot and rim are trimmed with gold. Limited to 250.

*478 *Adderley China* produced this delightful porcelain mug (10cm). A colour profile portrait of the Queen within a cartouche of gilded feathers and coloured flowers, together with coronation date in gold, are on the front, with a crowned cypher on the reverse. The slightly flared shape is enhanced by a moulded rim which, like the elegant handles is trimmed with gold.

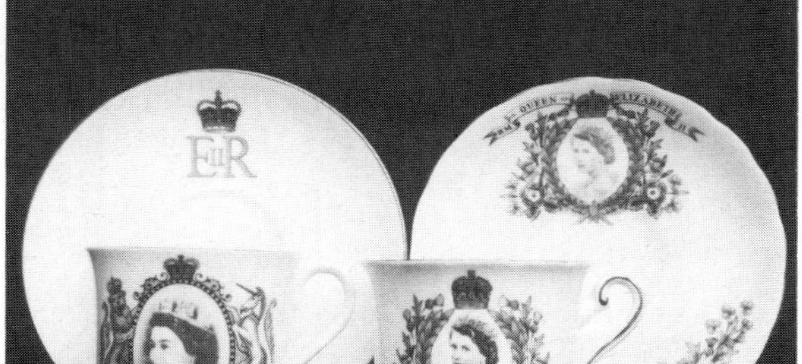

479 480

We illustrate a range of porcelain cups and saucers issued to mark the Coronation. Excellent printing and good quality were to be seen even at the cheapest level.

*479 This portrait of the Queen wearing a tiara is in sepia and framed by the royal Supporters printed in colour on a set (7.5cm) produced by *Shelley.*

*480 Another portrait of the Queen in light brown, with coloured wreath and flowers, decorates the example here from *Tuscan China*. On the reverse is a crowned cypher in laurel with "Coronation June 2nd 1953" in brown.

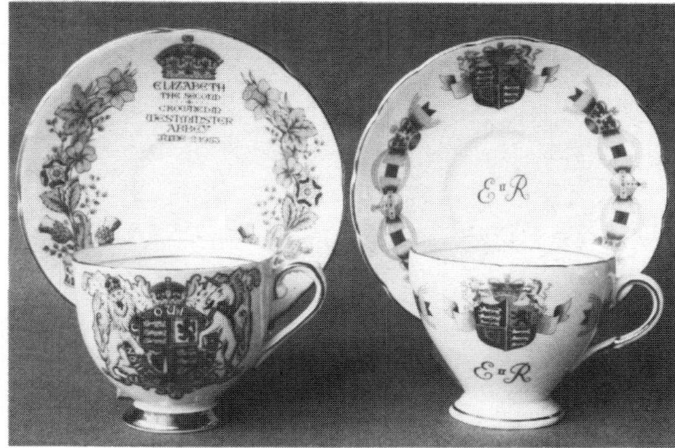

481 482

*481 A magnificent Royal Arms, with hand enamelling, dominates the front of this cup (7cm) from *Stanley China*. On the reverse are large national flowers with hand enamelling. Inscription is on the saucer. Many collectors regard this as the finest tea set.

*482 A different approach to using the Arms can be seen on this set from *Foley China*. The design, arms with crowns and orbs encircling the cup and saucer is printed in full colour. Distinctive and decorative.

*483 This cone-shaped cup (7cm) bears a very delicate full colour portrait of the Queen on a blue background, framed by national flowers. On the reverse two heralds' trumpets surmount "EIIR". The inscription runs both inside and outside the cup. *Gladstone China* made this set, but others also used this design.

*484 Whilst this printed design showing the Queen framed by lion and unicorn is frequently used on a variety of china and pottery wares, the example here (7.5cm) is distinguished by its gold handle with crown and the large bold transfer on the saucer. Unmarked.

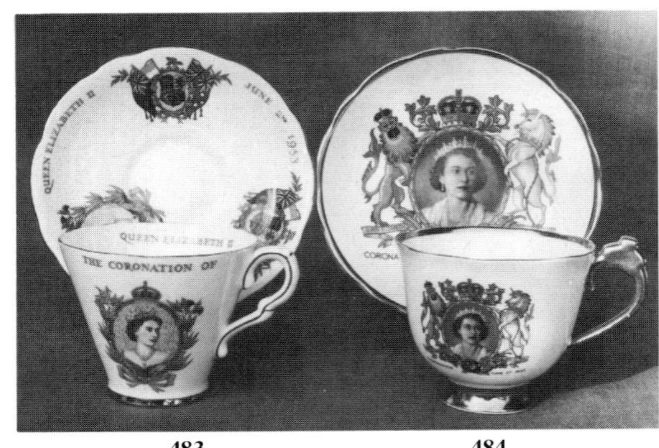

483 **484**

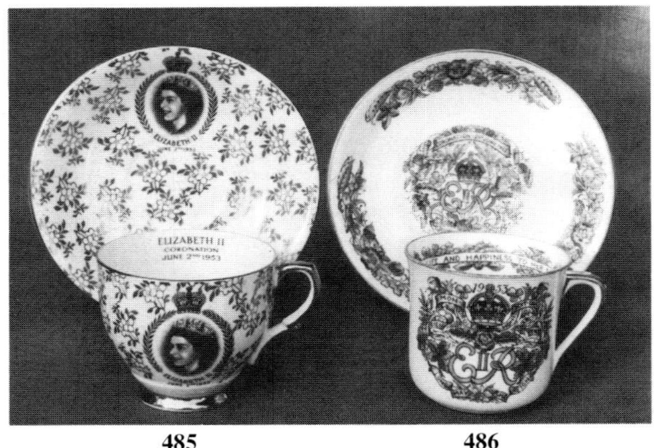

485 **486**

*485 A sepia portrait surrounded by green laurel is the main design feature of this porcelain cup and saucer (7cm) by *Taylor & Kent*. The crown has some hand enamelling. A fine overall floral pattern in gold provides the background. An EIIR cypher and crown completes the decoration. Coronation date is printed inside the cup.

*486 This porcelain cup and saucer (7cm) from *Hammersley* is dominated by a colourful, printed design incorporating the cypher in blue beneath a red rose and crown. National flowers are entwined with ribbons and inscriptions. On the reverse, the Coronation date and spray of national flowers. Inside, "Long life and happiness to her Majesty".

*487, *488 Two quality items from the *Minton* factory. The plate (27cm) bears a large royal coat of arms against a white ground. Geometric pattern panels in pale blue are interspersed with the ten royal beasts **(GG7)** to form the outer border. Limited to 1000. By contrast the pale green covered trinket box (10cm) is decorated in gold with an etched inscription around the rim of the cover. A stylized pattern of gold coloured roses and thistles decorates the base.

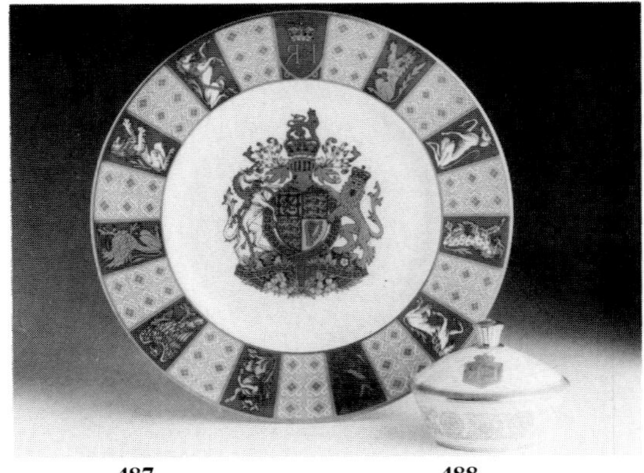

487 **488**

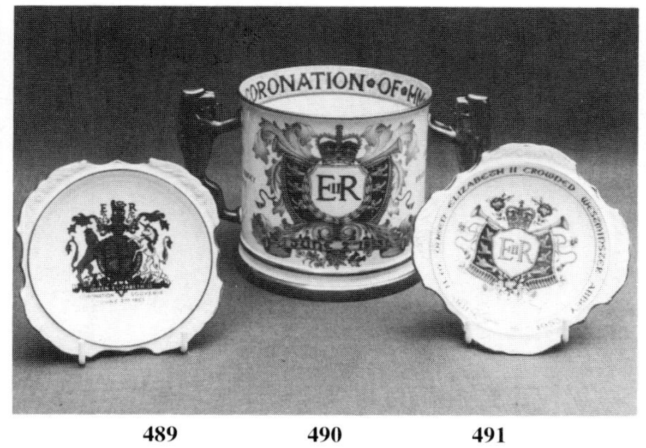

489 **490** **491**

*489, *491 Pin trays continue to be popular and those made by *Paragon* are particularly sought after. A variety of shapes and decorations were used of which two are shown (12cm). A traditional coat of arms in colour dominates that on the left, whilst a more imaginative design using enamelled banners and rim inscription is shown on the right.

*490 Gold lion handles and broad gold base rim enrich the loving cup (11.5cm). Reds, blues and purples decorate the front with similar colouring to a coat of arms on the reverse. Probably limited to 500 though not clearly marked as such.

*492 Thos Goode & Co Ltd who had created a reputation for commissioning fine comemmorative pieces, especially from the *Copeland* factory, issued this pottery tyg (14.5cm) in 1953. The shape was used previously in 1937 for the Coronation of George VI. The new piece shows the EIIR cypher on one panel, the Royal Arms on another and the third bears an inscription detailing Coronation date. The three lions peer over the rim which together with the handles are gilded. This is the last of this type produced. All later deluxe pieces from Copeland-Spode are in porcelain and have a quite different shape **(542)**.

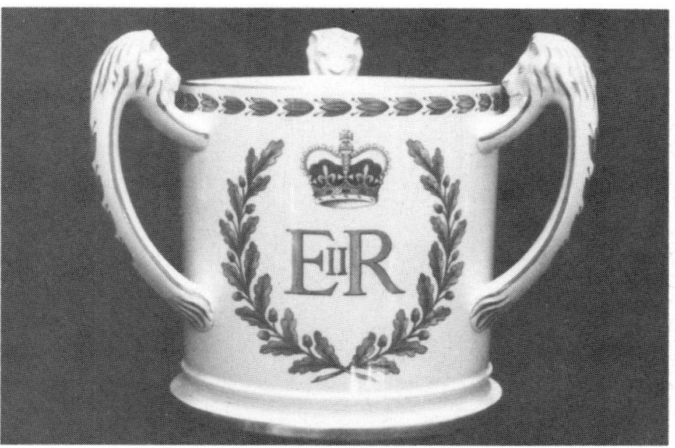

492

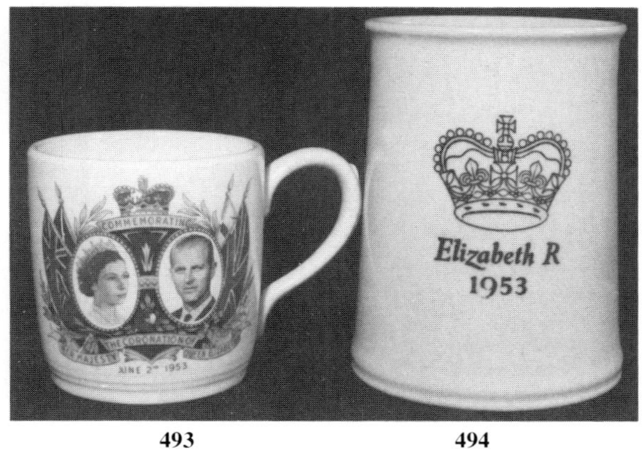

493 **494**

*493 There must be very few commemoratives for the 1953 coronation which show side by side portraits of Queen Elizabeth and the Duke of Edinburgh. This pottery mug (8.5cm) has no maker's mark but is stamped "Canada" and was made for the Canadian market. Sepia portraits are flanked by coloured Union flags and emblems. The reverse records the year of the coronation below a crown.

*494 *Royal Doulton* made this tall stoneware tankard (12.5cm) with a cream glazed ground. A large crown and inscription are printed in black. Items for the 1953 coronation were to be the last royal commemoratives **(FF3)** produced by the Lambeth factory before its closure a few years later.

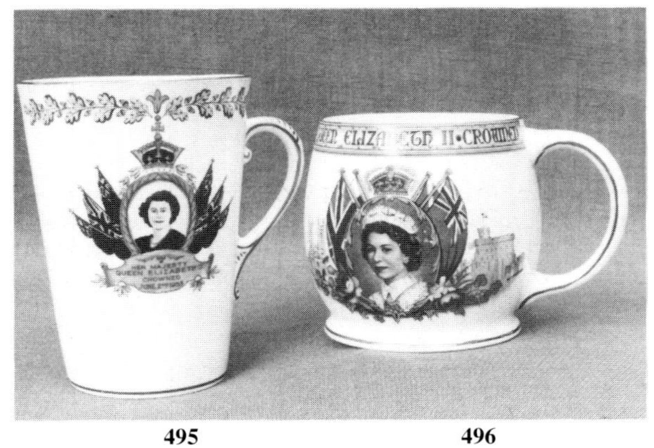

495 496

*495 This tall, flared porcelain mug (11.5cm) was designed by Scott-Jervis for *New Chelsea*. The informal portrait of the Queen is framed by hand enamelled flags and surmounted by a crown. Oak leaves encircle the rim and on the reverse is a crowned cypher and "Long may she reign".

*496 This chubby, barrel-shaped porcelain mug (8cm) is unmarked, but bears an Aynsley type decoration **(see DD1)**. A portrait of the Queen surrounded by flags with Westminster Abbey and Windsor Castle in the background is on the front whilst the reverse shows a colourful state crown.

*497 Both porcelain plates (26cm) show sepia portraits of Queen Elizabeth. *Burgess and Leigh* made that on the left with a coloured frame against a background of flags, Windsor Castle and Westminster Abbey. Roses, shamrocks and thistles in natural colours fill the border.

*498 The other by *Crown Devon* is on a cream ground and has a relief moulded border of emblems with a simple but effective decoration around the crowned portrait.

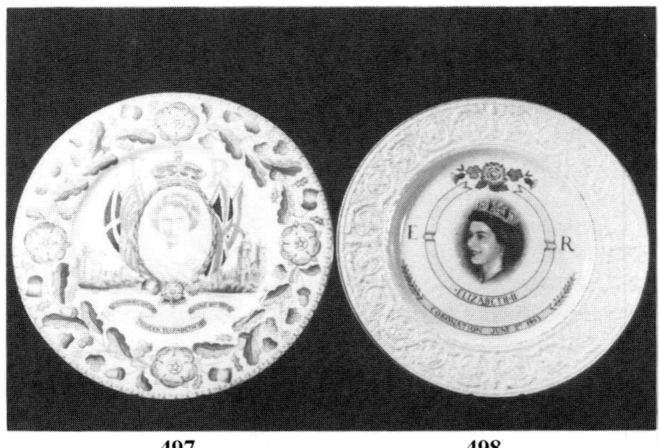

497 498

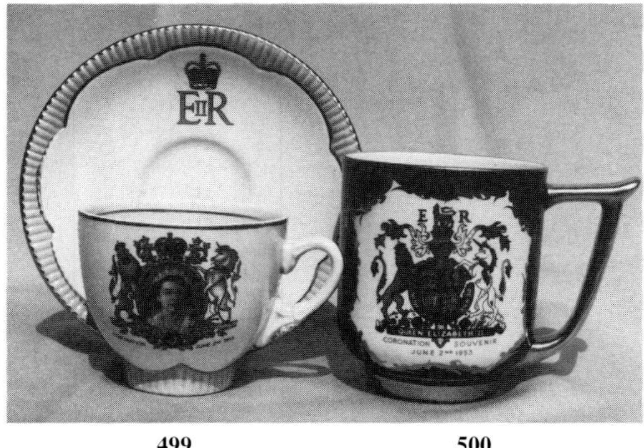

499 500

*499 In striking contrast to the designs we associate with Clarice Cliff, both these porcelain pieces reflect her later post war work. The cup (7cm) and saucer show a sepia portrait, coloured beasts and floral decoration. A pale blue ribbed border decorates the foot of the cup and rim of the saucer. Backstamp for *Newport Pottery Co,* Clarice Cliff.

*500 The mug (9.5cm) is in cobalt blue and gold. The shield is on a white background and is the approved design by the Council of Industrial Design **(454)**. Foot and handle are gold as is the cypher inscription on the reverse. Made by *Royal Staffordshire,* Clarice Cliff.

The Investiture of the Prince of Wales • 1969 •

Charles Philip Arthur George, the Queen's eldest son, was created Prince of Wales in 1958. On 1 July 1969 at Caernarvon Castle, Prince Charles was invested with the insignia of the title and received the Loyal Address from the people of Wales.

The title itself dates back to 1301 when Edward I was said to have presented his new born son to the Welsh chiefs at Caernarvon Castle as their very own prince. It is not the birth-right of the oldest son of the Sovereign to claim the title Prince of Wales and he must, in fact, await the favour of the Sovereign. Although the association of the title with the Principality goes back nearly 700 years, it carries with it practically no specific duties and the Prince has no land in Wales from which he may derive income. Edward VIII, who was Prince of Wales for nearly 25 years, took a particular interest in Welsh affairs, visiting the area many times and becoming very popular with the Welsh people. In preparation for his own investiture Prince Charles spent two months at Aberystwyth University studying the history and language of Wales.

Caernarvon Castle had been carefully renovated and gradually prepared for several years prior to the investiture day. Lord Snowdon was principally responsible for overseeing this and, in particular, for the arrangements of the day. In spite of the fact that some 4000 guests were to be accommodated at the ceremony, the natural open air feature of the castle was retained as much as possible, with only the orchestra and thrones under canopy cover. Needless to say, much of the ceremony was conducted in the native language in keeping with tradition.

Prince Charles had previously attracted no interest from the commemorative potters apart from a few examples at the time of his mother's coronation **(455) (473)**. It was to be expected that the Dragon of Wales and Prince of Wales Feathers would strongly feature in designs. Of those who chose a dragon that from Paragon **(521)** was of excellent quality. Caernarvon Castle was depicted on the Coalport goblet **(520)** in an imaginative way in gold. On reflection, the choice and quality of pieces offered was surprisingly limited considering that the occasion attracted a lot of public interest.

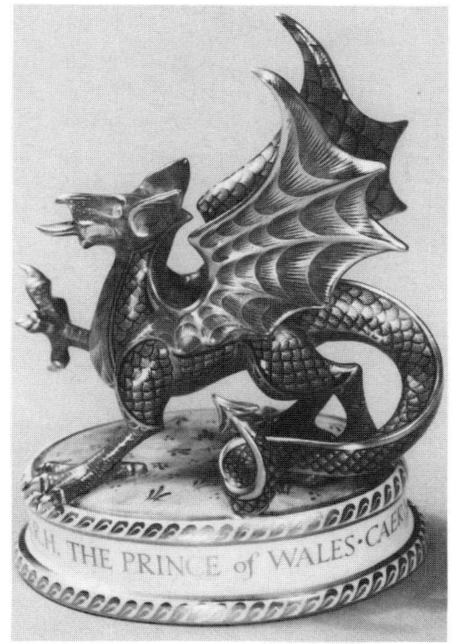

501

*501 *Royal Crown Derby's* Dragon was one of the few exceptional quality items we have seen. It was chosen as a memento to be presented to the 1st Battalion of the Welsh Guards for the part they played in the Investiture ceremony.

This beautifully moulded, porcelain Welsh Dragon (12cm tall), richly decorated with red and gilt stands on a green and white base on which is inscribed "The Investiture of HRH The Prince of Wales Caernarvon July 1969". The production was limited to 250.

*502 *Duchess China* issued this porcelain cup and saucer (7cm) decorated with the red dragon of Wales. Handle and rim are trimmed with gold.

*503 *Rye Pottery* has a reputation for creating interesting, well designed wares. This ivory coloured pottery mug (10cm) is no exception. Prince of Wales Feathers are on the front with 1969 on each side and "Charles Prince of Wales" beneath, all hand painted in blue. Orange yellow and blue lines circle the top, bottom and inside rim.

*504 The *New Devon Pottery* also chose the popular Welsh dragon for their pottery mug (9cm).

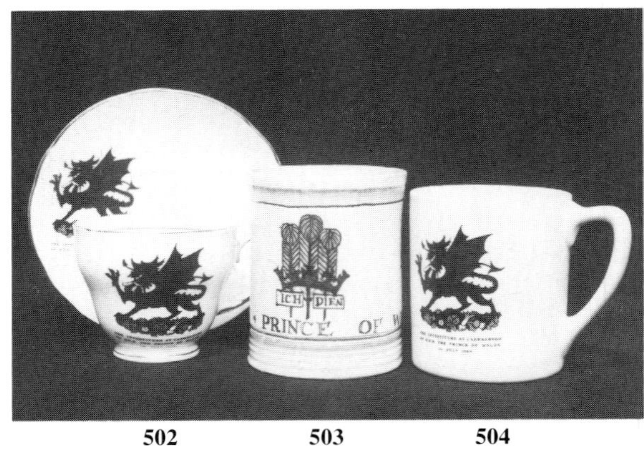

502 503 504

*505 *Crown Ducal* made this tall mug (9cm) in pottery. Prince of Wales Feathers and Welsh Dragon are incorporated in the mainly black and gold coat of arms. An inscription in Welsh reads "Y DDRAIG GOCH DDYRY CYCHWYN". Design approved by the College of Arms.

*506 The pottery mug (7.5cm) by *Weatherby,* shows a gold profile of the Prince against a white background. A green frame is flanked by coloured flags with Prince of Wales Feathers at the top. Daffodils are in evidence. An inscription records the event.

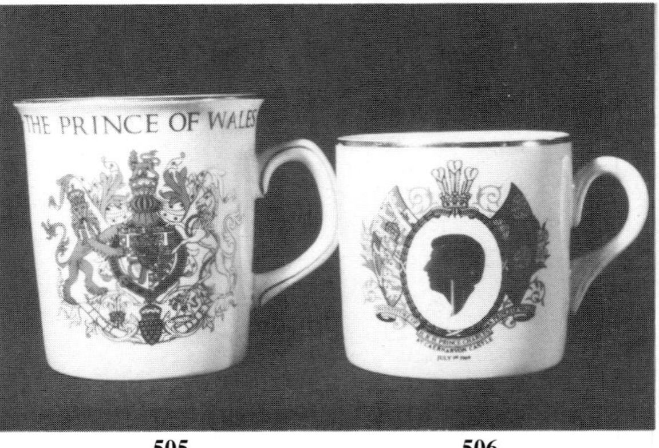

505 506

*507 A 19th century engraving of Caernarvon Castle is the basis for the interesting decoration on this pottery tankard (11.5cm) from *Wedgwood*. The view and inscriptions in black stand out very well on the cream body. Designed by Carl Toms.

*508 Also from *Wedgwood* comes another pottery tankard (10cm), the second in the royal commemorative series designed by Richard Guyatt. The design centres on the Welsh dragon and Prince of Wales Feathers. All printed in black with touches of gilding. "God bless the Prince of Wales" in gilt is inside the rim whilst outside its Welsh translation "Duw Gadwo'r Tywysog" and "Caernarfon 1969".

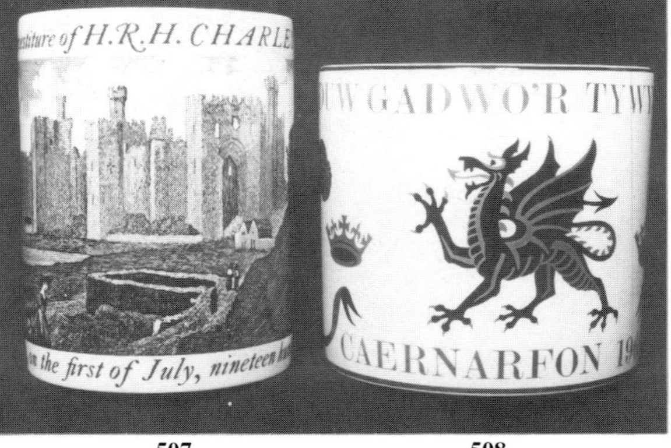

507 508

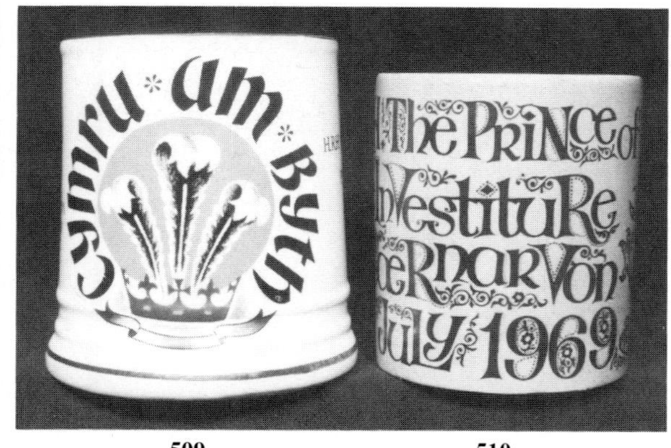

509 **510**

*509 Prince of Wales Feathers surrounded by "Cymru am Byth" (Wales for Ever) printed in black on a red background provide a bold decoration on the front of this cone-shaped pottery mug (9.5cm) from *Tryfan Design*. The inscription appears on each side in English and Welsh. James Broom Lynne MSIA is the designer.

*510 This pottery mug (8.5cm) has a royal blue body with an applied transfer print in light green consisting of "HRH The Prince of Wales. The investiture at Caernarvon 1st July 1969", in an interesting typescript, and a Welsh dragon. Made in several colours by *Staffordshire Potteries*.

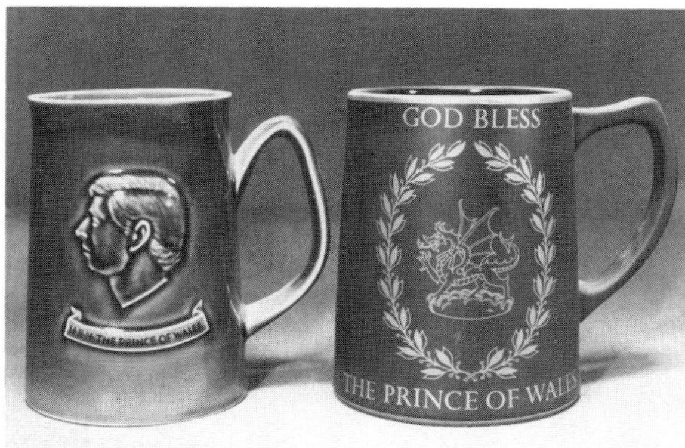

511 **512**

*511 A relief moulded profile of Prince Charles above "HRH The Prince of Wales" decorates the front of this grey, cone-shaped, pottery mug (11.5cm) from *Holkham Pottery* in Norfolk. The reverse has Prince of Wales Feathers and "Caernarvon July 1st 1969". Other colours also produced.

*512 Made in black basalt by *Wedgwood*, this tall mug (11cm) has the Welsh dragon within laurel leaves on the front with Prince of Wales Feathers on the rear. These, the inscriptions, handle and rim are printed in gold. Norman Wilson is the designer.

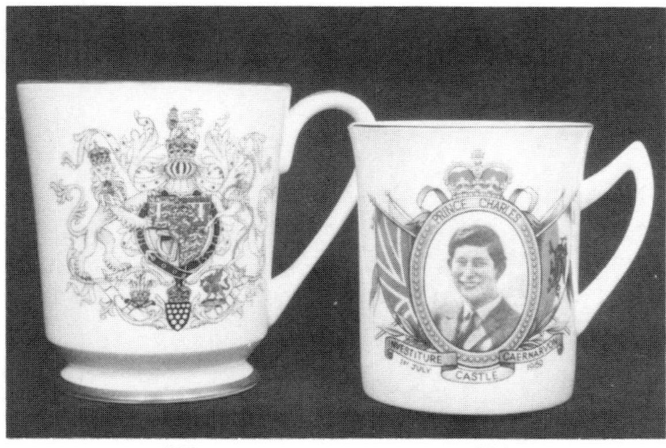

513 **514**

*513 This flared, footed porcelain mug (9cm) comes from *Aynsley*. Prince Charles' coat of arms together with the Welsh Dragon and Prince of Wales Feathers is on the front. The reverse lists all the Princes of Wales since 1301.

*514 The small, porcelain mug (8cm) shown here bears a portrait of Prince Charles, printed in sepia and surrounded by Union and Welsh flags in colour. Below, an inscription on a blue ribbon. The reverse shows the Arms of Cowbridge, Glamorgan. This transfer, the only one seen which used a photograph, was used by several makers.

*515, *516, *517, *518 As one might expect, red dragons and Prince of Wales feathers feature prominently on items made for the Investiture of Prince Charles at Caernarfon Castle on July 1st 1969.

The pottery mug (11cm) was made by *Lord Nelson Pottery* and uses the castle as a background to the red dragon. The cup and saucer show the same transfer.

Royal Winton made the porcelain footed dish (7cm) on the left featuring a slightly differently designed dragon. The small handles are in gold.

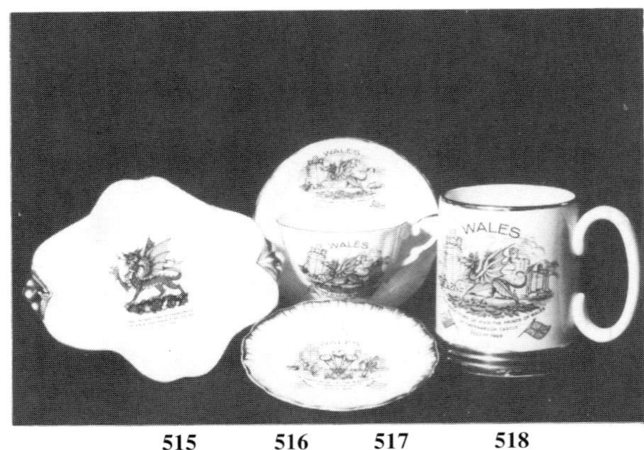

515 516 517 518

*519 A Welsh dragon and feathers are incorporated in the coat of arms which dominates the centre of this porcelain plate (26.5cm) by *Spode* commemorating the Investiture. A green patterned border decorates the inside rim. An inscription on the reverse reads "Charles Philip Arthur George Prince of Wales Caernarvon 1st July 1969".

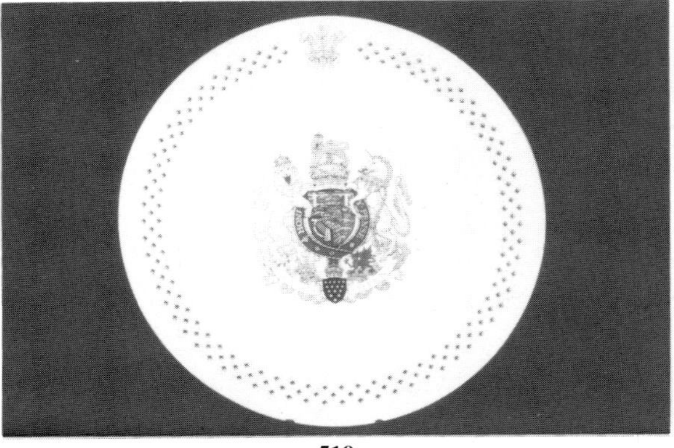

519

*520 A stylized presentation of Caernarvon Castle with pennants above and "Charles Prince of Wales 1969" below, all printed in gold on a white porcelain body makes this goblet (11.5cm) from Coalport a most appealing piece. This was the first Royal event for which Coalport produced this form of commemorative – they continue to this day. Another version is shown at **(EE6)**. These goblets take on an even more attractive presentation when seen as a series.

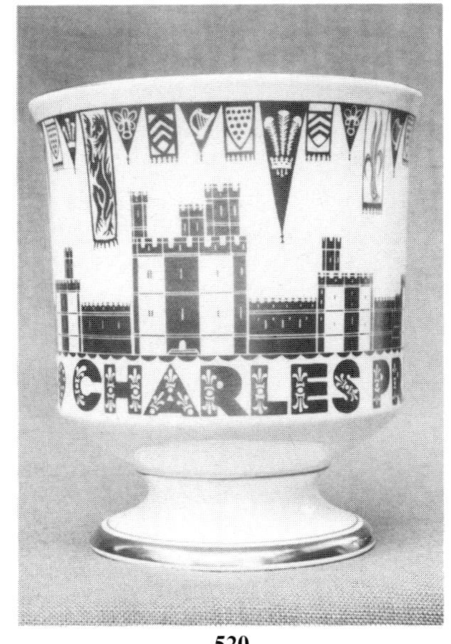

520

*521 This collection of fine quality items in porcelain was made by *Paragon* to commemorate the investiture of the Prince of Wales at Caernarfon in 1969. The simple but most effective design shows a large red Welsh dragon standing on a bed of thistles, roses, shamrocks and, of course, a leek. An inscription records the event.

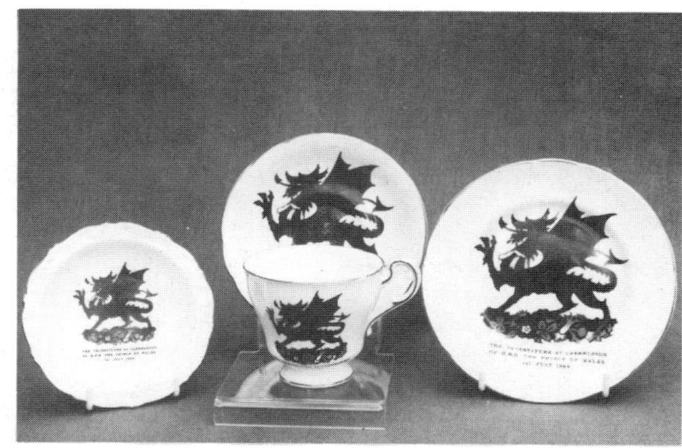

521

*522 *Bretby* created this pottery mantel ornament (11cm) in the shape of Caernarvon Castle. Well-modelled and painted in stone-grey and brown with the inscription on the base printed in black.

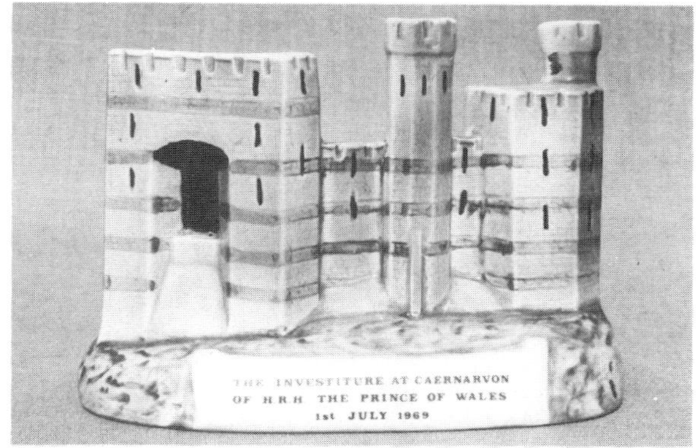

522

*523 This small, porcelain goblet (9.5cm) has the Prince of Wales Feathers printed on the front on a white oval set in a light blue body. Inside the rim is "HRH Prince Charles, Caernarvon, July 1969". Made by *Grosvenor China* for Jackson & Gosling Ltd.

*523A *Royal Crown Derby* made this porcelain bell (20cm) in a limited edition of 500. The main colour is maroon with hand gilded detail in burnished gold.

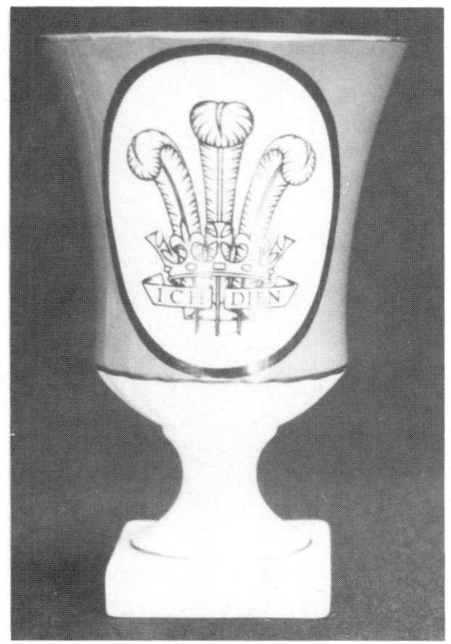

523

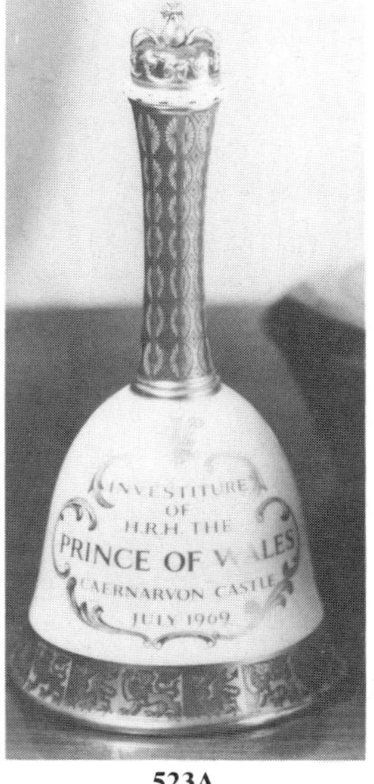

523A

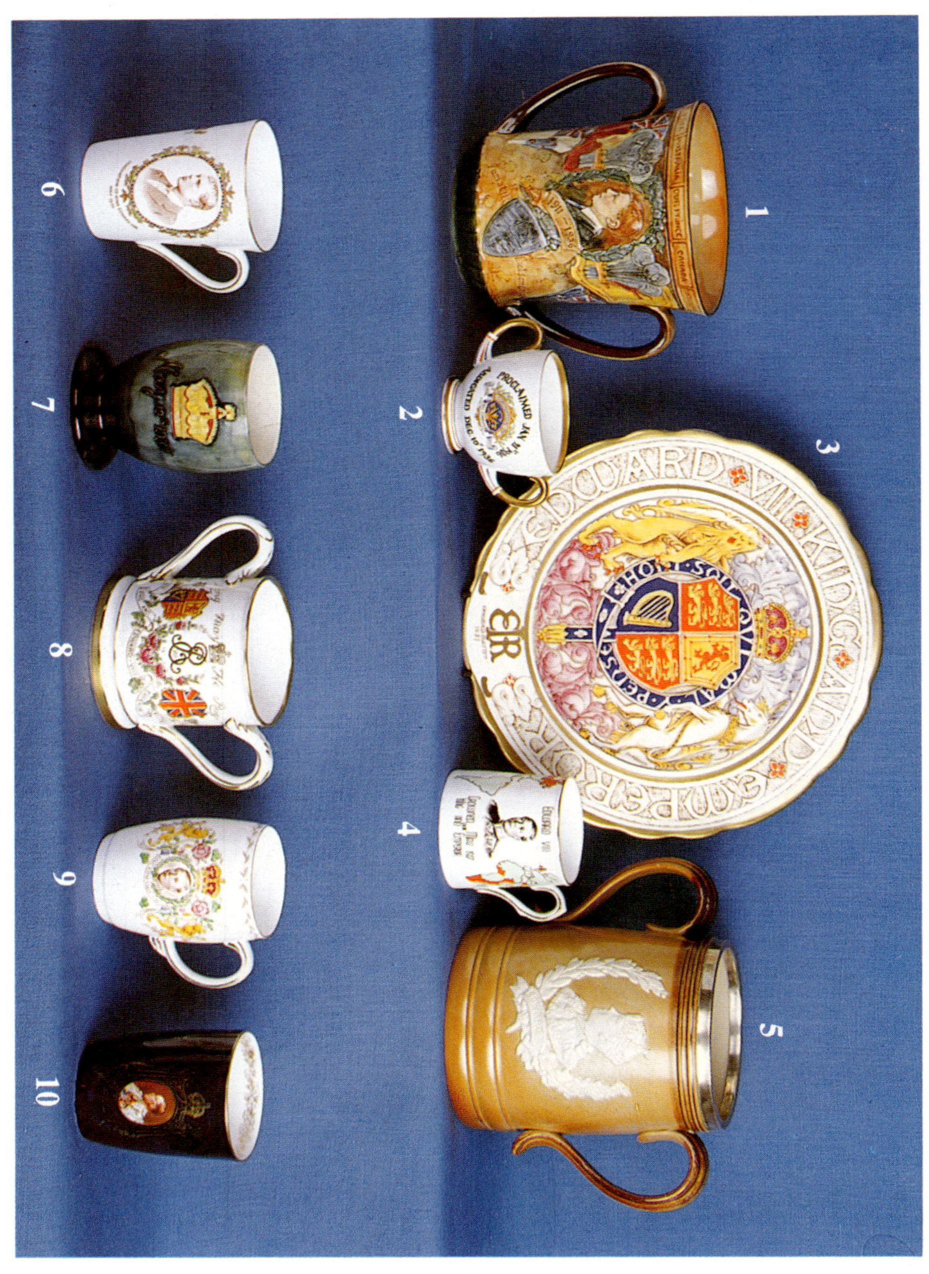

The "Proposed" Coronation of Edward VIII • 1937 •

Plate AA (see page 36)

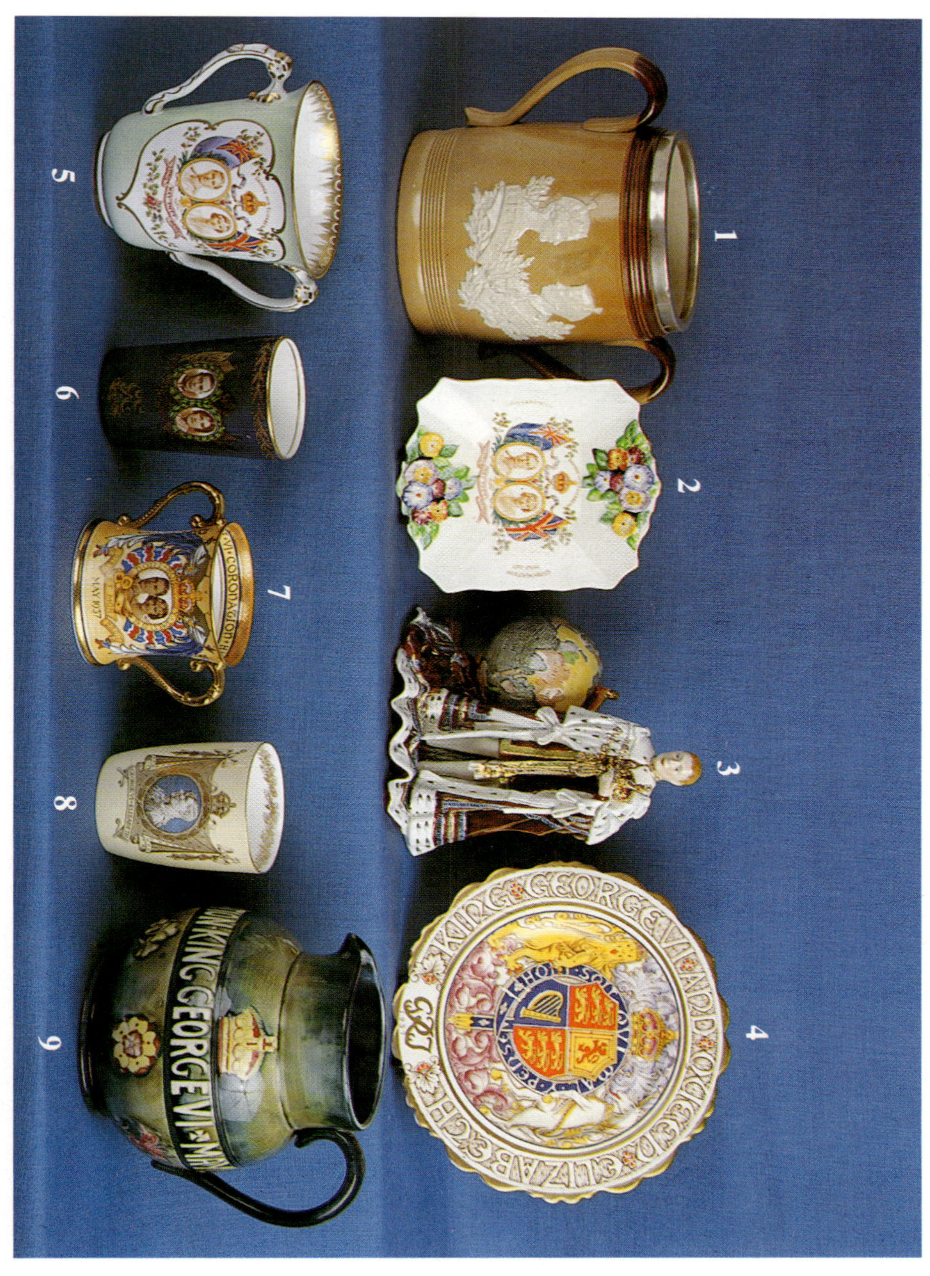

The Coronation of George VI • 1937 •

(see page 37)

Plate BB

Colour Plate AA (page 34)

The "proposed" Coronation of Edward VIII • 1937 •

AA1 A rare relief moulded loving cup (16.5cm) from the *Royal Doulton* factory commemorating the reign and abdication of Edward VIII. The front shows a coloured portrait of King Edward in relief flanked by the Prince of Wales feathers. An inscription reads "I am still the same man". Edward is again shown on the reverse but this time in coronation robes, flanked by flags and inscribed "God Save the King". The Doulton backstamp reads "To commemorate the reign of Edward VIII Jan/Dec 1936, long life and happiness. Limited edition of 2000. A similar loving cup was produced for the coronation but showed a facing head and shoulders portrait of Edward in mufti. This was redesigned for the abdication piece.

AA2 An unusual shaped loving cup (7cm) which shows a framed portrait of Edward VIII on the front. Collectors will be more interested in the reverse (seen here) which records the proclamation and abdication dates of his reign. Gold decorated handles, foot and rim with some red white and blue lining enhances the quality of this charming piece made by the *CWS*.

AA3 The design seen on this *Paragon* plate (18cm) was that used by the Company for the production of some 50 different articles **(248) (271)** commemorating the coronation of Edward VIII. Two months later the Company received permission to modify the registered design for the coronation of George VI and Elizabeth.

AA4 *Osborne China* manufactured this tapered porcelain mug (7.5cm) to commemorate the coronation. A sepia portrait of the King is shown together with a bold inscription. The remainder of the mug shows an outline map of the world in green with the principal countries of the Empire enamelled in red.

AA5 Unmistakably from the *Doulton* Lambeth factory, this silver rimmed loving cup (17cm) shows a relief moulded portrait of Edward VIII in white against the familiar Doulton brown glazed ground. St George and the dragon, again in white relief, are shown on the reverse. Inscribed on the base as a limited edition of 100, though it was almost certainly an incomplete order at the time of the abdication.

AA6 Informal portraits of Edward VIII seem to have been popular with potters both before and during his short reign **(259) (351)**. This one in sepia shows head and shoulders within an inscribed frame and the date of the coronation below. Made by *Grosvenor China*.

AA7 *William Moorcroft* designed this pottery beaker (11cm) for the coronation of Edward VIII, thus maintaining a factory tradition dating back to the coronation of Edward VII. The mottled blue/green ground is somewhat typical of the glaze used for commemorative pieces at this time **(399)** though a wide variety of colours and glazes have been used to striking effect.

AA8 The *Hammersley* loving cup (10cm) follows the same basic shape and design as that used for the Silver Jubilee of George V and Queen Mary **(214)**. Circumstances made it necessary to adapt quickly the Edward VIII pieces for the coronation of his brother **(278)**.

AA9 *Grafton China* produced this tall barrel-shaped porcelain mug (10.5cm). The sepia portrait is appropriately framed with emblems and flanked by gold coloured lions. A simple inscription on the reverse records the coronation date.

AA10 *Royal Doulton* produced for the coronation of Edward VIII four coloured beakers (9.5cm) in green, Rose du Barry, ivory and cobalt blue. The first three retailed at six shillings and sixpence but the cobalt cost the princely sum of nine shillings, possibly because it was a more difficult colour to fire. All are difficult to find but the cobalt blue has become a very rare item.

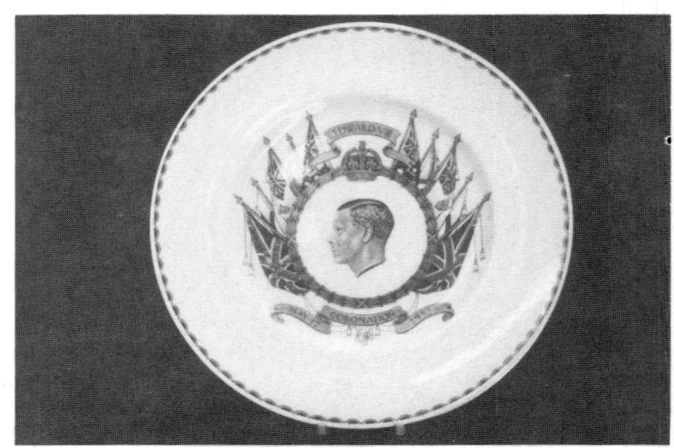

524

*524 This porcelain plate (22.5cm) bearing the mark *Royal Cauldon* has at its centre a printed crowned medallion portrait of Edward VIII printed in sepia. Coloured flags and laurel form a circular frame.

Colour Plate DD (page 39)

Commemoratives by Aynsley

DD1 This cup (6.5cm), saucer and plate in porcelain is found with a white ground as well as the pale green shown. The striking head and shoulders portrait of Queen Elizabeth in ermine robes is used by *Aynsley* on a number of other items **(CC3)**. A large crown, similar to that on the saucer, is repeated on the reverse of the cup.

DD2 Extensive hand painting and gilding contribute to the superb quality of this trophy vase (35.5cm) issued in a limited edition of 175 for the wedding of Prince Andrew and Sarah Ferguson. The front panel shows Westminster Abbey and entwined cyphers and inscription in gold record the occasion. This is just one of a number of trophy vases made by *Aynsley* to commemorate more recent royal events.

DD3 A wedding bell (12cm) in porcelain with gold loop handle commemorates the marriage of Prince Andrew and Miss Sarah Ferguson. The Royal Arms is shown on the front. Characteristically, family trees for Prince Andrew and Miss Sarah Ferguson are detailed on the reverse.

DD4 Royal Arms dominate the front of this porcelain mug (8.5cm) made for the Jubilee in 1977. A list of Kings and Queens of England with the dates of their reigns can be found on the back.

DD5 Details of the opening of the St Lawrence Seaway are contained within a broad band on the rim of this porcelain plate (22.5cm). The map showing the route of the seaway dominates most of the plate.

DD6 For the birth of Prince Henry on 15 September 1984 Aynsley made this porcelain loving cup (6.5cm) similar to one they produced for the birth of Prince William. A framed coloured picture of Balmoral Castle with an inscription below is shown to the front. The reverse reads "To commemorate the second child of their Royal Highnesses the Prince and Princess of Wales".

DD7 *Aynsley* have used the same transfer for this attractive chalice (12cm) as that on the loving cup **(D6)**. A cartouche with Royal Arms and emblems decorates the reverse, whilst shields representing the countries of the Empire circle the inside rim.

DD8 A gold inscription below portraits on this attractive porcelain mug (7.5cm) records the visit of George VI and Queen Elizabeth to Canada in 1939. Views of the parliament buildings in Ottawa are on the reverse.

DD9 To commemorate the Queen Mother's 80th birthday *Aynsley* produced this large porcelain plate (26.5cm) combining the coat of arms and Bowes-Lyon family tree as a central design. Clusters of national emblems form an attractive border with inner rim bearing the inscription.

*527 This waisted porcelain cup and saucer (6.5cm), made for the 1937 coronation, by *Aynsley*, has portraits of Their Majesties within frames of laurel supported by a lion and unicorn and surmounted by flags. The reverse has a throne from the House of Lords. On the saucer, Buckingham Palace, matching **(394)**.

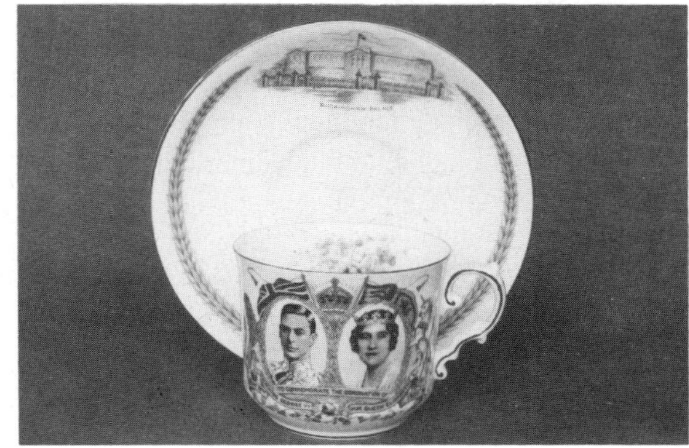

527

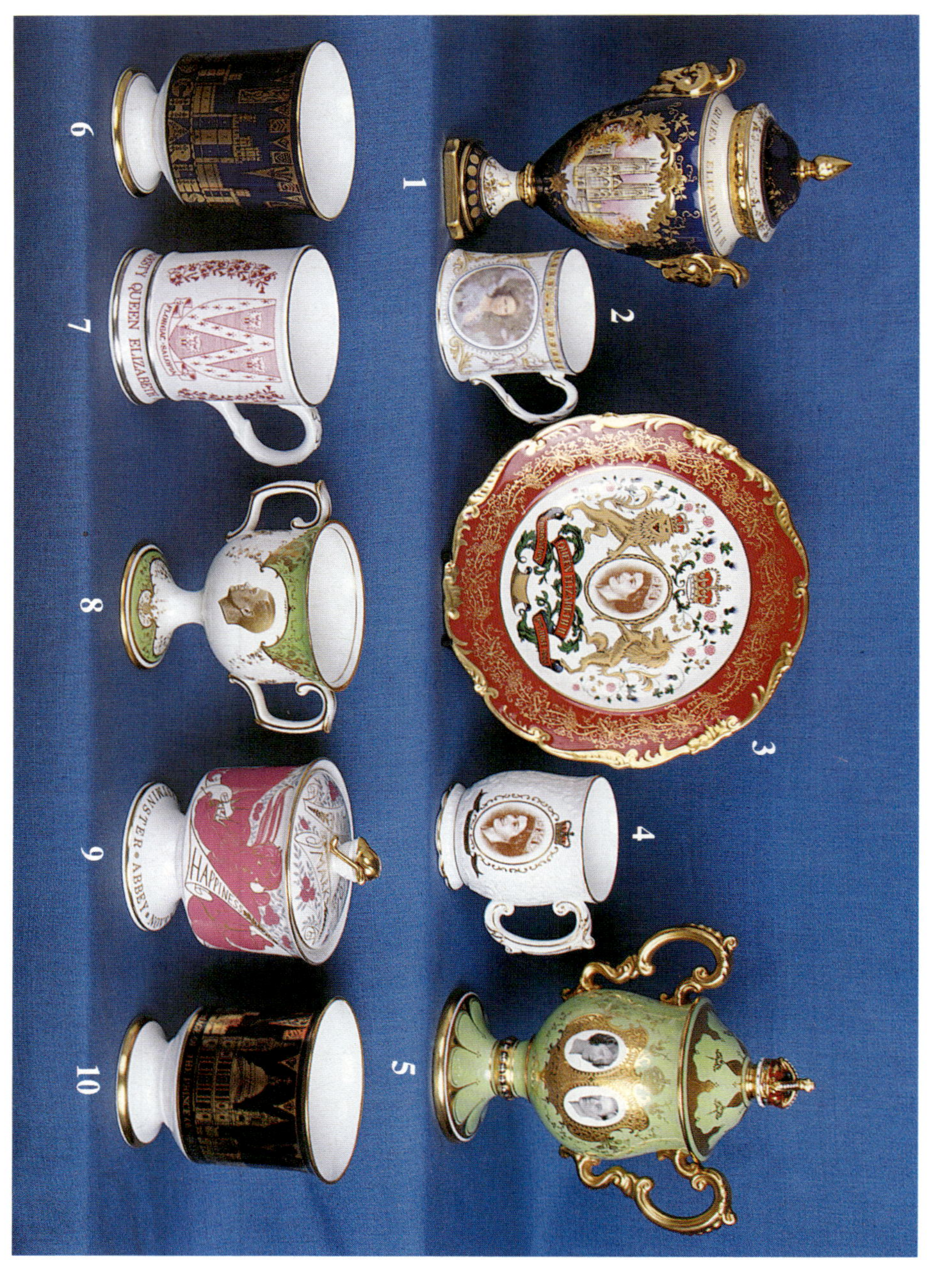

Commemoratives by Coalport

Plate EE

(see page 44)

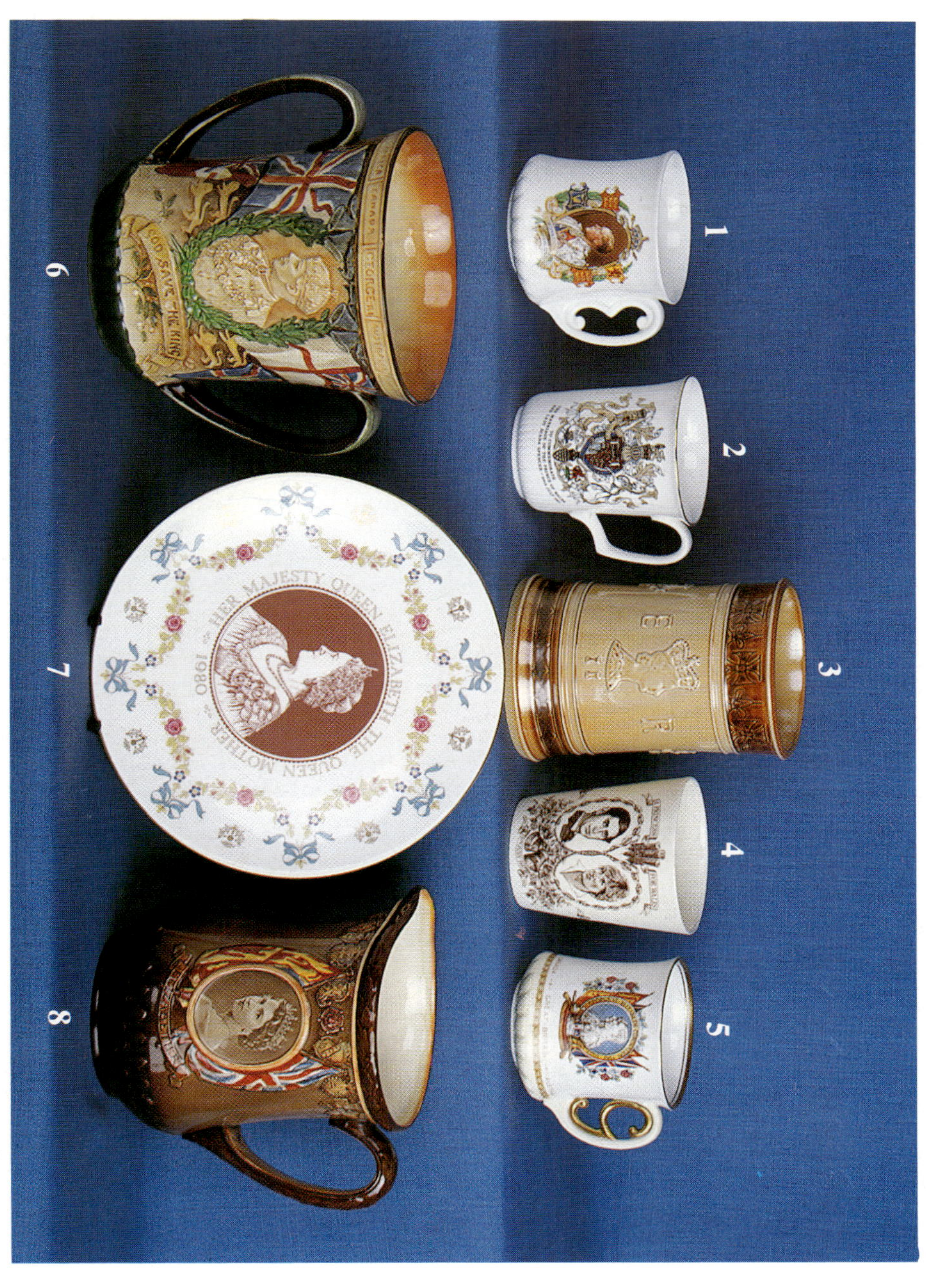

Commemoratives by Doulton

(see page 45)

Plate FF

Colour Plate EE (page 42)

Commemoratives by Coalport

EE1 The *Heritage Collection* commissioned this elegant "Rams Head" vase (25cm) for the Queen's Silver Jubilee in a limited edition of 200. The front shows the West Front of Westminster Abbey, painted and signed by J. Mottram, within a cartouche of raised gold leaves and flowers. The reverse has an intricate raised gold filigree pattern. "Queen Elizabeth II Silver Jubilee 1952-1977" is inscribed around the neck.

EE2 On 13 June 1987 Princess Anne was created Princess Royal. Several pieces were made to commemorate the event and this is one of the more popular items. The portrait has a misty quality and is supported by lions and unicorns, with a stylized cypher within a shield on the reverse.

EE3 A rich red border outlined with a moulded gold rim surrounds a central design against a white ground on this plate (22cm). The framed sepia portrait of the young Queen, crown and beasts dominate, with a ribbon inscription in red below. Made for the coronation of the Queen in1953.

EE4 Another 1953 coronation souvenir in the form of a shaped mug (9.5cm) using the same sepia portrait of the young Queen as before. The handle and body show some relief moulding and a gold cypher and crown decorate the reverse.

EE5 This two-handled lidded vase (22 cm), for the 1937 coronation, is of exceptional quality and shows portraits of King George VI and Queen Elizabeth. Extensive use has been made of gold for the decorated scrolled handles, foot and waist. A coloured crown surmounts the lid. The reverse shows a gold crown, cypher and date of the coronation. Only a very small number of these would have been made.

EE6 and EE10 *Coalport* produced this porcelain goblet (12cm) in both white and cobalt blue ground for a number of royal occasions **(520)**. That on the left shows Caernarvon Castle outlined in gold accompanied by decorated banners of dragons, daffodils and Prince of Wales feathers. A bold inscription reads "Charles Prince of Wales 1969". The backstamp records that Charles Prince of Wales was presented to the people by Queen Elizabeth II Caernarvon Castle 1st July 1969. Limited edition of 500. That on the right is in the same vein showing outlines of St Pauls Cathedral, Buckingham Palace and Windsor Castle. An inscription records the marriage of the Prince of Wales to Lady Diana Spencer. 2000 edition.

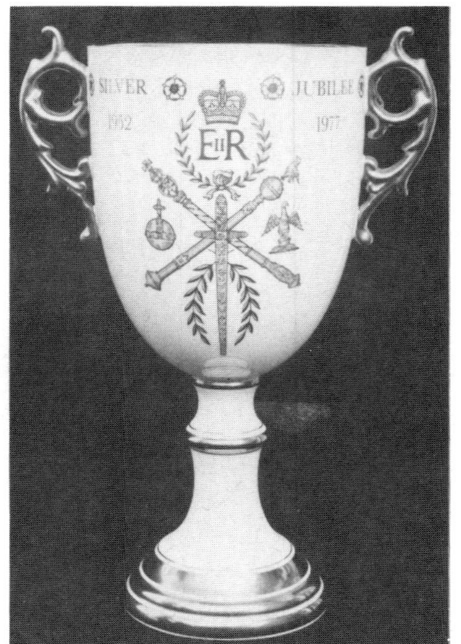

528

EE7 Commissioned in 1978 by the Ironbridge Gorge Museum Trust in a limited edition of 1000 to celebrate the 25th anniversary of the coronation. The front of this mug (10.5cm) bears the Shropshire coat of arms with an inscription on the reverse relating to the event.

EE8 An inscription on the base of this loving cup (12cm) reads: "Designed previous to the renunciation of the throne Dec 10 1936". The gold profile of Edward VIII is shown against a white ground with a pale green and gold decoration. Crown, cypher and coronation date in gold against the white ground are shown on the reverse. A rare item.

EE9 One of the more attractive pieces made for the wedding of Princess Anne and Captain Mark Phillips in the form of a covered vase (14cm). A special feature is the equestrian flavour conveyed by the gold riding hat and crop which form the finial of the lid.

*528 The reverse of the *Coalport* goblet (22.5cms) celebrating the 1977 Silver Jubilee illustrated on the cover. The ornate decoration of coronation regalia is all in raised gold. Limited to 1000 pieces.

Commemoratives by Royal Doulton

FF1 *Royal Doulton* produced this shaped porcelain mug with ungilded "E" handle using the transfer decoration as on **(257)**. The same "E" handle mug was employed for the 1953 coronation **(451)** and was also used for a mug featuring Princess Elizabeth in 1937 **(529)**.

FF2 This flared porcelain mug (9.5cm) for the 1981 Royal Wedding has a rather unimaginative decoration of colour printed coat of arms and inscription on the front with Prince of Wales feathers on the reverse. A caption on the base indicates it was produced solely for Doulton employees.

FF3 In 1956 the Lambeth pottery finally closed its doors. This brown, stoneware tankard (14.5cm) marking the Coronation of Queen Elizabeth in 1953 is the last royal commemorative piece from this most famous factory. It was designed by Agnete Hoy, the last head of design at Lambeth, whose monogram is on the base. Whilst not stated, the piece was limited to 500.

FF4 Another 1981 Royal Wedding piece, this pottery beaker (9.5cm) recalls one of the most famous shapes to come from *Doulton,* the so-called "Burslem beaker" first seen for the Golden Jubilee of Queen Victoria, and issued subsequently for many events including the Diamond Jubilee **(43, 45, 47)** the Coronation of Edward VII **(132)** and George V **(179, 186)**. The Silver Jubilee of 1935 marked its last previous use. The brown printed design is also in the same tradition as its predecessors.

FF5 Possibly one of the scarcest items produced by the company for the Coronation of George VI is this waisted china mug (8.5cm) which has the "standard" transfer decoration. It is the "G" handle trimmed in gold that makes it something different. The same body shape was also used for the Edward VIII mug **(FF1)** and for a 1953 Coronation piece **(451)**.

FF6 Limited edition relief moulded jugs were a popular product of the *Doulton* factory during the 1930's and were mostly designed by Charles Noke and Harry Fenton to celebrate historical and literary occasions. The front shows King George VI flanked by flags, whilst the reverse similarly shows Queen Elizabeth and Scottish flags. Limited to 2000 (16.5cm).

FF7 To celebrate the Queen Mother's 80th Birthday, *Doulton* produced this attractive plate (21cm). A brown printed profile portrait in the centre is surrounded by a colourful border of roses and thistles tied by pale blue swags.

FF8 A framed portrait of Queen Elizabeth II and coloured flags in low moulded relief is set against a brown treacle glaze on this unlimited edition pottery jug (16cm). Windsor Castle on the reverse and moulded shields complete the decoration.

*529 *Doulton* first produced their "E" handle mug for the proposed coronation of Edward VIII **(FF1)**. The shape was repeated with a gold lined handle for Princess Elizabeth at the time of her father's coronation and again for her coronation in 1953. A Marcus Adams portrait in sepia is on the front and "HRH Princess Elizabeth of York, 1937" is inscribed on the reverse. This was made in much smaller numbers than for the 1953 coronation and is now very difficult to find.

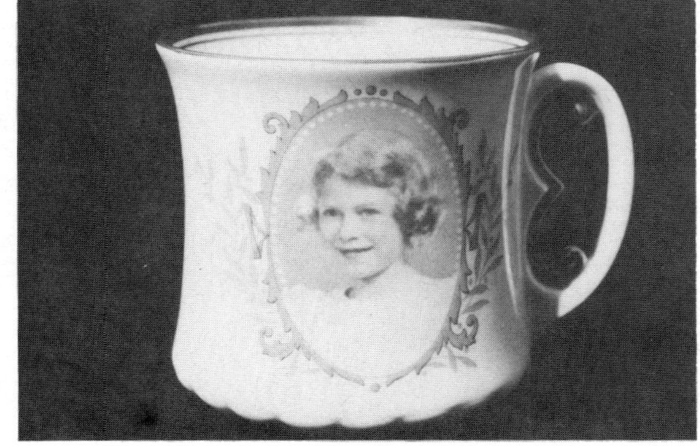

529

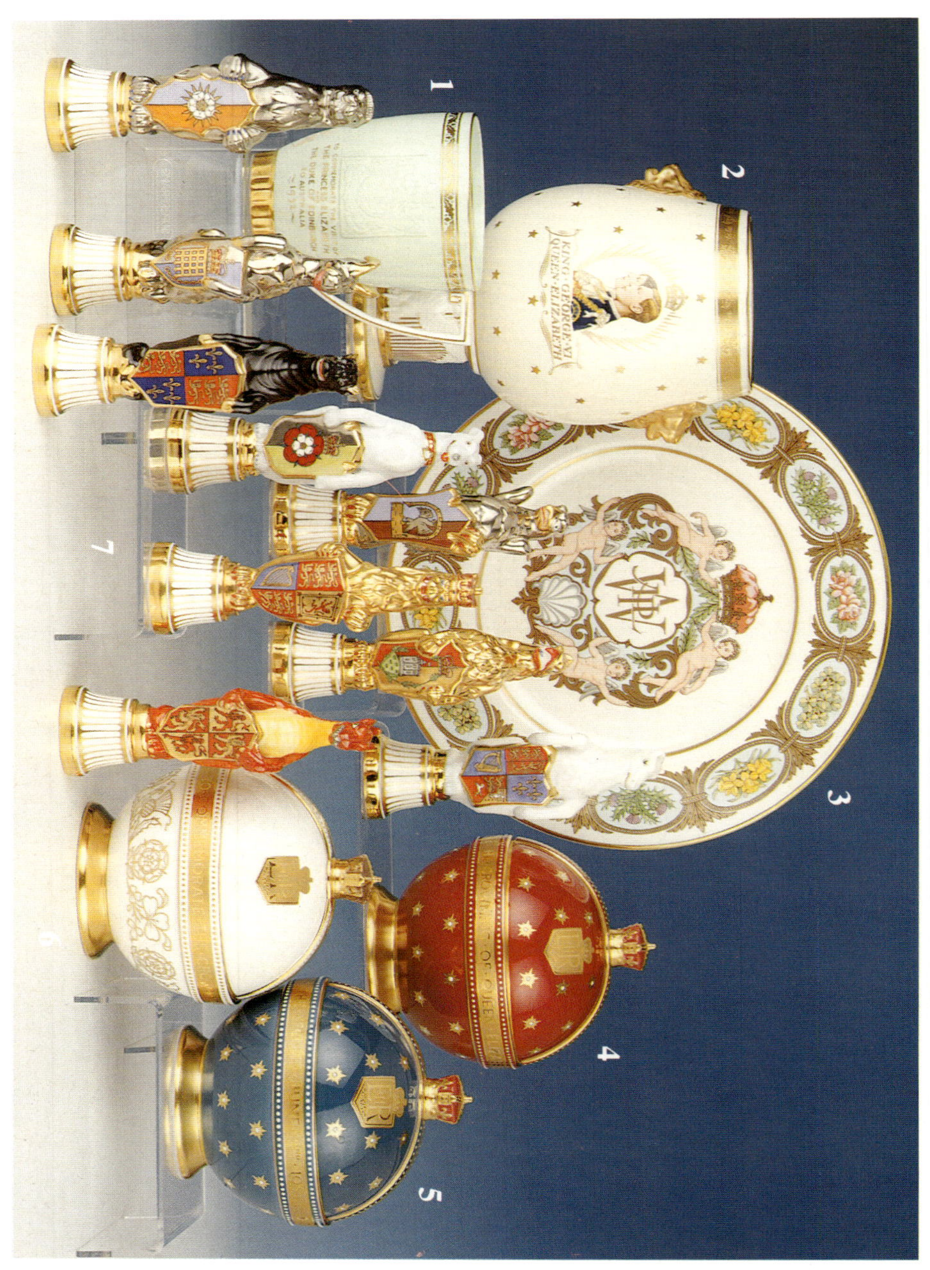

Commemoratives by Minton

Plate GG (see page 48)

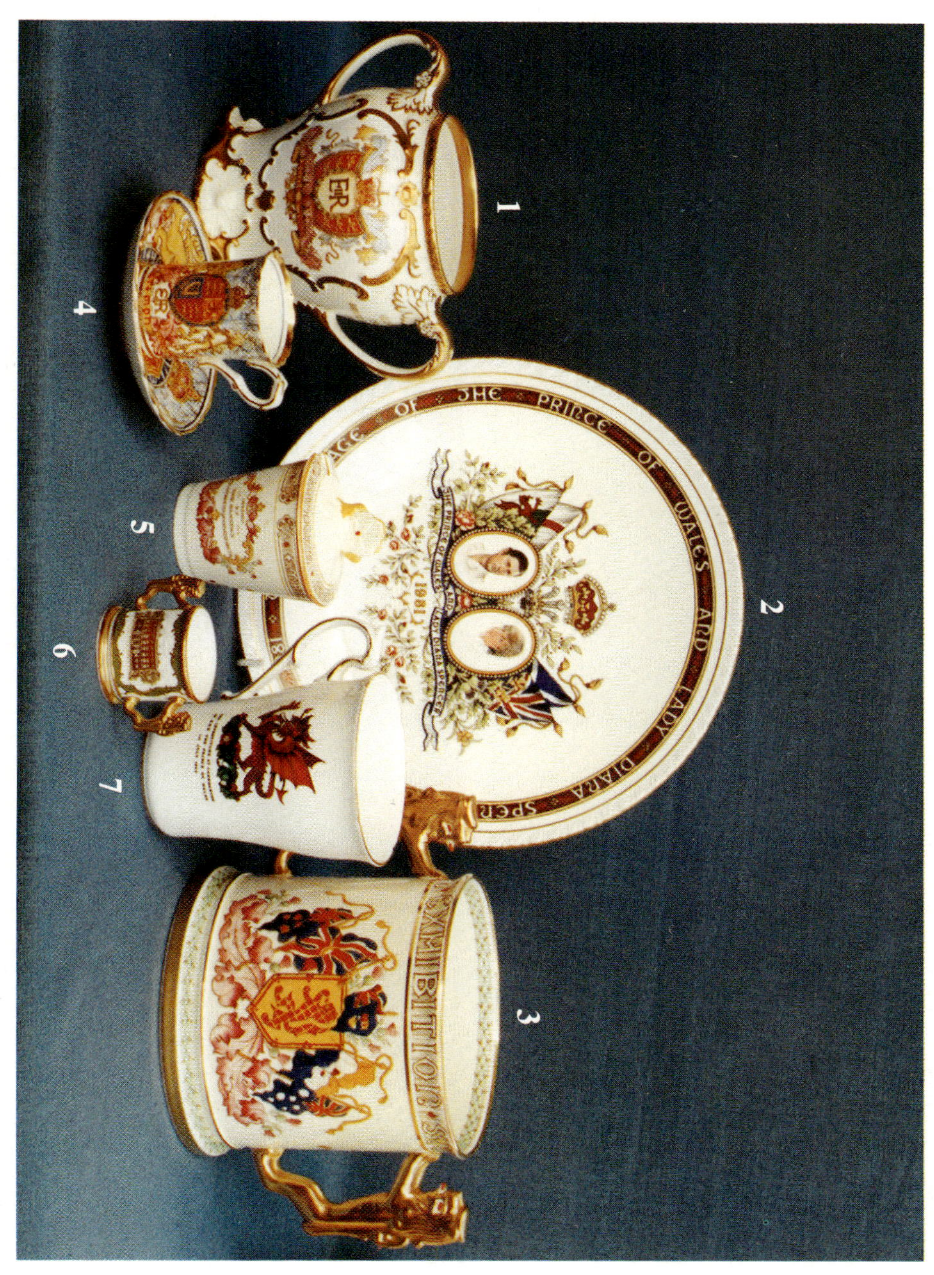

Commemoratives by Paragon

(see page 49)

Plate HH

Colour Plate GG (page 46)

Commemoratives by Minton

GG1 In 1952 Princess Elizabeth and the Duke of Edinburgh were to visit Australia. John Wadsworth designed this handled beaker (11cm) in a small limited edition of 100 to commemorate the event. The pale green ground has a gold coat of arms of Australia and inscription recording the details.

GG2 A large goblet (20cm) commemorating in 1939 the first visit of a reigning sovereign to the United States. The design bears some similar features to the beaker **(RR9)** together with raised moulded eagles in white around the stem and two gold lion handles. Made exclusively for W.H. Plummer, New York, and limited to 3000.

GG3 Produced in a limited edition of 750 to commemorate the christening of Prince William on 4th August 1982. Bunches of roses, thistles, daffodils and shamrocks decorate the outer border with an elaborately framed cypher dominating the centre of the plate (27cm).

GG4, 5, 6 John Wadsworth, Art Director of *Minton*, was responsible for many of the items made by the company for the 1953 coronation. Three coloured orbs (15cm) were designed in red, turquoise and cobalt blue, in a limited edition of 50 each. The white was limited to 600. The rich colours used have been complemented by the use of gold decoration and acid etched legend on the rim.

GG7 Reference has been made elsewhere **(526)** to the part played by *Mintons* in the design and production of the Queen's Beasts for the Queen's Vase, so it is no surprise that sets of the beasts (15.5 cm) should be subsequently made to commemorate the 1953 coronation. They were modelled by James Woodford OBE, RA, and were similarly rich in brilliant colours, with generous decorations of burnished gold. Each beast held a shield, as detailed below:

1 The Lion of Mortimer with the livery of the House of York and white rose.
2 The Yale of Beaufort with the Beaufort colours and crowned portcullis.
3 The Black Bull of Clarence with the Royal Arms from 1405 to 1603.
4 The White Greyhound of Richmond with Tudor livery and a crowned Tudor rose.
5 The Falcon of Plantagenets with the livery colours of the House of York.
6 The Lion of England with the Royal Arms of the United Kingdom.
7 The Griffin of Edward III with the badge of the House of Windsor.
8 The Red Dragon of Wales with arms associated with Wales.
9 The White Horse of Hanover with the Royal Arms of the United Kingdom from 1714 to 1800.
10 The Unicorn of Scotland with Royal Arms of Scottish Kings.

Each model bears the *Minton* backstamp, the name of the beast and the modeller James Woodford. A selection is shown.

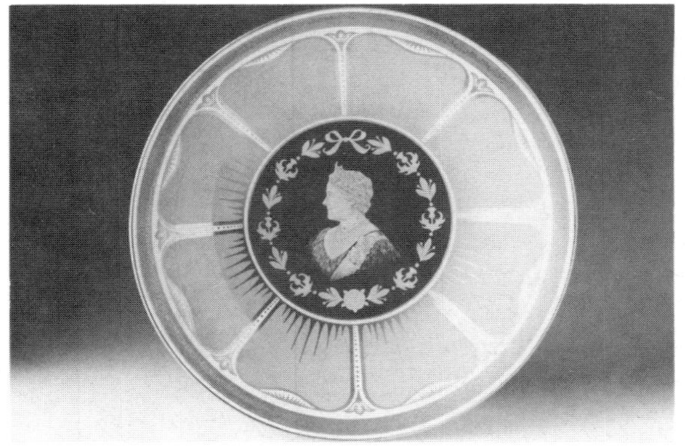

530

*530 *Minton* made this bowl (29cm) appropriately in a limited edition of 80 to celebrate the Queen Mother's 80th birthday. The portrait is framed against a deep red background with a broad border of pink. The rim is embellished in gold.

Colour Plate HH (page 47)

Commemoratives by Paragon

HH1 An outstanding example of the quality we have come to expect from *Paragon*. This Grecian urn (12cm) celebrates the coronation of Queen Elizabeth II and was probably made in a limited edition of 500, though not inscribed as such. Heavy gilding decorates the moulded frame, handles and foot. A

coat of arms is contained within a similar frame on the reverse.

HH2 This plate uses the same basic design as the loving cup **(607)** and commemorates the wedding of the Prince of Wales and Lady Diana Spencer. The intricate design, coupled with the rich colours, makes this one of the better plates produced for this occasion.

HH3 In 1938 King George VI and Queen Elizabeth opened the Scottish Exhibition at Bella Houston Park, Glasgow. A number of commemorative items were produced including some by *Paragon*. The loving cup (14cm) shows a Scottish lion within a shield with an inscription on the reverse. Also seen on a plate, pin tray and honey pot **(688A)**.

HH4 Considered by some *Paragon* collectors to be one of the most attractive pieces made, this coffee can (6cm) and saucer commemorates the coronation of Edward VIII and is almost identical to that later made for George VI **(E5)**.

HH5 A honey pot (9.5cm) commemorating the Scottish Exhibition in 1938. The rim of the lid is inscribed with the details of the event and the back (shown) records that it was opened by King George VI and Queen Elizabeth. Front the same as **(HH3)**.

HH6 A series of miniature loving cups (4cm) were sold in 1983/1984 in complete sets of 12 to commemorate royal birth places. Norfolk House, birthplace of George III is shown. Limited to 293 complete sets.

HH7 The tall mug (10.5cm) produced for the investiture of Prince Charles in 1969 is a companion to items shown in **(521)** and incorporates the shaped handle used for the cup.

*531 For the wedding of Princess Anne in 1973, *Paragon* issued this large (13cm) porcelain loving cup in an edition of 500. The front has a coloured design of entwined A and M in a floral frame, under which is designer A. Johnson's facsimile signature. The reverse bears the Princess' Arms, heralds' trumpets and wedding bells. Details of wedding dates etc are given under each gold lion handle. Unusually, this was the only piece issued by *Paragon* for the wedding.

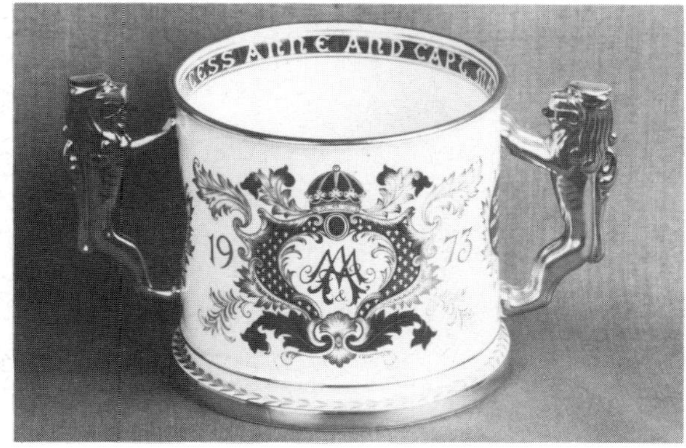

531

The Silver Wedding of Queen Elizabeth and Prince Philip • 1972 •

Princess Elizabeth as she then was, had married Lt. Philip Mountbatten on the 20th November 1947, just as Britain was emerging from the effects of the second World War. It was still a time of austerity with the production of decorative china for the home market still suspended. As mentioned elsewhere this resulted in few commemoratives being issued to mark the wedding.

Strangely, twenty five years later, despite the popularity of the Queen and her Consort, remarkably little commemorative china was produced to mark their silver wedding. The last time a Royal silver wedding had been significantly commemorated in ceramics was in 1888 – that of the Prince and Princess of Wales **(K1, K7)**. George V's anniversary fell in 1918 and George VI's in 1948 when on both occasions the country was still in the aftermath of a World War.

It was, however, a busy year for the Queen and Prince Philip. In February they travelled to the Gulf States and the Far East, visiting Bahrain, Malaysia, Singapore and Thailand. Princess Anne, already deeply involved with the Save the Children Fund, and who had been to Hong Kong earlier that year on her first "solo" official overseas assignment, accompanied them. Queen Juliana and Prince Bernhard of the Netherlands paid a State Visit to Britain in April. In May a State Visit to France took place, during which the Queen, Prince Philip and Prince Charles visited the Duke and Duchess of Windsor. This was the first time they had been so visited, and it was to be the last, for the Duke died shortly after, on May 28th 1972 **(803)**.

The Anniversary was marked by a State drive to the Guildhall and a Thanksgiving Service in Westminster Abbey to which were invited as many of the 100 couples who had been married on the same day as could be located.

*532 *Royal Worcester* produced two delightful pieces for the celebration of the silver wedding, one of which is this exquisite porcelain bowl (22.5cm). On the inside, a fine engraved medallion portrait of the Queen and Prince Philip surrounded by a floral wreath is on the base whilst ornate cyphers, coats of arms and an inscription encircle the inside. On the outside are detailed views of Buckingham Palace, Windsor Castle and Balmoral together with floral panels. The black and gold decoration combine to make this an outstanding example of the factory's work. Limited to 500. (The other piece is a sculpted group of doves produced in an edition of only 25.)

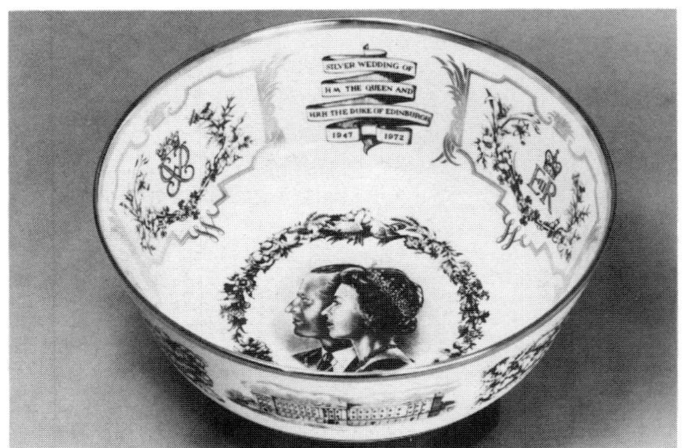

532

*533 Gilt silhouette portraits of the Queen and Prince Philip in a frame of lion and unicorn, printed in chocolate brown, are on the front of this waisted, porcelain mug (11cm) from *Crown Staffordshire*. A crowned EIIR and Prince Philip's cypher in gilt decorate the reverse. The edition is "limited".

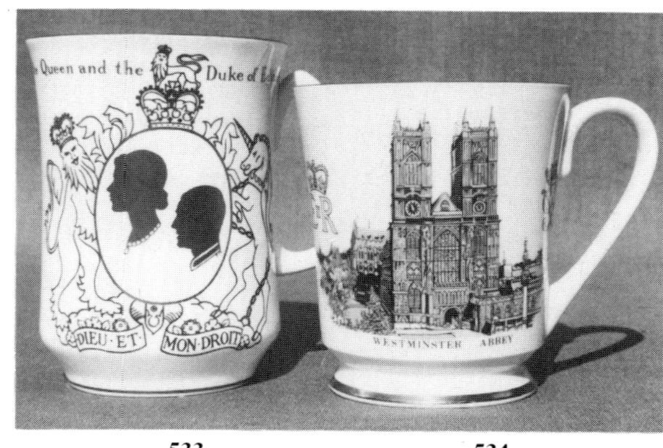

533 534

*534 A delightful colour print of Westminster Abbey and the cyphers of the Queen and Prince Philip decorate the *Aynsley* flared, porcelain mug (9.5cm). A commemoration of their wedding is on the reverse. Inside the rim is another marking the 25th Anniversary. Perhaps one of the prettiest of the modern *Aynsley* designs, always popular with collectors.

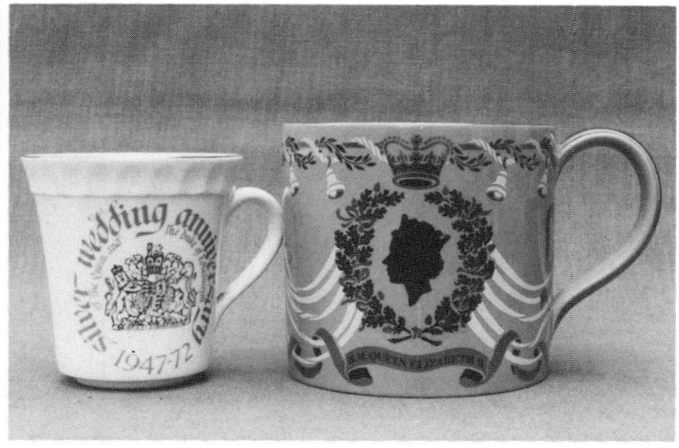

535 536

*535 *Wilsons* of Paignton made the shaped porcelain mug (9.5cm) showing a rose coat of arms contained within a blue inscription.

*536 The piece on the right is readily recognisable as a Richard Guyatt designed mug (10.5cm) for *Wedgwood* using the familiar pint size shape on a drab ground. The silhouette portrait of the Queen is in black with other decorations in gold and silver. The Duke of Edinburgh is shown on the reverse in a similar fashion. Made in an unlimited edition.

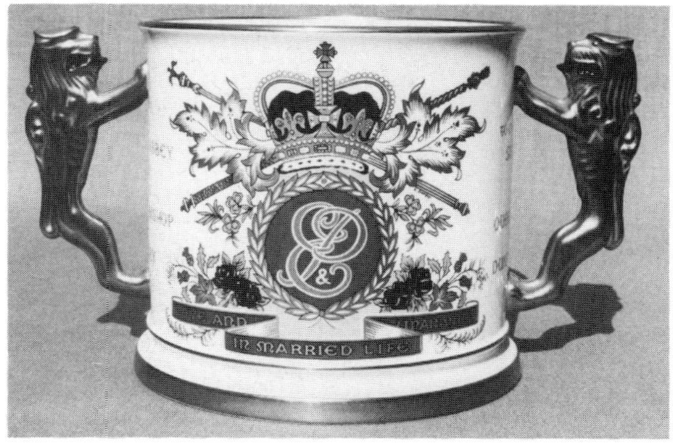

537

*537 This large porcelain loving cup (13cm) from *Paragon* is the only one in the series not to have the typical gold lion handles. These are in silver in honour of the Silver Wedding anniversary. The 1935 piece **(plate L)** had "plain" handles. The front bears entwined E and P beneath crown and sceptres, and above the inscription "Love and Unanimity in married life". On the reverse are the Royal Arms and on each side there are inscriptions commemorating the Wedding and Silver Wedding. The design is printed mainly in silver and blue with some colour added. A further inscription is inside the rim. The edition is of 750 and each piece is numbered.

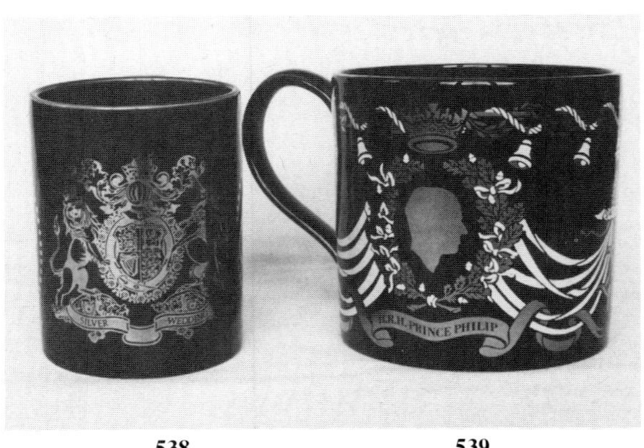

538 539

*538 *Portmeirion Pottery* produced this pottery mug (10.5cm) which has a deep blue body on which are the Royal Arms, the cyphers of Prince Philip and the Queen all printed in silver. An ornate handle completes the decoration of this distinctive mug.

*539 This pottery mug (10.5cm) designed by Richard Guyatt for *Wedgwood* is one of the series produced in glazed black basalt. The design is the same as that on **(536)**, but here is printed in white with raised gold. Limited to 500.

*540 Shown here is the small (8cm) porcelain loving cup from *Paragon*. It has silver handles and the same design as **(537)** but was issued in an unlimited edition. The reverse is illustrated.

*541 This heart-shaped porcelain box (10cm) is made by *Aynsley*. The top has a colour picture of Westminster Abbey whilst the cyphers of the Queen and Prince Philip decorate the front. A full commemoration is on the base.

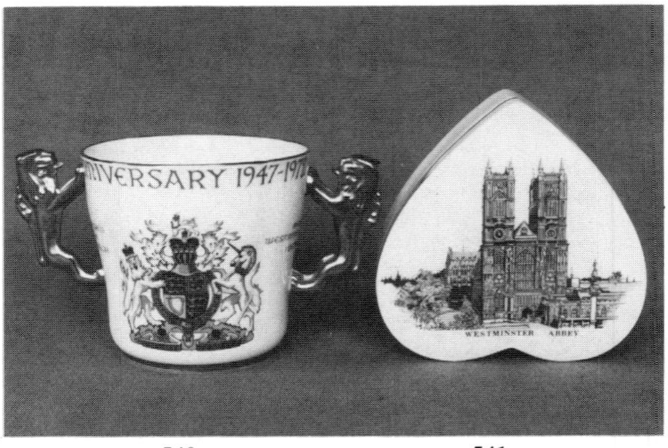

540 541

*542 The porcelain loving cup (16 cm) produced by *Spode* for this occasion, is the first in their series of royal commemoratives to use this body and shape. Later issues in 1977 **(JJ8)** and 1980 **(Cover)** continued the same style. This piece has portraits of the Queen and Prince Philip in ovals surrounded by raised, gilded scrollwork. On the reverse are the Arms of the Queen and Philip framed in garter belts. The cup is mainly maroon with highlighting in gilt. Inside the rim a further inscription commemorates the Silver Wedding. The edition is of 500 with each piece numbered.

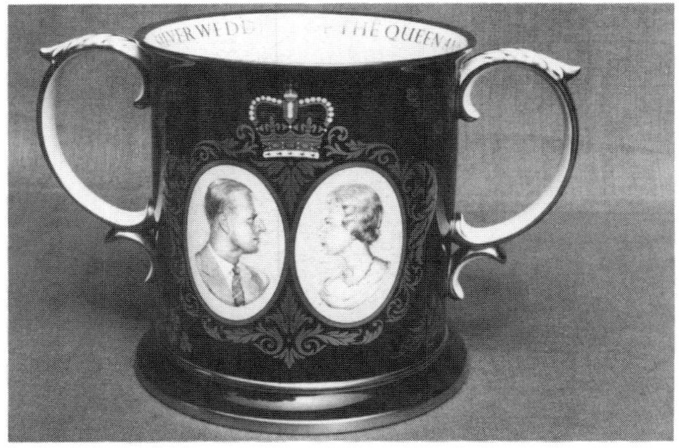

542

The Wedding of Princess Anne & Capt. Mark Phillips • 1973 •

HRH The Princess Anne, second child and only daughter of Queen Elizabeth and Prince Philip, married Captain Mark Phillips at Westminster Abbey on November 14th 1973. The date was chosen by Princess Anne, it is said, as a special compliment to Prince Charles who celebrated his 25th birthday on the same day. Captain Phillips was an officer in the 1st Queen's Dragoon Guards. The couple shared a common interest in equestrianism, he becoming a member of Great Britain's 1972 Olympic team which won a Gold medal and Princess Anne, a 1972 winner at Burghley, and later also an Olympic team member.

Princess Anne was the first of the Queen's children to marry, and the ceremony was shown in colour on television. Anne however had determined that the wedding was to be restrained in tone and she had only two attendants, Lady Sarah Armstrong-Jones as bridesmaid and Prince Edward as pageboy.

Despite the popular interest, there was not a great selection of commemorative ware produced. *Wedgwood* issued a Guyatt Queensware mug **(548)** and two blue jasperware items, whilst *Royal Doulton* only produced a black basalt bust **(544)**. Paragon produced a large loving cup in their traditional manner **(531)** but did not issue a small version. However those pieces that were made available showed a refreshing diversity ranging from the very "designy" mug from *J & J May* **(547)** to the simple but effective "free hand" portraits on the *Crown Staffordshire* plate **(553)**.

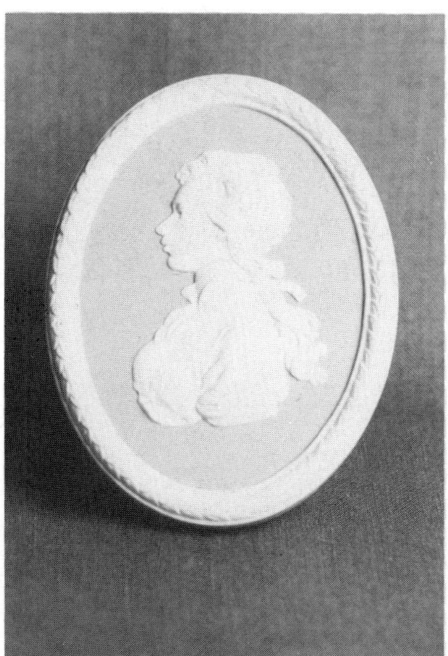

543

*543 This light blue jasperware plaque (11cm) with applied moulded decoration is in the long tradition of *Wedgwood* plaques issued to commemorate impor - tant events and personages. This example, in an edition of 2000, has a very fine, detailed bust of the Princess within a border of laurel.

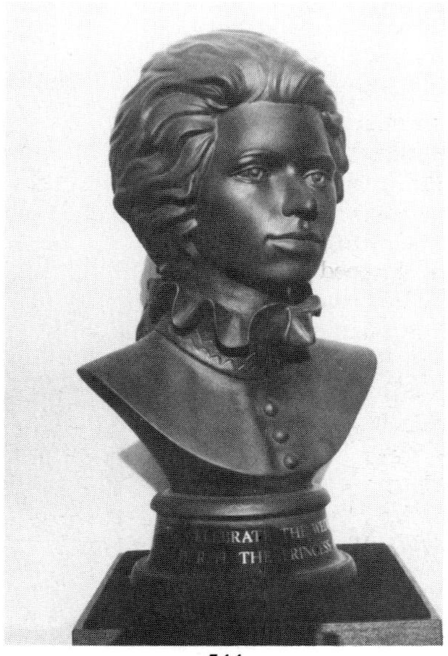

544

*544 *Royal Doulton* produced this black porcelain bust (29cm) of the Princess in an edition limited to 750. An inscription in gilt "To celebrate the wedding of HRH The Princess Anne...November 14th 1973" is on the base. The princess is depicted in a high collared blouse with lace trim. No matching bust of Captain Phillips was made.

*545, *546 Both these betrothal mugs (9cm) are a matching pair since they only vary in small detail. That on the left shows the hands in blue with inscription in red whilst the other shows the horseshoe and riding crop in red with inscription in blue. In both cases the reverse records the birth dates of Princess Anne and Lt Mark Phillips in blue and red respectively. A broad moulded rim is gold lined. Produced by *Wilson's* Paignton.

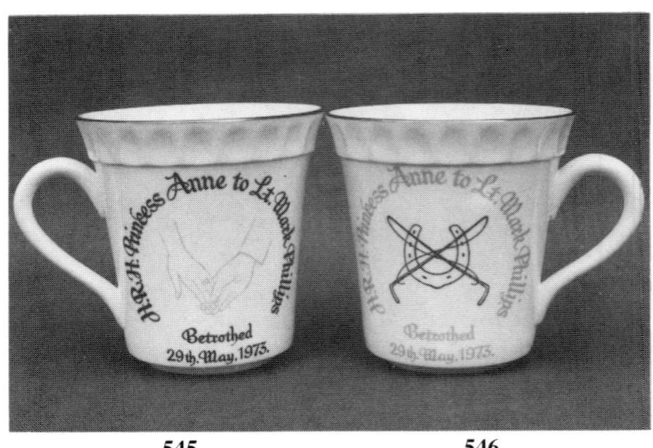

545 546

*547 Clifford Richards designed this stylish pottery mug (9cm) for *J & J May*. Red hearts contain profiles of Anne and Mark on one side and wedding details on the other. Horse riders encircle the foot beneath Westminster Abbey and the Houses of Parliament. An orange sun rises over the scene, which has an almost oriental look. This example has an overprint on the base "Preserved from assasination 20th March 1974".

*548 Gold wedding bells hang from garlands whilst red and blue swags link the date in blue, with black profiles of Anne and Mark in separate laurel frames. A gold bow ties the ribbons at the handle. *Wedgwood* pottery mug (10.5cm) designed by Richard Guyatt.

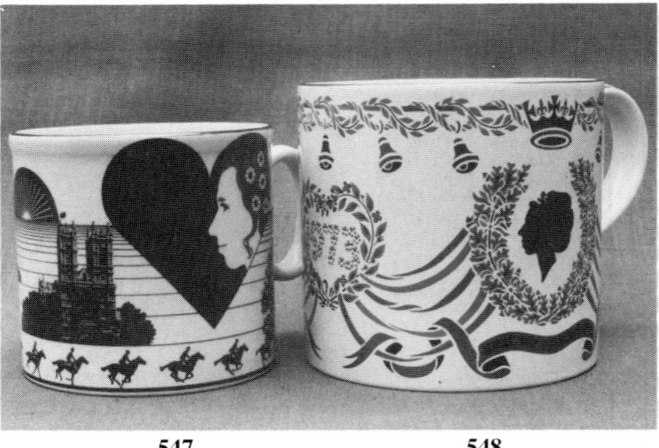

547 548

*549 A colour transfer print of Anne and Mark in oval frames of laurel, surmounted by wedding bells decorates the front of a porcelain mug (9.5 cm) from *Aynsley*. On the reverse an inscription with horseshoe and bells. "The marriage of Her Royal Highness the Princess Anne" is inside the rim.

*550, *551 Two porcelain mugs (both 9.5cm) by *Crown Staffordshire*. In the centre a flared shape with moulded body, on which are light brown silhouettes, within green laurel. Coloured horseshoe/whip and bells are on the reverse. Marked "Royal Wedding souvenir. A limited edition". The other mug of waisted form has "drawn" profiles in light brown in a colourful frame. A full inscription is at the back.

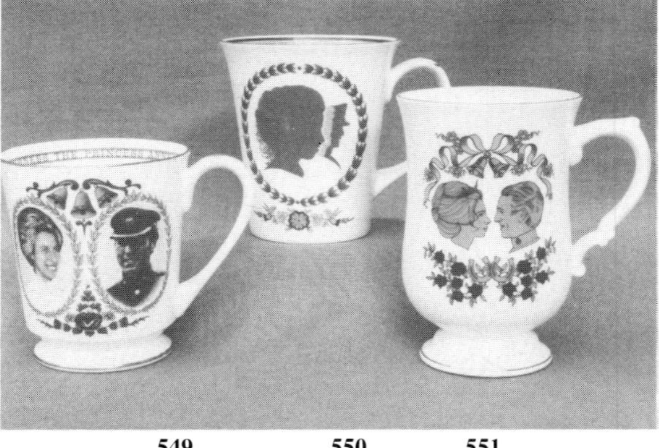

549 550 551

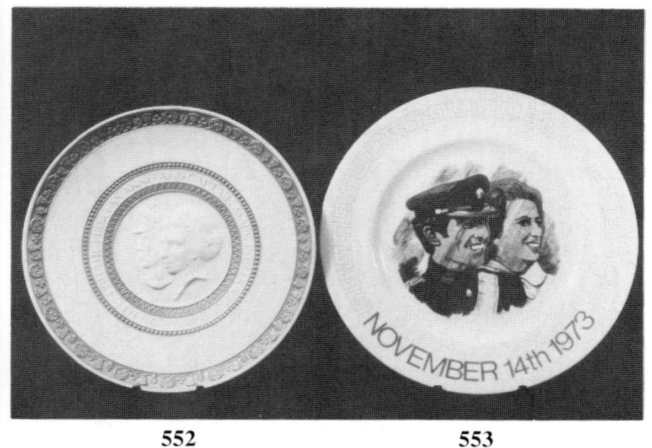

552 553

*552 The Heritage Collection commissioned this pretty porcelain dish (19cm) from *Hutschenreuther* of Germany. The body is a soft pink with relief moulded profiles of Anne and Mark and wedding inscription in the centre. Rim decoration of national flowers, and the two circular frames for the portraits are gilded. This restrained use of colour results in elegant simplicity. Limited to 125.

*553 An interesting approach to the portraits can be seen on this pottery plate (20cm) from *Crown Staffordshire*. "Freely drawn" in sepia this informal picture captures a very happy couple. With minimum of colour and decoration, a striking effect is obtained. Marked "A limited edition".

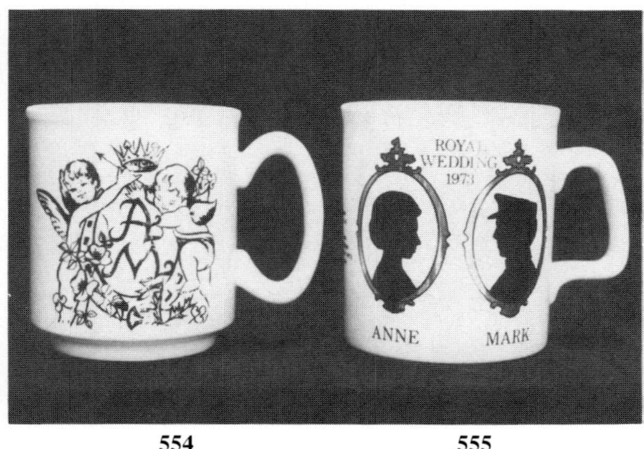

554 555

*554 Illustrated here are two "cheap and cheerful" pottery commemoratives which have a certain appeal. The unmarked mug on the left (9cm) has a pair of cupids holding arrow, coronet and horseshoe over entwined "A" and "M". On the back is a wedding inscription. The print here is black on a blue body, also seen in other colours.

*555 This example (9.5cm) has silhouette profiles of the couple in black within gold oval frames. On the reverse they are seen mounted on horseback. A wedding inscription is at the side. Made by *Staffordshire Potteries*.

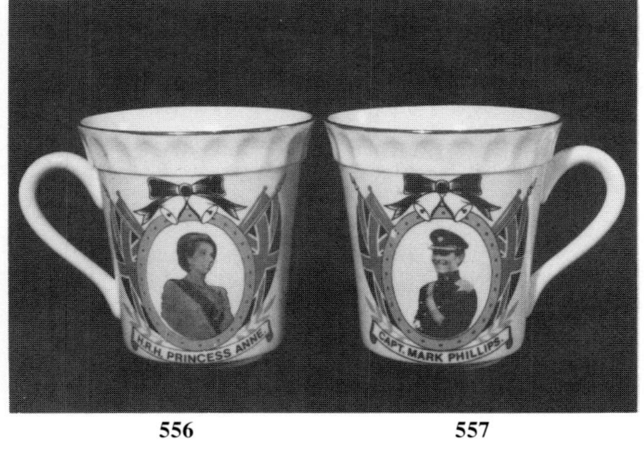

556 557

*556, *557 An interesting pair of matching shaped mugs made for the wedding of Princess Anne and Captain Mark Phillips by *Wilson's* Paignton. The portraits are in black and white, flanked with flags and wedding bells above. A black and white picture of Westminster Abbey is featured on the reverse with an inscription which reads "November 14th 1973, to commemorate the wedding of Princess Anne and Captain Mark Phillips". The broad moulded top rim has a silver edge. A similar matching pair of mugs were produced for their betrothal **(545) (546)**.

Queen Elizabeth II Silver Jubilee • 1977 •

The first 25 years of the "new Elizabethan era", as some have dubbed it, produced unparalleled progress in science and technology, rapid changes in social attitudes and advances in communications which increasingly placed the royal family under the scrutiny of the popular press. Constitutionally the monarchy embraced the emergence of a Commonwealth from the old style Empire and the implications of closer links to Europe with Britain's entry into the Common Market **(591)**. On a more personal level, Prince Andrew and Prince Edward were born, Prince Charles became Prince of Wales and Princess Anne was married **(547)** and gave the Queen and the Duke of Edinburgh their first grandchild in Jubilee year **(728)**.

Considerable interest and enthusiasm was shown for the Jubilee events which took place throughout the year. As well as the overseas tour and home countries visits of Her Majesty and the Duke of Edinburgh **(580)**, an abundance of gala concerts, sporting events and civic functions took place, culminating in the royal procession on Jubilee Bank holiday. Exhibitions with a royal flavour were popular with two in particular of interest to the ceramic collectors. The Commemorative Collectors Society staged an exhibition of items made for the Jubilee and, at the Bethnal Green Museum, pieces from the Blewitt Collection were on show. Both produced catalogues titled "Jubilee Royal" and "Jubilation" respectively, which have become increasingly useful as reference material for collectors.

Restrictions on the use of royal coats of arms and cyphers on souvenirs were relaxed but commemoratives had to be in good taste and free from advertisement or implication of any royal patronage. Though the Design Council mounted an exhibition of souvenirs in January 1977, there was nevertheless no officially approved list and in the "Jubilee Royal" catalogue more than 200 ceramic pieces were itemised. All the major manufacturers were involved as well as many of the small factories. A special Jubilee appeal fund was launched and contributing manufacturers were allowed to use a special emblem **(574)** on their wares.

Predictably, with such a large number of items produced, the quality and design covered the full spectrum. Portraits **(570)** **(575)** and coats of arms **(562)** **(577)** were predominant, with some of the other more interesting ideas coming from the cheaper end of the market. In keeping with tradition, and with collectors in mind, Coalport **(572)** and Wedgwood **(JJ10)** repeated popular shapes. There was no shortage of pieces for the more expensive taste with a trophy vase **(DD2)** from Aynsley and lavishly decorated loving cups from Paragon and Spode. Something different was a boldly designed vase **(605)** from Poole Pottery and a pair of delightful candlesticks from Minton. In all a vast selection which perhaps spoiled the collector for choice.

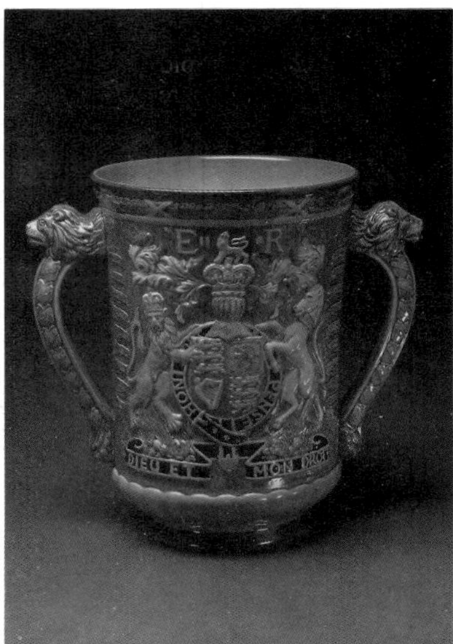

558

*558 *Royal Doulton* produced this beautiful large porcelain loving cup (26.5cm) in an edition of 250. The reverse shown here has the Royal Arms with cypher above. On the front is a half length portrait of the Queen in coronation robes framed within flags and inscriptions. The handles are decorated with lions' heads and small shields contain names of Commonwealth countries. All details on the loving cup are moulded and coloured with rich enamels. Designed by Reginald Johnson.

*559 This *Crown Staffordshire* plate (27cm) was designed by J.A. Bailey and limited to 1500. A large coloured portrait against a black background is embellished with a broad white and gold border.

*560 The *Aynsley* plate (27cm) shows a coloured coat of arms below which is the familiar "Kings and Queens of England" list used by this manufacturer **(460)**. A broad pale blue border is decorated in gold and contained within an outer and inner gold band with the latter bearing an inscription.

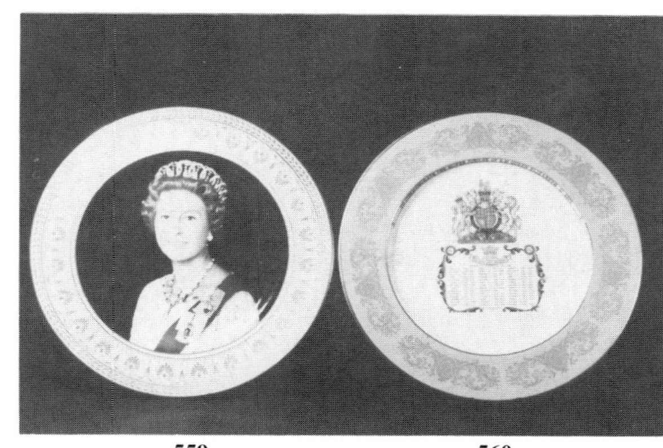

559 560

*561 Both *Spode* and *Royal Doulton* have chosen a coat of arms in the design of their Jubilee mugs (10cm). Extensive use of gold, red and blue is used by *Spode* with the emblems on the upper border in purple, pink and green. A broad gold band extends around the base and on the moulded handle.

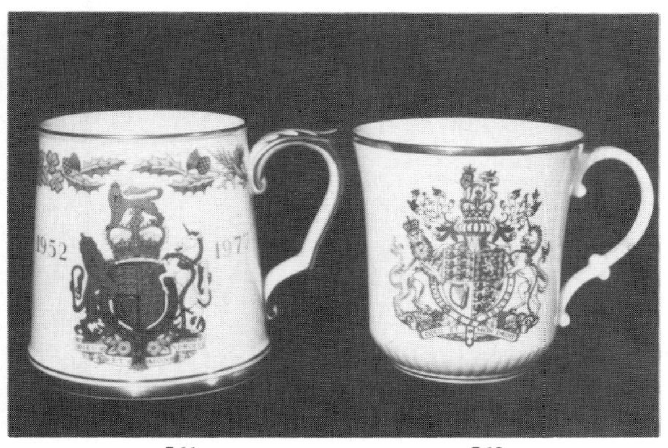

561 562

*562 By contrast, *Royal Doulton* have only used gold for their Arms with a gold inscription recording the Jubilee event on the reverse. A fluted base and flared top presents a less traditional design.

*563 *Royal Staffordshire* made this porcelain loving cup (9cm) bearing a colourful coat of arms and inscription. Gold lining to rim, foot and the ornate handles adds to the quality. A transfer the same as that used by *Carlton* on the front of the kneeling mug **(574)** is on the reverse. It is, of course, not unusual to find the same transfer repeated by different manufacturers.

*564 Moulded handles lined in gold and bearing the accession and jubilee dates are a particular feature of this porcelain loving cup (8cm) made by *Aynsley*. Similar shaped handles were used again for the Aynsley 1981 wedding mug **(638)**. The front shows a coloured coat of arms whilst the reverse lists the Kings and Queens of England **(560).**

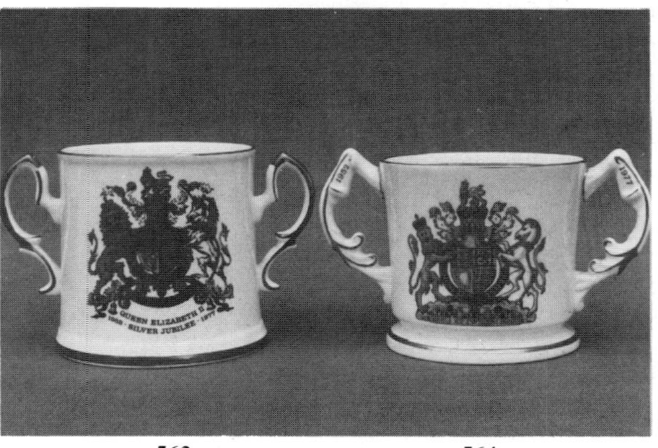

563 564

*565 Two very different Silver Jubilee items. On the left is a jug (22cm) made by *Burleigh* and shows the crowning ceremony in relief, against a pale turquoise ground. Westminster Abbey, also in relief, is shown on the reverse. Historical details of the Gothic chair and reference to the artist, E.T. Bailey, are incorporated into the backstamp.

*566 The other is a vase (22cm) from *Crown Devon* bearing a coloured royal coat of arms on white against a cobalt blue ground. Rims to foot, waist and top are gilded.

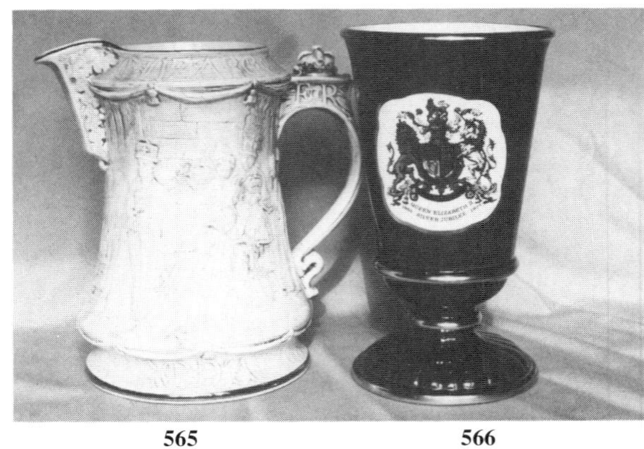

565 566

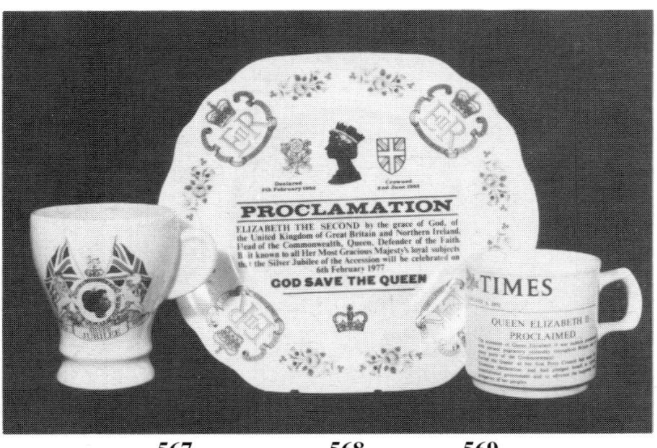

567 568 569

*567 This pottery mug (10.5cm) which has a colour transfer on the front and an ear for a handle, tells its own story on the rear; "This Jubilee mug was presented to you by Ovaltine and Woman's Own because you were born in the week February 6th-12th 1977 ,the Silver Jubilee of Queen Elizabeth II"

*568 The porcelain plate (23cm), made by *Newcastle upon Tyne China*, carries the proclamation statement for the Jubilee as well as the Accession and Coronation dates, all printed in black.

*569 The masthead of the "Times" for 9 Feb 1953 together with an excerpt from the Court Circular printed in silver is the unusual decoration on this pottery mug (8cm) by *Kaleidoscope*.

*570 To celebrate the Silver Jubilee review of the army in July 1977 *Wedgwood* produced this mug (12cm). A formal coloured portrait with inscription decorates the front, with the reverse showing a Union Flag and NATO flags together with a dated inscription. Limited to 15000 it was widely distributed to the British Army of the Rhine.

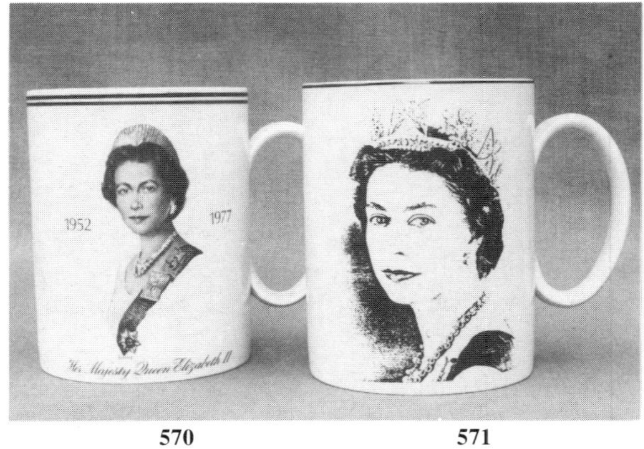

570 571

*571 Lord Snowdon designed this 1 pint mug (12cm). The overall front and back decoration is in black with a royal coat of arms and inscription on the reverse. Also from the *Wedgwood* factory.

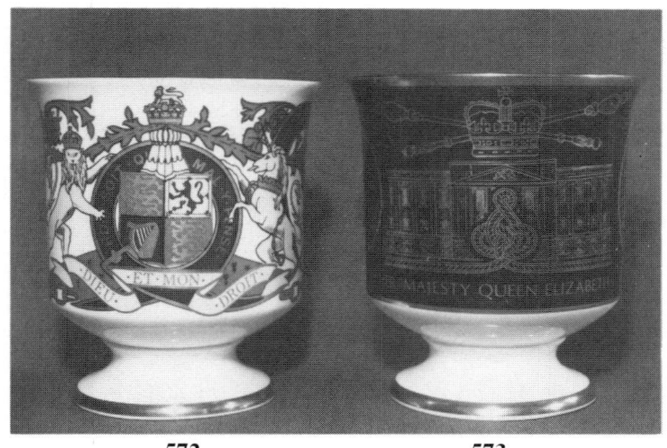

572 **573**

Coalport produced a variety of items for the occasion including three versions of their porcelain goblets (12cm). Two are shown here. Both in numbered editions of 2000.

*572 The Royal Arms, together with three garter belts containing the rose of England, profiles of Elizabeth and Philip, and national emblems with "Tria Juncta in Uno" symbolising the United Kingdom form a continuous design. Blue and ivory with gilt highlights. An inscription is inside the rim.

*573 This example has a cobalt blue ground with gold design featuring Westminster Abbey, Buckingham Palace and Caernarvon Castle. Profiles of the Queen, Prince Philip and on the reverse Prince Charles are included.

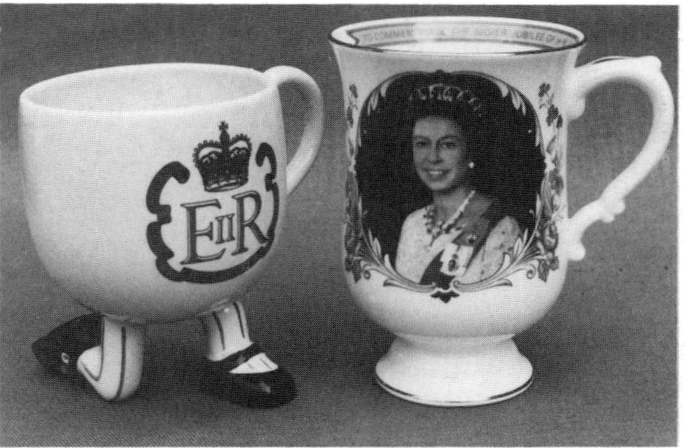

574 **575**

*574 This novelty pottery kneeling mug (10.5cm) was made by *Carlton Ware* who designed mugs in a similar vein for the 1981 wedding **(608) (655)**. A cypher, crown and inscription is the only decoration apart from black strapped shoes.

*575 This porcelain mug (12cm) shows a formal head and shoulders portrait of the Queen surrounded by coloured national emblems. An inscription in pink reads "1952 Silver Jubilee 1977" on the reverse with a similar inscription on the inside rim. Made by *Crown Staffordshire*.

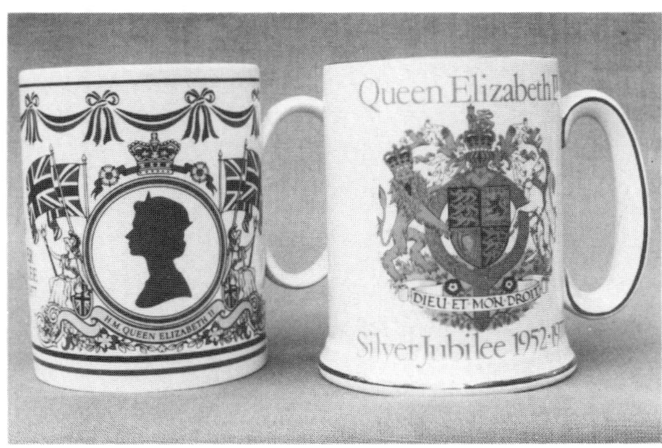

576 **577**

*576 A straight-sided pottery tankard (12cm) with a very colourful design. Silhouettes of the Queen and Prince Philip are in frames, supported by Britannia and flags. Designed by Keith Williams for *Wedgwood*.

*577 There is a rather heavier body to this pottery tankard (12cm) from *Wood and Sons*. The Royal Arms in colour decorate the front whilst the reverse carries the official Silver Jubilee emblem in blue.

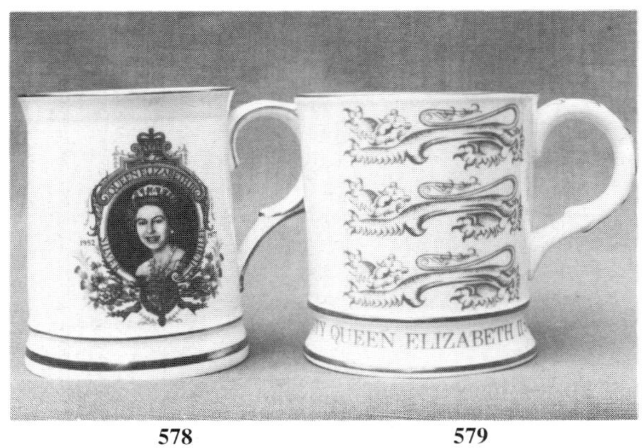

578 **579**

*578 There is little of intrinsic merit in this porcelain mug (11cm). It illustrates, in our opinion, the sad decline of one of the most collectable names in royal commemoratives – *Hammersley.* This example uses the same commonly-met printed transfer on both front and rear, and has some silver trim on rim, foot and handle.

*579 The Ironbridge Gorge Museum Trust commissioned this interesting porcelain mug (10.5 cm) from *Coalport.* The three lions of England dominate the front whilst the message "Success to Trade, Peace & Plenty, Coalport for ever. God Save the Queen" are printed in script on the reverse. All in purple on white. Edition of 1000.

These two pottery mugs were produced to mark the Review of the Fleet by the Queen at Spithead on June 28th. Both are 9 cm tall with the same printed transfer on the front as that on the *Hammersley* piece above **(578)**.

*580 From an un-named pottery shows a colour print of HM Yacht Britannia.

*581 *The Lord Nelson Pottery* example, has HMS Tiger (venue for talks on Southern Rhodesia Independence). There is a fleet of ships on the front. Printed in black on a brown ground this design was also produced on a tankard and plate and with various ships and naval crests.

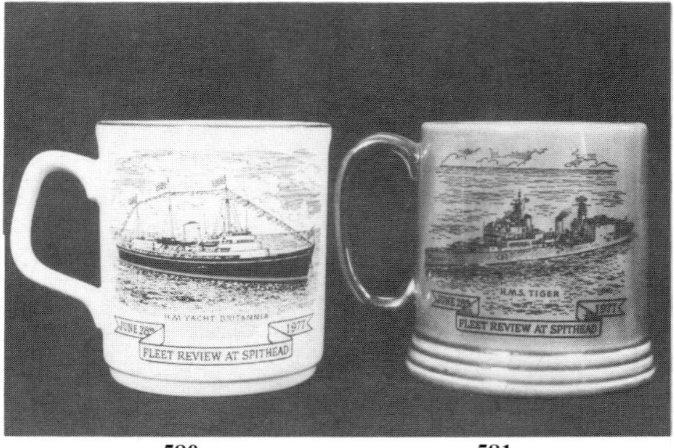

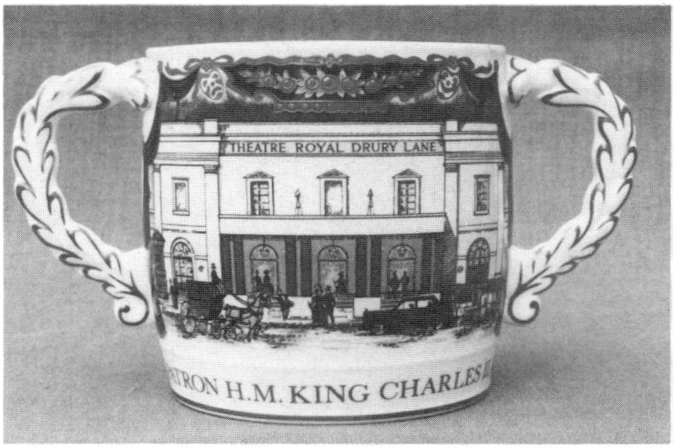

580 **581**

582

*582 *Coalport* made this highly decorative, porcelain loving cup (10.5cm) to a commission from the Royal General Theatrical Fund Association in an edition limited to 1000. On the reverse, shown here, is a beautiful colour print of the Theatre Royal Drury Lane. In gold "1st Patron HM King Charles II 1663". The front is at **(JJ5)**.

*583 A cheerful, informal portrait of the Queen and Duke of Edinburgh within a frame of laurel appear on this distinctive pottery mug (9cm) from *Tamsware*. On the reverse a printed EIIR cypher.

*584 A full colour transfer of the Union flag, and national flowers surmounted by a crown together with a sepia portrait of the Queen decorate the front of this unmarked pottery mug (7.5cm). The reverse has a colour transfer showing a viking ship with the caption "Gods Port our haven".

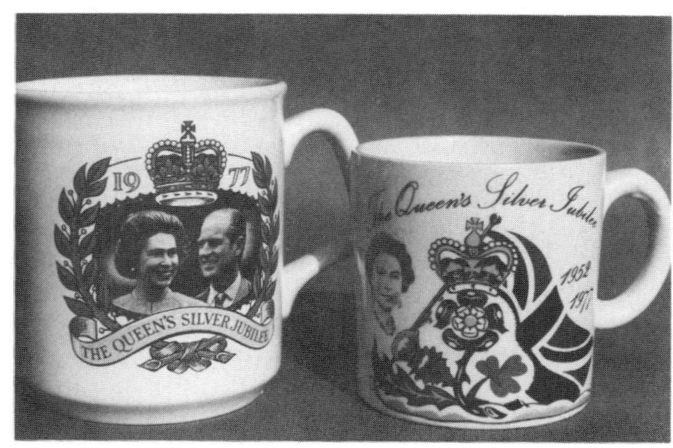

583 584

*585 A gold crown and EIIR cypher both on a deep red background with an ornamental black printed cartouche and inscription decorate the front of this porcelain cup and saucer (7.5cm) from *Springfield*. A gold crowned cypher and inscription are on the reverse.

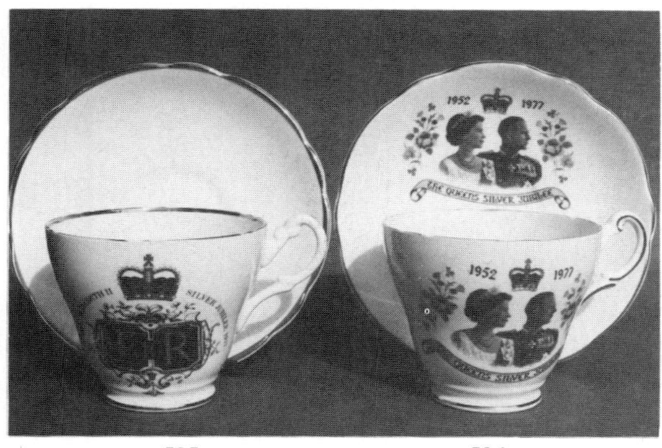

585 586

*586 This porcelain cup and saucer from *Regency China* is the same as **(585)** with different decoration. Here there is a full colour portrait of the Queen and the Duke, national flowers and inscription. The reverse has a crown, 1977 and "Jubilee Year". These two sets are typical of the inexpensive but attractive teaware produced for the occasion.

*587 *588 Illustrated here are two examples of the many attractive studio pottery pieces issued for the event. They are hand made, often with very individual designs but are perhaps not appreciated yet as much as they should be. The dish on the left (17.5cm) has a dark green body with the piped decoration in yellow. Embossed monogram "MW". On the right another dish (16.5cm) has a body colour of ochre with the piped decoration in dark brown. Monogram "DX".

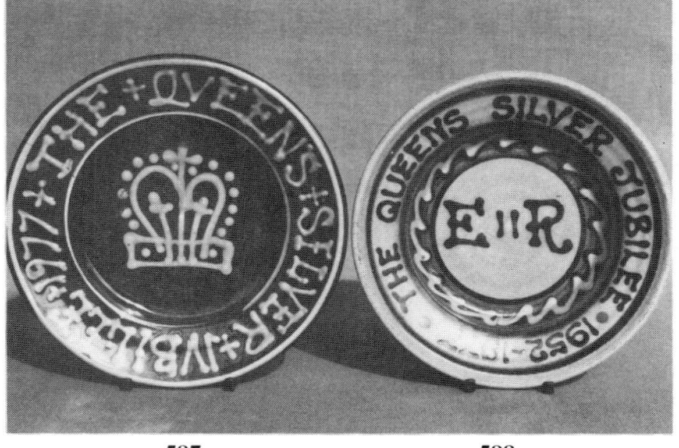

587 588

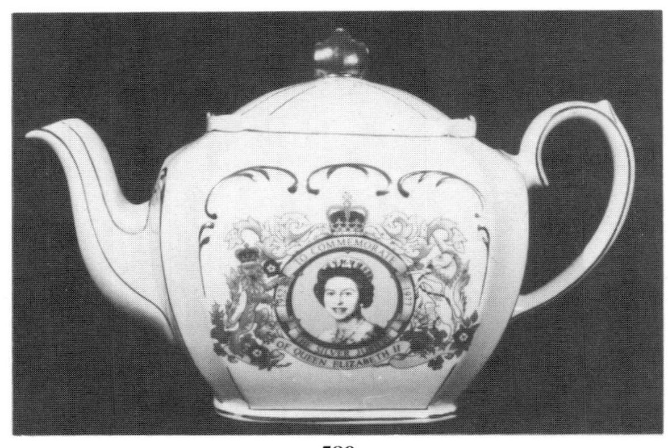

589

*589 This pottery teapot (15cm) has a colourful printed design with a portrait of the Queen in a circular frame supported by lion and unicorn, decorative scrollwork and national floral emblems. The reverse has a crown and flowers in colour. All the moulded, raised lines on the body, handle and spout have been picked out in silver, as has the crown finial on the lid. Made by *Sadler* who have given a very decorative treatment to this commonly met transfer.

Two porcelain plates (both 27cm) from *Mercian China*.

*590 The Commemorative Collectors Society commissioned a series of nine plates to mark the Jubilee. This one has a full colour transfer illustrating the Queen surrounded by her senior Legal Lords. The plate was designed by A. Kitson Towler and produced in a limited edition of 60.

*591 Similar in style, this plate has a colour transfer showing the Queen together with other Heads of State of the European Community. The border has the flags of the member states. The matching plate of the pair shows the Heads of Government. Only 25 sample plates were produced as the full scale project fell through.

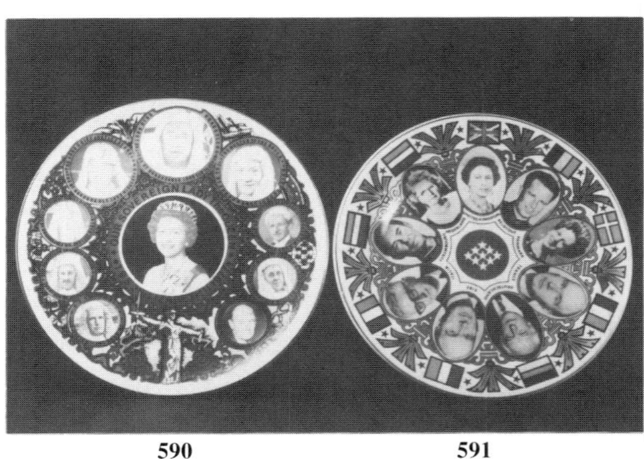

590 **591**

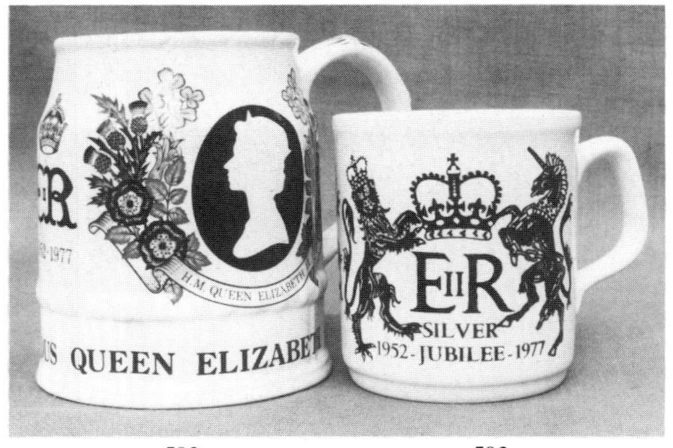

592 **593**

*592 *Masons* produced this tall (11.5cm) pottery tankard. The design, printed in red, has a crowned cypher on the front, with white medallion profiles of the Queen and Prince Philip in red ovals on either side. Coloured national flowers frame the portraits.

*593 Another striking design consisting of the lion and unicorn supporting a crowned cypher, all in red, decorates this unmarked pottery mug (9cm). Simple yet well designed.

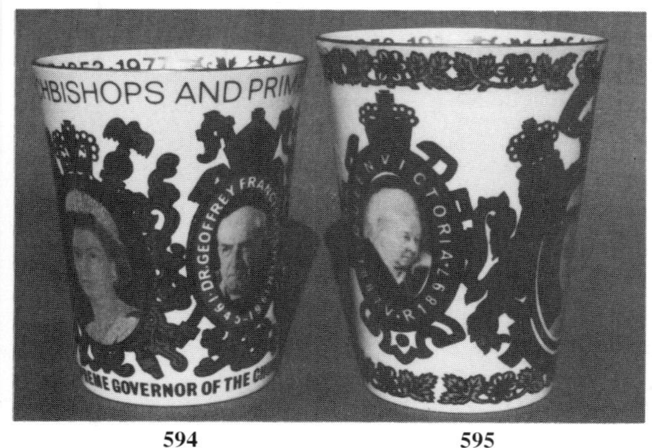

594 595

*594 Illustrated are two from the set of four porcelain beakers commissioned from *Mercian China* by the Commemorative Collectors Society. That on the left (10cm) records the three Archbishops and Primates of all England between 1952-1977.

*595 "Jubilees Royal" is the title of the other (11cm) which records three previous monarchs who had celebrated Jubilees: George III, Victoria and George V. Two other beakers featured Masters of the Queens Musick and Poets Laureate. Designed by Kitson Towler.

*596 A really cheerful pottery mug (8.5cm) from *Adams*. A very pretty black print of Pearly Kings and Queens dancing, forms a continuous decoration with the title "Jubilee greetings from the Pearly Kings and Queens of London". Signed Polly. On the base "Derived from an original design by Pearl Binder...".

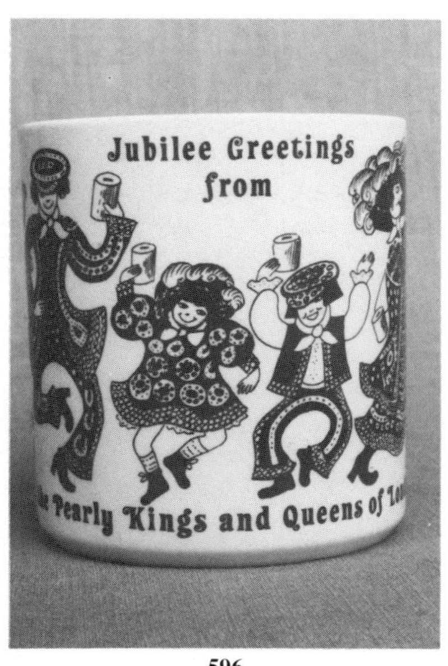

596

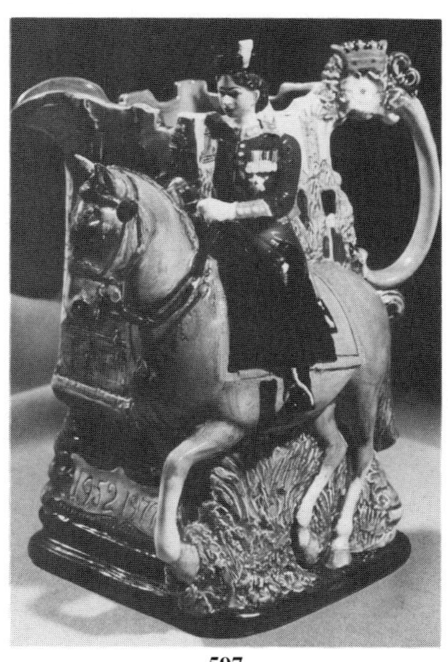

597

*597 This pottery jug (27.5cm) is another example of the interesting items made by *Burgess & Leigh* **(see 439)**. Designed by Ernest Bailey in an edition of only 25 pieces, the jug features Her Majesty on horseback at the Trooping of the Colour ceremony. St Pauls Cathedral, Westminster Abbey and the Palace of Westminster are on the reverse. A detailed inscription on the base explains the reasons for the ceremony, celebrating the Queen's official birthday.

*598 *Royal Worcester* produced this elegant porcelain plate (25cm) in an edition limited to 2000. The Royal Arms and inscription in the centre are in gold whilst the wide rim is in pale blue and black.

*599 *Holkham Pottery* made this Jubilee mug (11cm) in a limited edition of 250 for Scotts China Shop, King's Lynn. The royal family has a close association with the town it being so near to Sandringham House. A gold cypher, crown and inscription is mounted against a blue ground glaze.

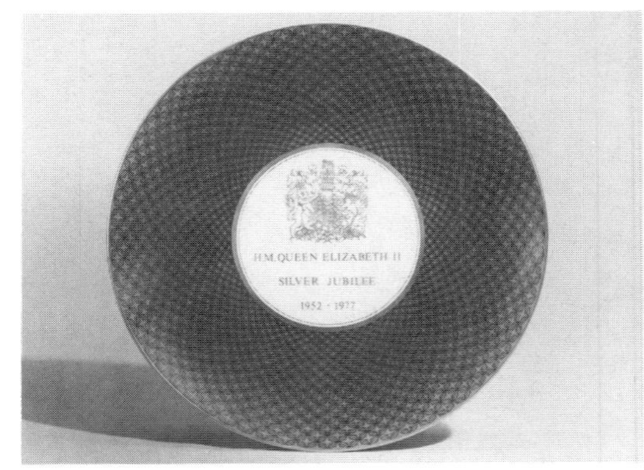

598

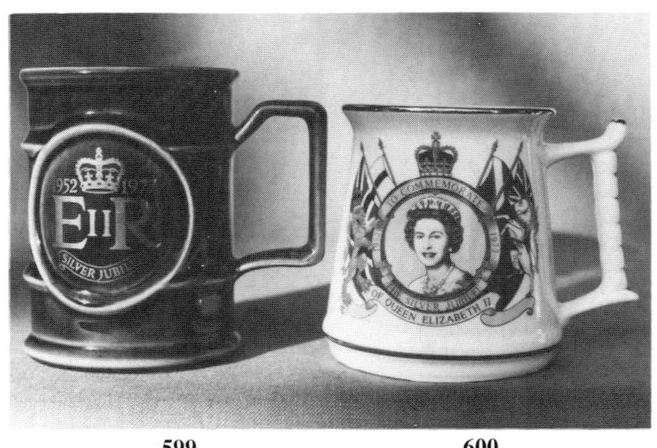

599 600

*600 Multi-coloured flags surround the sepia portrait of the Queen on this porcelain mug (10cm). A banded inscription is flanked by the royal beasts. No potter's mark is shown but the reverse is inscribed "Old English Night Delamare Lodge No 8529 Bro Allan Oakes W.M. 1st November 1977". A collectable Masonic item of the future.

*601 Another in the series of pottery mugs (10cm) designed by Richard Guyatt for *Wedgwood*. This example has a gold and black printed design featuring profiles of the Queen and Prince Philip in heart shaped frames with lion and unicorn on either side. "God Save the Queen" in gold is printed inside. A similar version all in black with platinum trim was issued as well as a black basalt edition limited to 500.

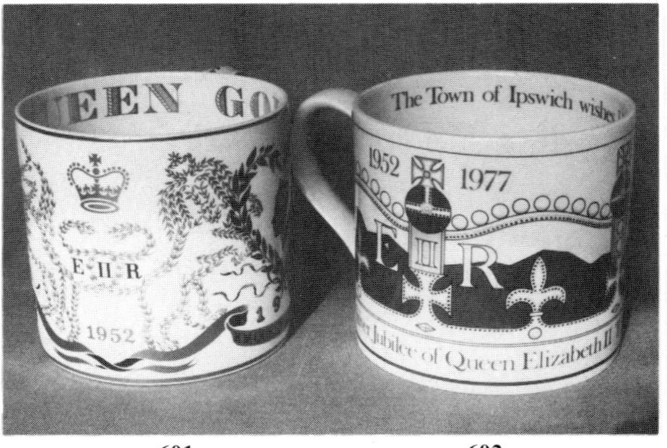

601 602

*602 This pottery mug (10cm), designed by the Suffolk College of Higher and Further Education, commemorates the Queen's visit to Ipswich in her Jubilee Year. A printed purple crown forms a continuous design round the mug, with dates and inscription. Inside "The Town of Ipswich wishes Her Majesty a long, happy and peaceful reign".

*603 *Wedgwood* produced this very colourful, pottery plate (26cm) which has a blue printed silhouette of the Queen in the centre surrounded by Guards, Household Cavalrymen and Heralds in full colour. The border has the first verse of the National Anthem in white beneath a frieze of Maltese crosses. Panels of national flowers separate the figures.

*604 This much simpler, porcelain plate (21cm) comes from the *Elizabethan* company. A well printed, full colour Royal Arms decorates the centre whilst Silver Jubilee cyphers are placed around the ivory coloured border. The rim has a silver line.

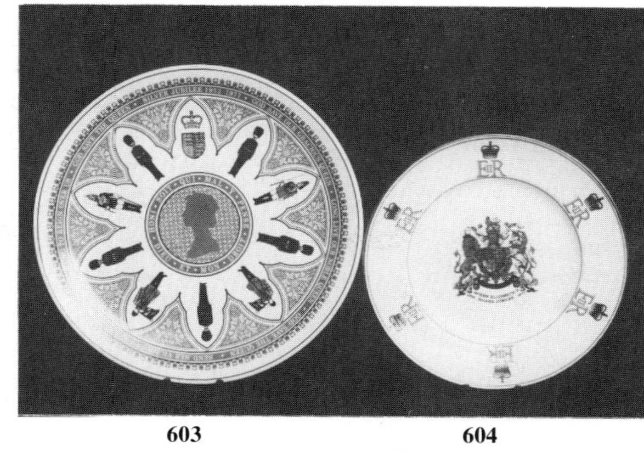

603 604

*605 *Poole* has produced here a most unusual and impressive vase (25cm). It has a "bronzed" finish with very detailed moulded lion and unicorn on front and rear which are highlighted in black. The rim is encircled with flowers and EIIR cypher and 1952-1977.

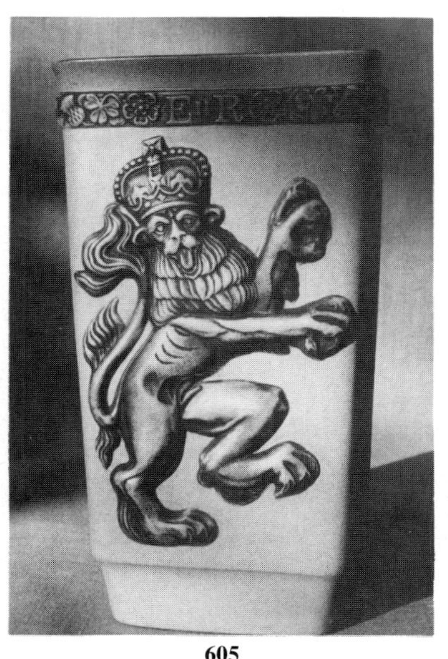

605

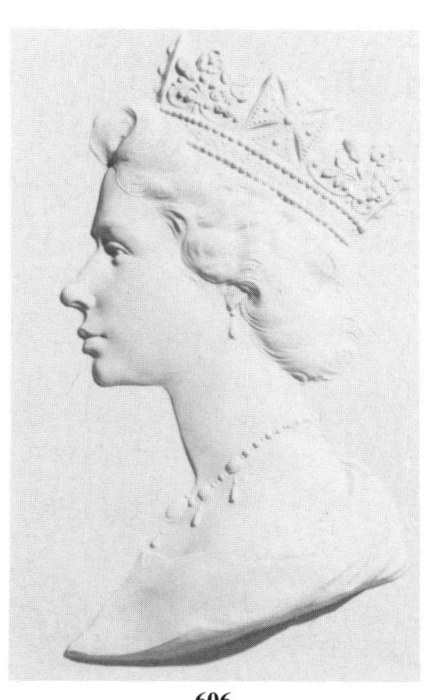

606

*606 *Royal Worcester* produced this ivory coloured porcelain plaque (55cm) designed in bas-relief by Arnold Machin. A very similar crowned profile of the Queen, by Machin, had become world famous as that used on British definitive postage stamps from 1967 until 1990. The plaque was limited to 1000 pieces.

The Wedding of Prince Charles and Lady Diana Spencer • 1981 •

On 24 February 1981 the Queen and Duke of Edinburgh announced the betrothal of the Prince of Wales to Lady Diana Spencer, thus ending months of speculation from the press and heralding what was to become the most public wedding of all time. After the engagement Lady Diana attracted immense attention from the media with a plethora of material produced on almost every aspect of her life.

Historians were quick to link the Royal House of Windsor with the Spencer family through lines of succession dating back to Henry VII in 1457. It also emerged that a very much more recent association was formed with Diana and the royal children when, as a child, she lived in Park House next to Sandringham House. It was several years later that Prince Charles and Lady Diana were to renew their acquaintanceship.

The marriage was planned for 29 July 1981 at St Pauls Cathedral, a somewhat surprising choice of venue. All attention in the ensuing months was focused on the arrangements and details of that one important day. Prince Andrew and Prince Edward were to be his supporters (best men) in keeping with royal tradition, and there would be five bridesmaids and two page boys. The Royal Naval Cookery School was commissioned to make the cake and the wedding dress was designed by two comparatively unknowns, Elizabeth and David Emanuel.

The day itself lived up to all expectations, with every aspect of the royal procession and ceremony described in graphic detail and seen by millions on colour television throughout the world.

In true tradition, souvenirs of all kinds were sold in the months leading up to the event. The Commemorative Society, in association with the Observer Newspaper, organised an exhibition at the Guildhall, Windsor, of royal wedding commemoratives dating back to Queen Victoria's marriage in 1840. Of course the potters were equal to the occasion with every major manufacturer making a contribution. Improved technology enabled them to reproduce bold clear photographic portraits **(615)** **(652)** which gave pieces a "modern feel". A method of applying a photographic portrait to ceramics, developed by Patrick Boston, was favoured by Panorama **(629)** and the inevitable coats of arms and Prince of Wales feathers were incorporated to a greater or lesser extent in almost every design.

Photographs taken at the time of the betrothal **(650)** were popular with even the engagement ring receiving special attention **(615)**. A few more enterprising manufacturers chose to wait for the post-ceremony pictures of Princess Diana in the much talked about wedding gown **(632)**. Of the quality items, a covered chalice **(KK7)** a loving cup **(607)** and vase **(FC6)** immediately come to mind. But finally the grand public occasion was given a sense of proportion by the fun pieces produced by *Carlton* **(610)**.

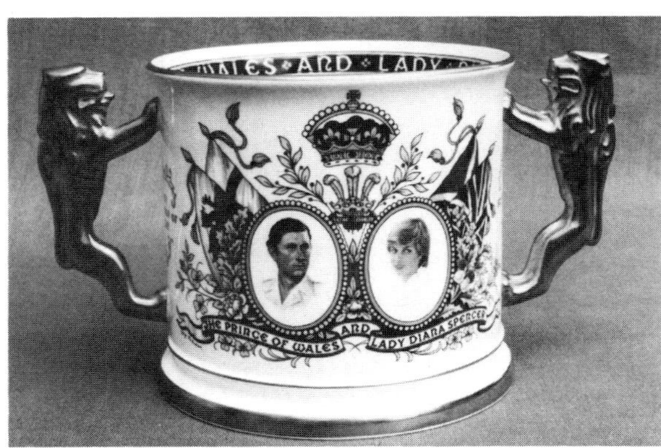

607

607 *Paragon* have used the same shape for this loving cup (13cm) as for that used to celebrate the Queen Mother's 80th birthday **(MM8)**. Portraits, national flags, crown and inscription are in suitable colours. On the reverse a coloured coat of arms incorporates the three feathers and dragon. Lion handles, foot and rim are all in gold. Limited to 750.

*608 Three fun pieces from *Carlton* which, because of their novelty, must become collectors' favourites in the future **(655)**. The pottery mug (11cm) in the centre shows conjoined portraits against a background of coloured emblems. On the reverse a red dragon is mounted similarly against national emblems. Entwined hearts form the handles.

*609 *610 A matching pair of standing pottery mugs (13cm) show separate portraits of the couple. Coloured ribbons and hearts decorate the sides, whilst the boots are coloured white and black respectively. An inscription on the reverse details the event.

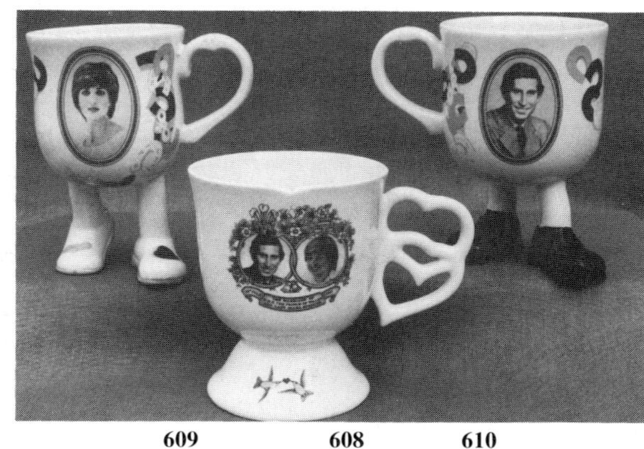

609 **608** **610**

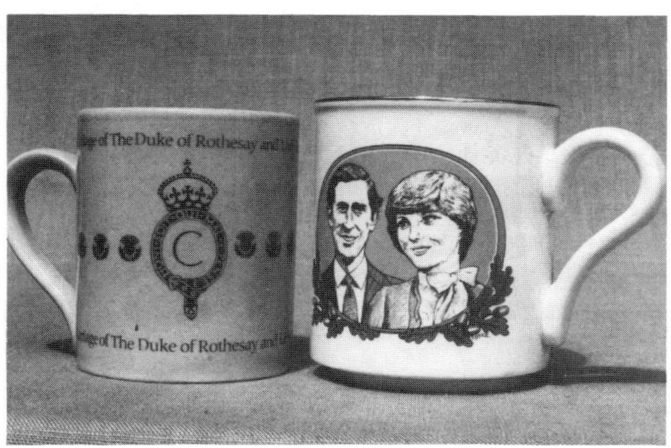

611 **612**

*611 Two unusual pottery mugs which mark the wedding of the Prince under his other titles. That on the left (9cm), a brown bodied mug from National Trust of Scotland marks "the Marriage of the Duke of Rothesay and Lady Diana Spencer". Blue printed thistles and a "C" within a garter belt together with inscriptions are the sole decoration.

*612 The one from *Arthur Wood* (9cm) has a black printed portrait of the couple on a blue ground on the front whilst the inscription on the reverse offers loyal greetings to "The Duke and Duchess of Cornwall" on the occasion of their wedding.

*613 Issued in a limited edition of 5000 this porcelain loving cup (8cm) by *Doulton* shows sepia portraits of Charles and Diana framed within a gold decorated heart. A similar heart frames a spray of daffodils on the reverse. An inscription in gold is shown on the inside rim.

*614 *Highland Fine China* produced this small unusual porcelain mug (7.5cm). Gold profiles of Charles and Diana are shown against a blue background within a circular frame. The reverse shows the Prince of Wales feathers in blue. A broad blue patterned border between narrow gold bands and a gold lion handle complete the design.

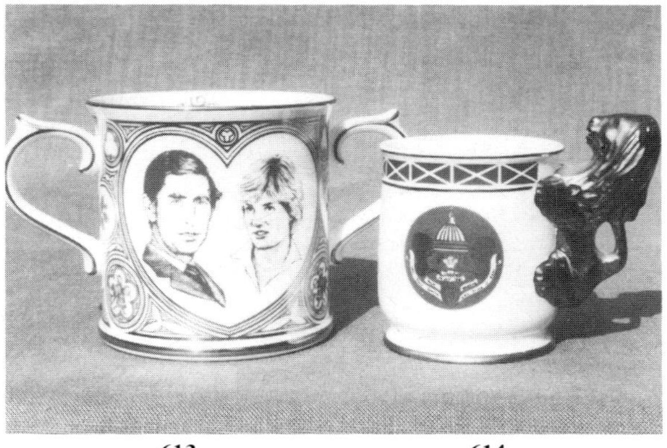

613 **614**

*615 Charles and Diana's portrait is printed in colour and framed by national flowers in gold on this flared porcelain beaker (10cm) from *Caverswall*. The reverse has a close-up of Diana's engagement ring. There are also doves, national flowers and C and D with coronets all in gold. This "Royal Betrothal Beaker" was issued for the engagement on 24th February 1981.

*616 The matching *Caverswall* beaker celebrates the wedding. Sepia portraits of Charles and Diana are surmounted by Prince of Wales feathers and doves. The reverse has boldly coloured shields carrying the Arms of Prince Charles and the Spencers.

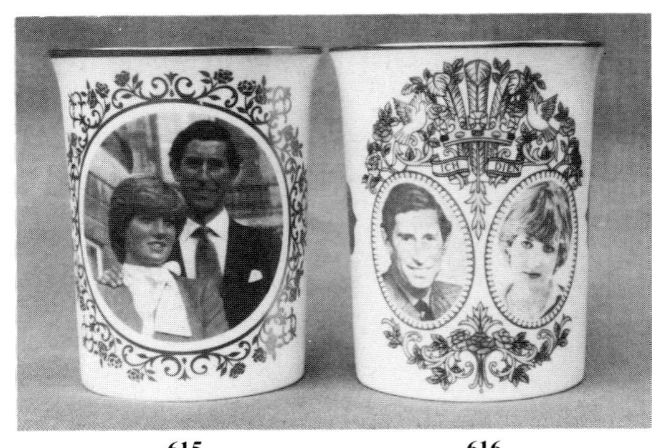

615 **616**

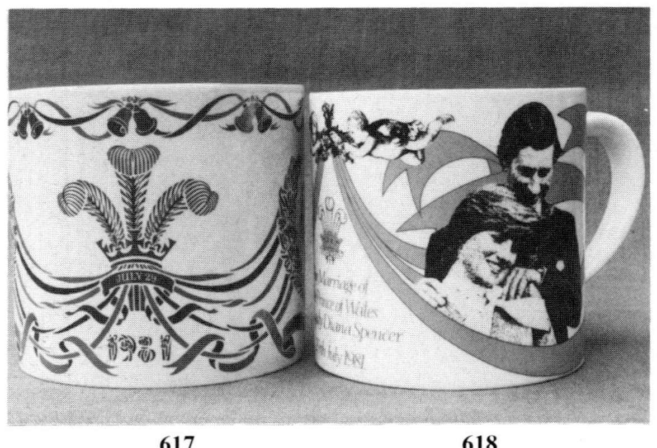

617 **618**

*617 *Wedgwood* issued three versions of the mug (10.5cm) designed by Richard Guyatt. The designs are the same, consisting of the Prince of Wales feathers flanked by profiles of Charles and Diana in frames of laurel. Ribbons and bells encircle the rim. Illustrated is the Queensware version with the design in blue, in an edition of 3000. Another, in blue and gold, was limited to 1500. The black basalt edition was 250.

*618 "The Observer" commissioned this pottery mug (10.5cm) from *Crown Staffordshire*. Black printed portraits of Charles and Diana are on either side of mustard coloured swags, held by cupids, which frame the wedding inscription. Designed by Guyatt and Jenkins

*619 The Commemorative Collectors Society commissioned this porcelain plate (27cm) from *Coalport* in an edition of 500 pieces. Colour portraits of Charles and Diana are surmounted by Prince of Wales feathers and date of the wedding. The rim shows dragons, entwined C and D, and the Arms of Charles and the Spencer family.

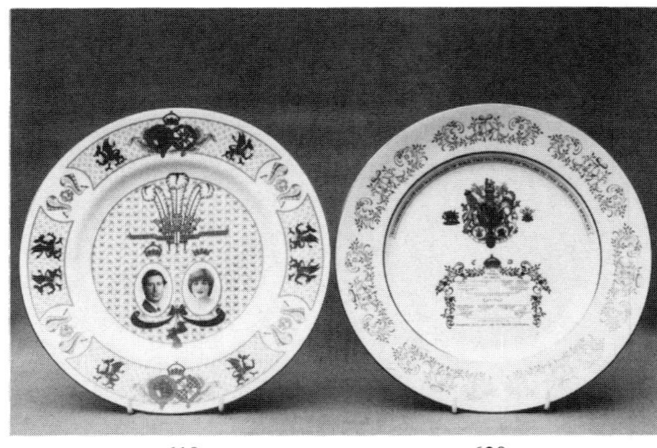

619 **620**

*620 The personal Arms of Prince Charles in full colour over the family trees (as far back as grandparents only) of Charles and Diana are the key features in the design of this porcelain plate(27cm) by *Aynsley*.

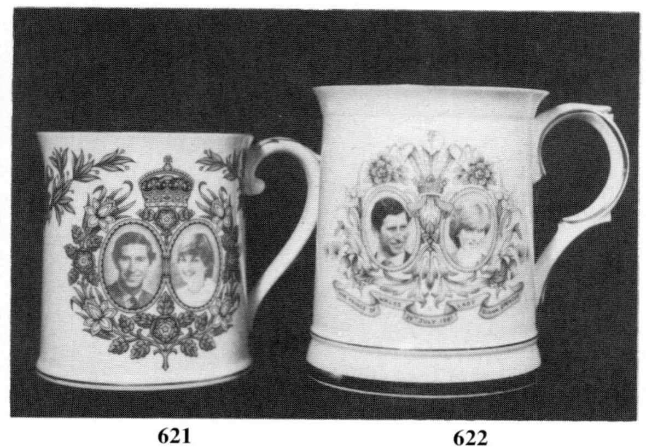

621 622

*621 Two informal sepia portraits are framed within a garland of foliage, roses and daffodils and surmounted by a crown on this porcelain mug (9cm). An inscription on the back reads "To celebrate the wedding of His Royal Highness Charles Prince of Wales to Lady Diana Spencer, St Pauls Cathedral 29th July 1981". Backstamp for *Spode*.

*622 This tall mug (11cm) by *Hammersley* shows framed coloured portraits of Prince Charles and Lady Diana dominated by the traditional three feathers. Emblems in shades of pink, blue and yellow complete the design. A suitable inscription records the event on the reverse. Gold lining to base and handle enhance the quality.

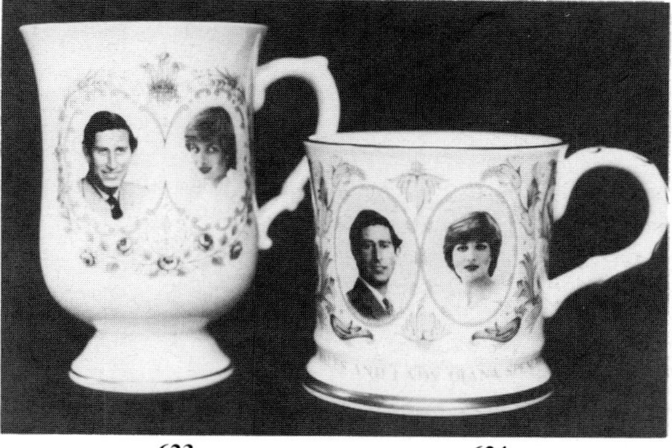

623 624

*623 Informal portraits of the bride and bridegroom are shown against a floral design comprising the national emblems in yellow, pink and green. Individual coats of arms appear on the reverse. An inscription on the inside rim records the date. *Crown Staffordshire* produced this tall porcelain mug (12cm).

*624 Framed coloured portraits against a white ground decorate this attractive porcelain mug (8cm) from the *Coalport* factory. Extensive use is made of gold lining to the foot, rim and moulded handle, with an inscription around the base.

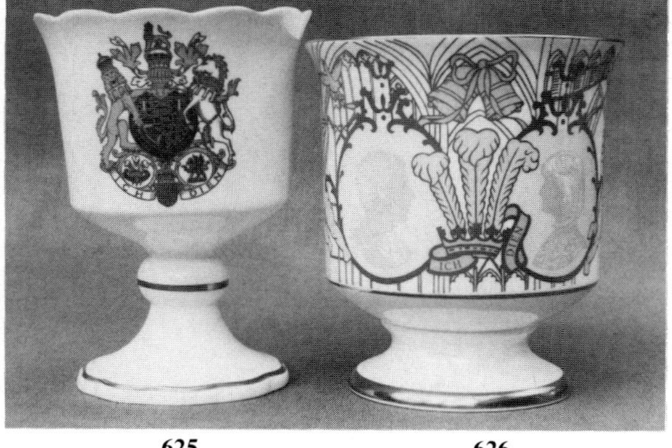

625 626

*625 A raised gold Royal Arms decorates the front of this very pretty porcelain goblet (13cm) from *Royal Worcester.* A print of St Pauls with inscription is on the reverse. Inside the scalloped rim "A toast to long life and happiness" in gold.

*626 This white, porcelain goblet (11.5cm) by *Coalport* was issued in an edition of 2000. Turquoise profiles of Charles and Diana are separated by Prince of Wales feathers, and surmounted by bells and doves. A stylised garter belt and cupids are on the reverse. All the delicate filigree work is in raised gold.

*627 Lord Snowdon and Carl Toms designed this pottery mug (12cm) for *Wedgwood* in a limited edition of 5000. The Prince of Wales feathers and foliage are predominantly in green. An inscription and cyphers complete the design.

*628 *Wedgwood* made this pottery mug (8.5cm) for one year only. An elaborate design in blue, together with a red heart, frames black and white profiles of Prince Charles and Lady Diana. Similar hearts frame the traditional three feathers and cyphers.

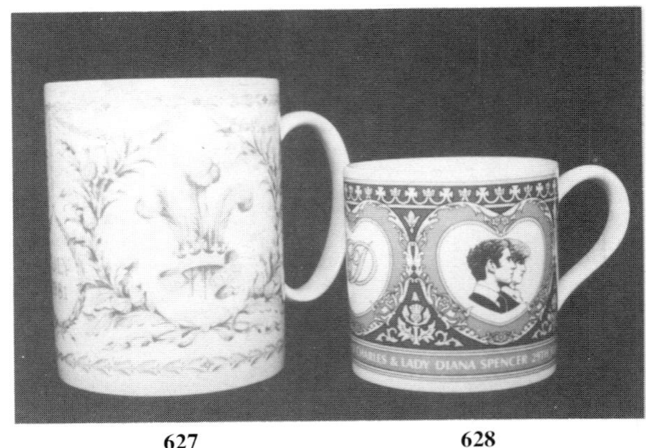

627 628

*629 *Panorama Studios* produced this porcelain mug (10cm) which is full of interesting detail. The front has a printed portrait of Charles and Diana (which we have not seen used elsewhere) set within a Garter belt. Dragons, Prince of Wales feathers and C and D cyphers encircle the rim. On the reverse is given a list of participants in the ceremony including groom's supporters, bridesmaids and pages. Edition of 500.

*630 This pottery goblet (11.5cm) from *Prinknash* has small black printed portraits surrounded by an inscription, bells and Prince of Wales feathers in gold.

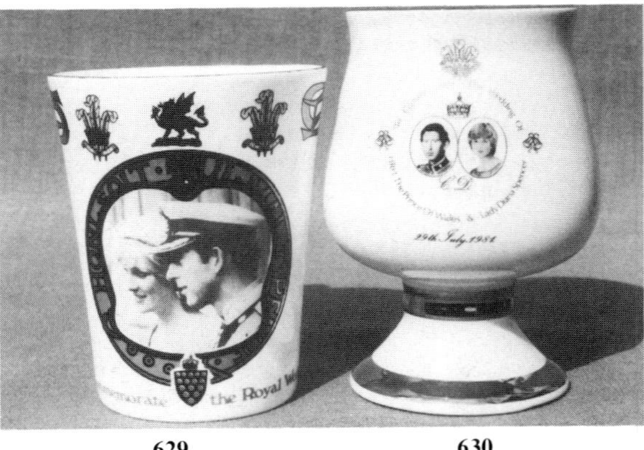

629 630

*631 Parian busts and figures of royalty **(161) (C3)** have been popular subjects for manufacturers for more than 150 years and have again become firm favourites with collectors recently. *Poole Ltd* produced these busts (11.5cm) for the wedding in a limited edition of 2000. The back of each bust bears the Prince of Wales feathers in relief.

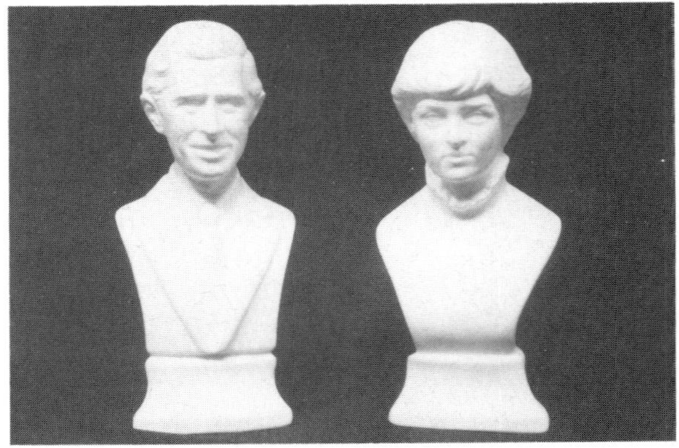

631

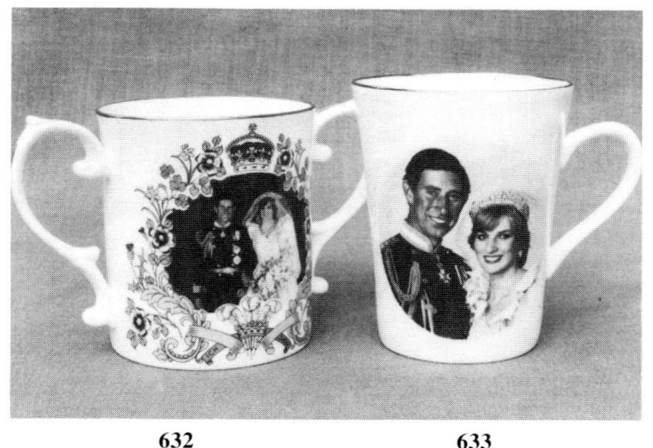

632 633

*632 A full length portrait of Charles and Diana after the wedding ceremony within a colourful frame of flowers is on the front of the porcelain loving cup (9.5cm) from *Caverswall*. On the reverse "Long live the Prince and Princess of Wales" is supported by the Union Flag and a Royal Standard.

*633 Another close up photograph (taken by Lord Lichfield) of the couple after the wedding covers the front of this flared porcelain mug (l0cm) from *St Georges China*. The reverse carries wedding details.

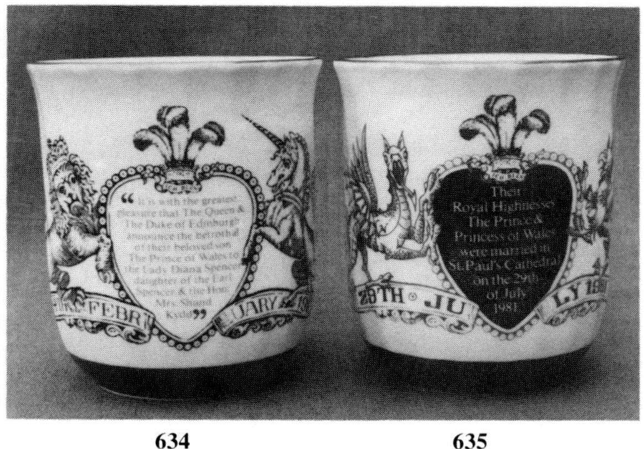

634 635

J & J May "The Commemorators" produced this elegant pair of fluted, porcelain mugs (9cm each) to commemorate the engagement and wedding.

*634 On the front of this mug is the full statement announcing the betrothal, printed in blue, within a heart-shaped, beaded frame supported by a lion and unicorn all in rose. "24th February 1981" in gilt completes the design.

*635 The matching mug has a similar design. Here the heart in deep red contains the wedding details. "The Welsh Dragon and the Spencer Griffin support the Royal Marriage" proclaims an inscription inside the rim and indeed these beasts are seen as supporters on the front!

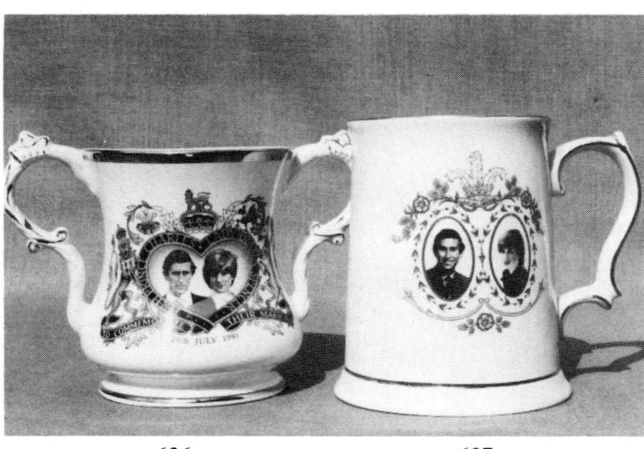

636 637

*636 This waisted, pottery loving cup (11cm) comes from *Old Foley,* (James Kent). The front has a printed, colour transfer of Charles and Diana in a heart shaped frame supported by a lion and unicorn. The elaborate handles have moulded crowns picked out in gold. The reverse shows Prince of Wales feathers.

*637 *Royal Winton* produced this cone shaped, pottery tankard (12cm). A simple colour printed design of Charles and Diana framed by flowers decorates the front whilst the reverse gives wedding details beneath a Welsh dragon and national flowers.

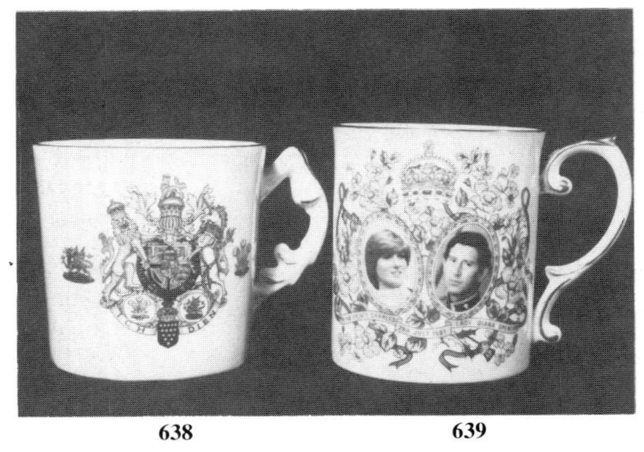

638 639

*638 Two contrasting designs are used by these manufacturers to commemorate the wedding. That on the left was made by *Aynsley* and shows a partly enamelled coloured coat of arms incorporating the Welsh dragon and Prince of Wales feathers. On the reverse is a royal family tree similar to other designs used by this manufacturer.

*639 The second mug, which was in a limited edition of 5000, bears the *China Craft* backstamp. Coloured portraits are contained within an elaborate design in pink, blues and greens. The reverse shows a picture of Highgrove House and the the moulded handle is lined in gold.

*640 This straight sided, pottery tankard (12.5cm) by *Wood & Sons* has a colourful Arms of the Prince of Wales on the front with blue printed details of the Wedding on the rear. Wood made similar pieces for the Coronation and Silver Jubilee **(577)**.

*641 In complete contrast to the piece shown at **(621)** is this pottery mug (8cm) also from *Spode*. Here we have an informal portrait of Charles and Diana in a cartouche with surrounding floral emblems and Prince of Wales feathers. The reverse carries details of the wedding. The complete design is printed in blue.

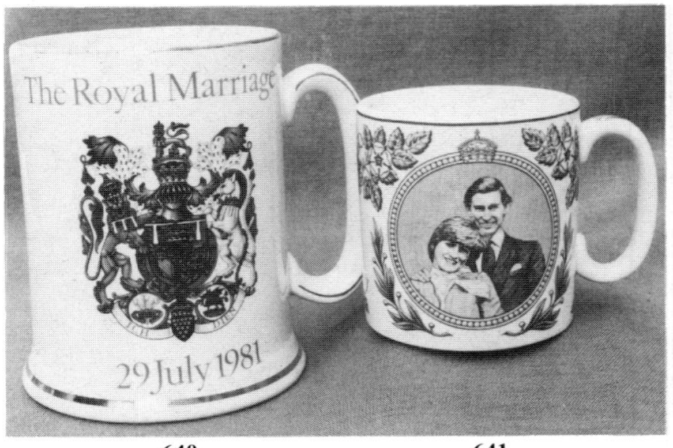

640 641

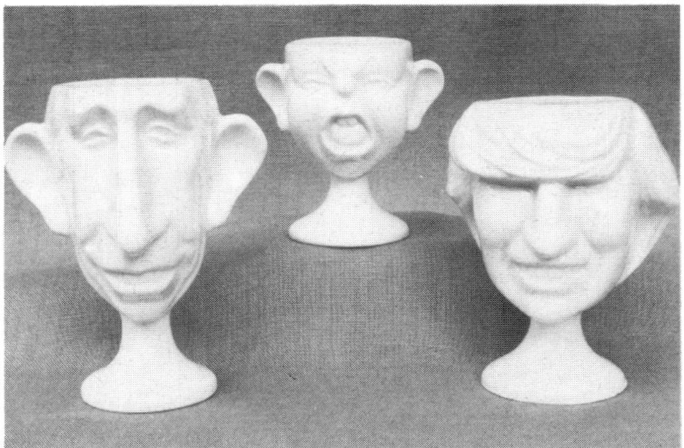

642

*642 These three pottery "character" pieces were produced by Luck & Flaw (the team behind the Spitting Images TV show). Charles (10.5cm) and Diana (9.5cm) were issued in 1981 and Prince William (7.5cm) in 1982. Like the Marc mug **(KK5)** these are pieces very much of their time. Interesting, if not everyone's favourite commemoratives!

*643 This pottery mug (9cm) from *Sunshine Ceramics* is a good example of how a "cheap and cheerful" piece can nonetheless be unusual. Colourful, flag-waving, typical London characters (and a Welsh lady and a Scotsman) form a continuous design.

*644 Majestic commissioned *Caverswall* to make this porcelain plate (21cm) in a "limited edition". Portraits of the Prince and Princess are surrounded by an inscription and a blue border containing views of Buckingham Palace, Highgrove House, Althorp and Caernarvon Castle.

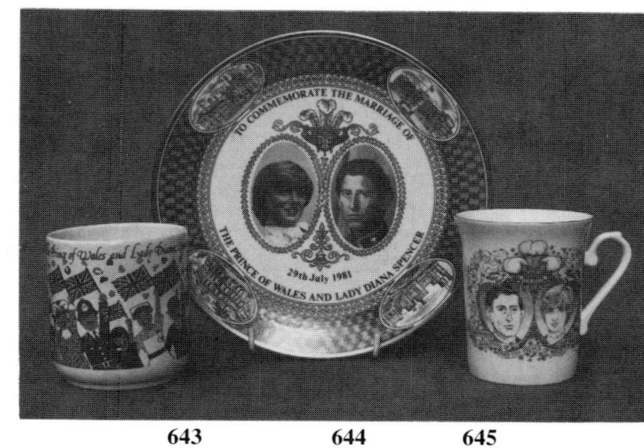

643 **644** **645**

*645 *Coronet* produced this porcelain mug (9cm) for Britannia. Sepia portraits within a rose pattern of cherubs and Prince of Wales Feathers are on the front with entwined C and D on the reverse.

This group of porcelain thimbles includes one *646 from *Highland China* which has a blue printed design of Prince of Wales Feathers and inscription. *647 from *Royal Worcester* which has bells on the front and Prince of Wales Feathers on the reverse. And a pair by *Caverswall* *648 for the Betrothal, with portraits and *649 for the wedding with Prince of Wales Feathers.

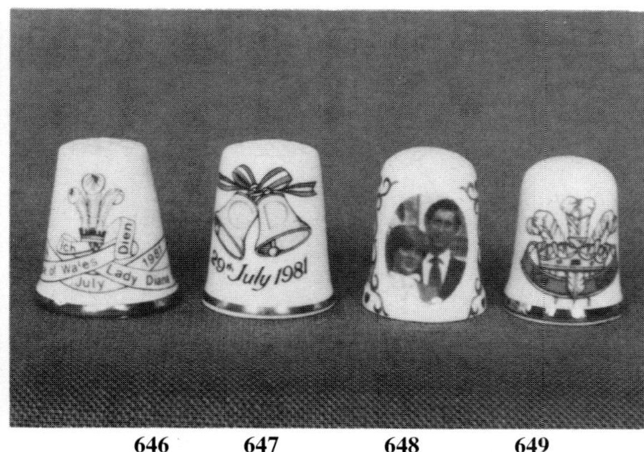

646 **647** **648** **649**

*650 Large numbers of plates were produced by many different manufacturers for the royal wedding. These two show contrasting designs. That on the left (21.5cm) uses modern technology to show a fine sepia photographic portrait of the royal couple bordered by an inscription. made by *Royal Kent*. Stafford.

*651 The other (22.5cm) designed by Richard Guyatt shows entwined ribbons framing the silhouette type portraits and feathers. Overall in dark blue against a white ground. Made by *Wedgwood* in an unlimited edition.

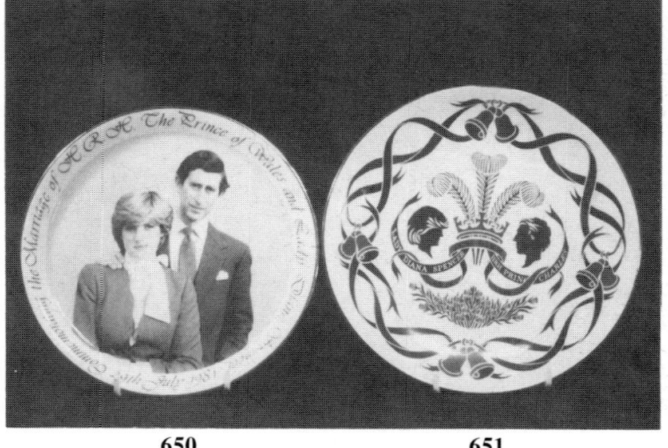

650 **651**

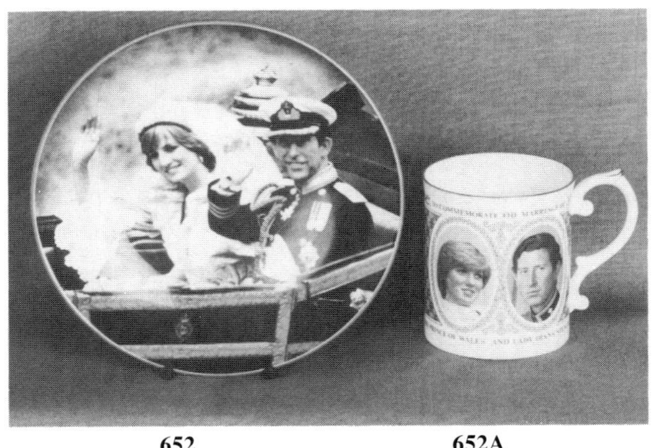

652 652A

*652 *Coalport* produced this Royal Wedding plate (20cm) exclusively for the North American market. A coloured picture of the happy couple taken on their carriage ride through London after the ceremony dominates the whole plate.

*652A Two more serious coloured portraits of Prince Charles and Lady Diana are seen on the mug (9cm) made by *Caverswall* for Majestic. Inscriptions border the top and bottom rims with the inevitable three feathers shown on the reverse against a white ground. Backstamp reads "Marriage beaker 29th July 1981".

*653 A typical "cheap and cheerful" pottery mug (9cm) from *Kiln Craft*. Black printed portraits of Charles and Diana are on either side with the Arms of Prince Charles and inscription on the front. Produced at all speed to hit the mass market early. A similar betrothal mug was made.

*654 Sepia portraits of Charles and Diana are framed by colourful national flowers and flags on this porcelain mug (l0cm) by *Hammersley*. Whilst this piece shows some improvement on the company's design for 1977 (**578**), it still fails to match the splendid designs of Hammersley's earlier days.

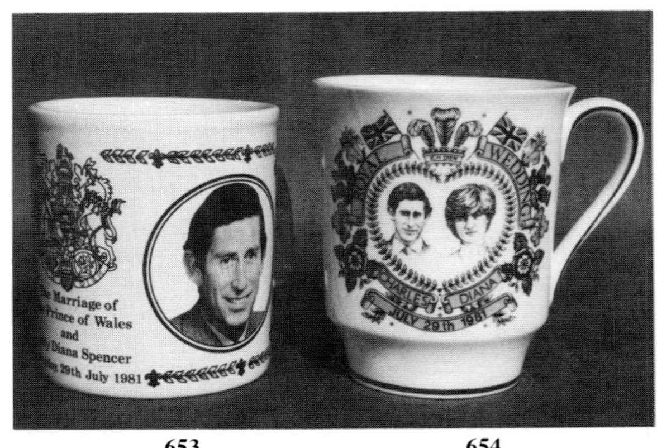

653 654

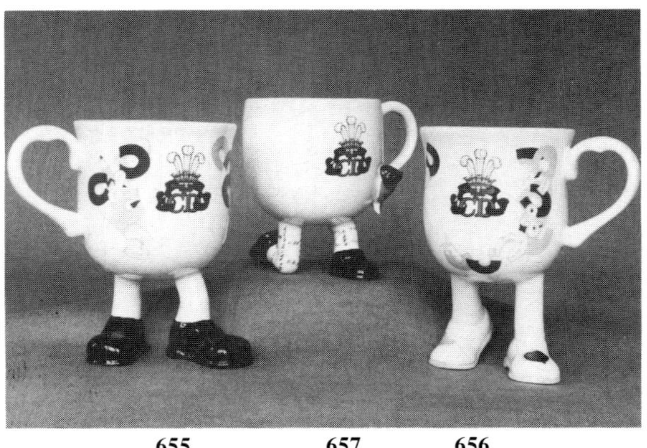

655 657 656

*655 *656 *657 Three more examples of the entertaining series of pottery "leg mugs" from *Carlton Ware*. All have "C D" beneath Prince of Wales Feathers whilst the pair in front (13cm) also have confetti spotted around. A heart and bow are on each of Diana's feet and there is a full commemoration on the reverse. The "kneeling prince" mug (10.5cm) carries a red rose and is sporting tartan trews.

The Wedding of Prince Andrew and Miss Sarah Ferguson•1986 •

Prince Andrew, the third child of the Queen, was born on 19 February 1960. He was educated at Gordonstoun like his older brother and father before him and, after a short stay at a school in Ontario, entered the Royal Naval College, Dartmouth, from which he embarked on a Naval career. As a helicopter pilot he subsequently served with distinction in the Falklands war of 1982. While pursuing his Naval career he was not expected to fulfil many official royal engagements. His public image was one of a typical young bachelor officer with a somewhat debonair approach to life and a healthy interest in the opposite sex. Needless to say, his private life was closely followed by the popular press and was of more than passing concern to his parents. It came as some surprise when, on 19 March 1986, the Queen announced to a gathering of Privy Councellors Prince Andrew's engagement to Miss Sarah Ferguson, the daughter of the polo manager to the royal family. As someone who was well known to them she was a popular choice with the family. Her vitality and bubbly personality seemed well suited to Prince Andrew's temperament.

The wedding was set for 23 July 1986 with the venue reverting to the more traditional Westminster Abbey. It was an altogether more relaxed affair than his brother's as it did not carry the same constitutional implications. No public holiday was declared but, as expected, the occasion attracted worldwide media coverage.

Prince Andrew was created Duke of York by the Queen just an hour or so before the ceremony, giving the potters another event to celebrate. Like his older brother, Prince Andrew had attracted just about no interest from the commemorative market before his wedding although he did appear on one piece to celebrate his 21st birthday **(786)**.

Engagement pictures of the happy couple **(675)** were popular though, like the 1981 wedding, some preferred to wait for the wedding photographs **(663)** taken on the steps of the Abbey or in the 1902 state landau **(664)**.

Almost without exception the naval theme was worked into designs with some being more evident than others **(LL4)**. At least one manufacturer **(666)** managed all three notable dates on the one piece. The 1981 wedding had introduced many newcomers to the commemorative market and retailers reported brisk business. Guyatt enthusiasts were disappointed when a limited edition mug **(LL8)** soon sold out. Wedgwood were quick to gauge the public demand and issued a conferment mug **(659)** in a slightly increased limited edition which, in our opinion, was the more pleasing of the two designs.

*658 Gold lion handles are a special feature of this porcelain loving cup (8.5cm) by *Finsbury China*. Two coloured portraits of the happy couple are shown above a blue ribbon inscription. Entwined initials and wedding bells decorate the back, and a fine gold line around the upper rim adds to the overall quality.

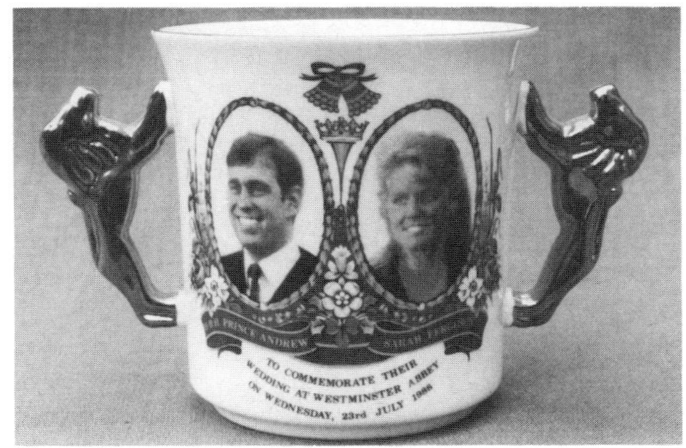

658

*659 This porcelain loving cup (10cm) celebrates the conferment of the title "Duke of York" on Prince Andrew. Profiles of the Duke and Duchess are in black within blue frames. The reverse is inscribed "Created on 23rd July 1986 at 10.0 a.m. Duke of York, Earl of Inverness, Baron Killyleagh". *John Pierce*. Limited to 50.

*660 *Wedgwood* produced this Queensware mug (10cm) to commemorate the Duke of York's conferment and was designed by Richard Guyatt in a limited edition of 1000. Shields and beasts are principally in black and gold with simulated waves in blue. Profiles in black of the Duke and Duchess are shown either side of the handle.

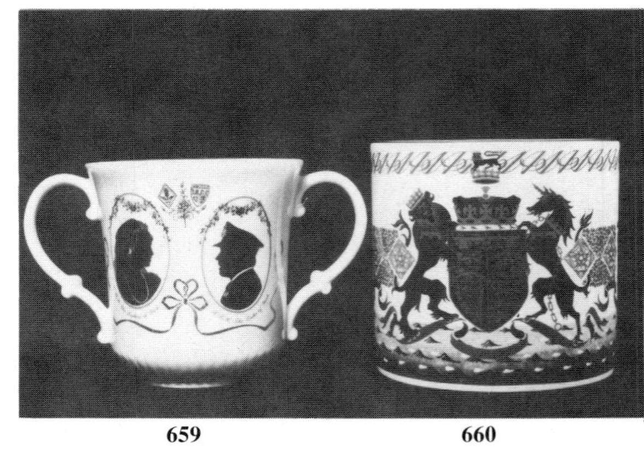

659 **660**

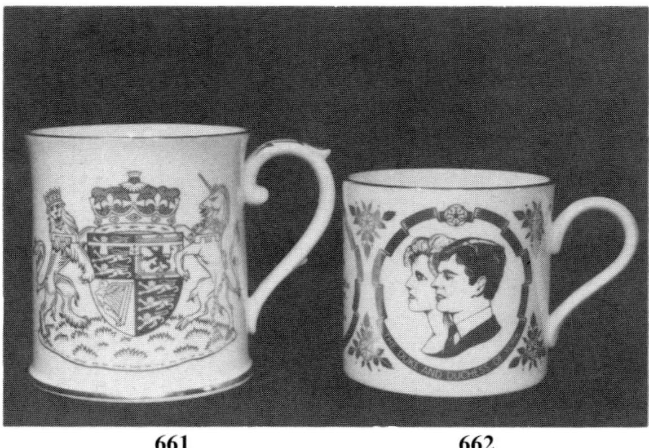

661 **662**

*661 This porcelain mug (9cm) by *Spode* celebrates the wedding of Prince Andrew and Miss Sarah Ferguson and is inscribed as such with a gold frame on the reverse side. A crowned shield in gold dominates the front. This same shape was used for Charles and Diana's wedding **(621)**.

*662 Two somewhat severe artist drawn portraits in profile dominate the small porcelain mug (7cm) from the *Wedgwood* factory to commemorate Prince Andrew's conferment as Duke of York. Stylized roses formally decorate the piece which is inscribed for the event within a similar frame to that used for the portrait.

*663 Wedding day pictures dominate both these pieces. The mug (12cm) made exclusively for Peter Jones Collection by *Sutherland*, has gold lion head handles. The coloured picture is within a frame of coloured emblems. The reverse contains details of the event. Limited edition of 500.

*664 *Sheltonian China* have used a most attractive coloured portrait of the Duke and Duchess of York to commemorate the day. The porcelain mug (9cm) is suitably inscribed below with the names on green ribbons and the reverse has a lucky horseshoe in colour. Fine gold lining has been added to the rim.

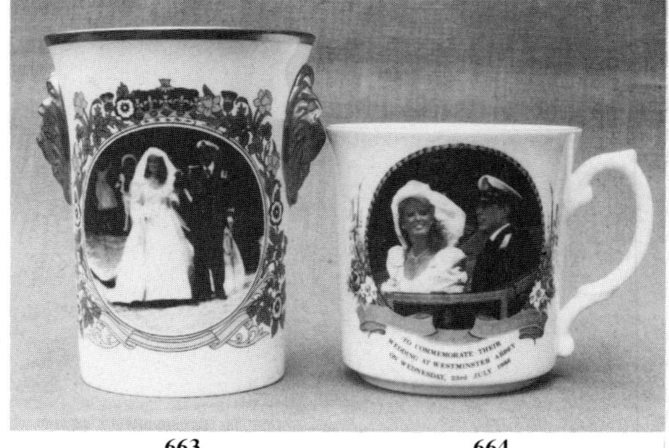

663 **664**

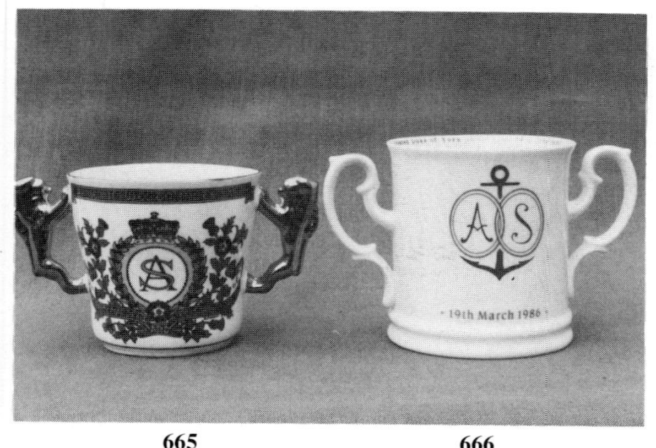

665 666

*665 Gold lion handles decorate this porcelain loving cup (8cm) by *Paragon* to celebrate the marriage of Prince Andrew and Miss Sarah Ferguson. Coloured emblems surround the entwined cypher. The reverse shows a coat of arms, lion and unicorn and inscriptions record the happy event.

*666 *Wiltons Dorincourt* produced the pretty taller loving cup (9cm) in porcelain. A gold anchor supporting the cyphers gives a nautical flavour to the design. Besides the details of the event recorded on the reverse, the inside rim is inscribed "Created Duke of York 10.0 a.m. 23rd July 1986". Limited to 100. Also found without the rim inscription.

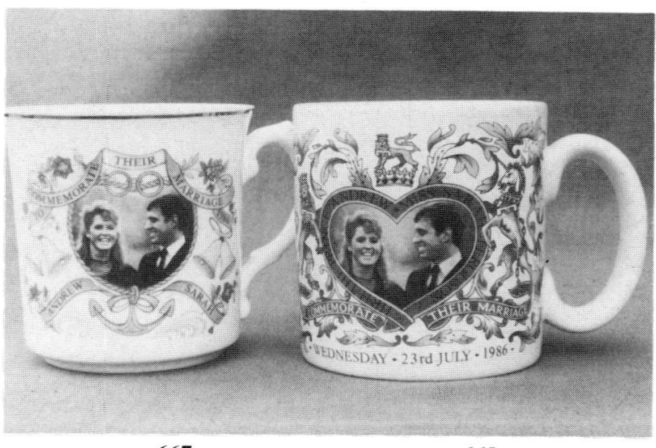

667 668

*667 Two mugs (8.5cm) use the same coloured portraits of Andrew and Sarah. That on the left has a naval theme with ropes and anchors together with the more traditional wedding bells. Colours are in pale blue, pink and yellow. The reverse gives the date 23 July 1986. Made by *Mayfair*.

*668 An inscribed heart frames the portraits on the other mug made by *John Buck*, with the lion and unicorn in support. A black and white picture of Westminster Abbey is shown on the back. The inner rim is inscribed with the young couple's names.

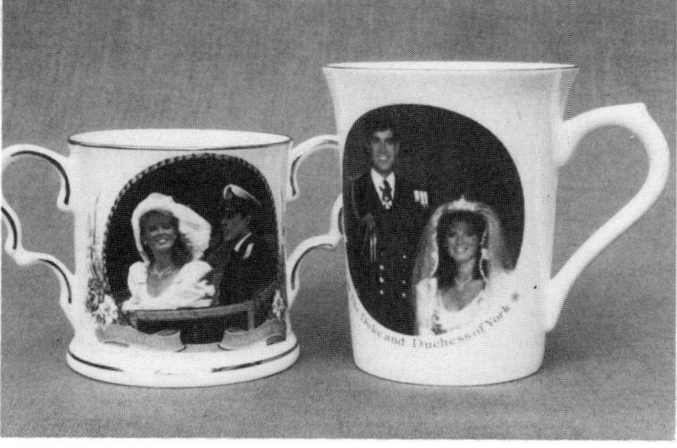

669 670

*669 The front of this small, porcelain loving cup (7cm) shows the couple in the carriage returning to Buckingham Palace. Whilst the caption here says "The Duke and Duchess of York", on the reverse they are described as HRH Prince Andrew and Sarah Ferguson. *Fenton China*.

*670 *Coronet* pottery makes the position clear on their porcelain mug (10cm). The front has an unusual photograph of the couple, entitled The Duke and Duchess of York, in which Andrew is standing next to Sarah. The reverse explains that he was created Duke of York on the morning of his marriage. Also listed are the previous Dukes of York.

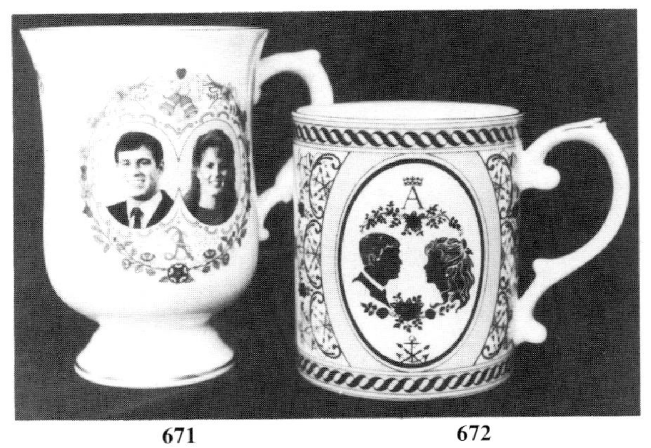

671 672

*671 This waisted porcelain mug (12cm) was issued by *Coalport*. Previously this shape and general treatment had the Crown Staffordshire name **(575, 623)**. Portraits of the couple within a conjoined oval frame surrounded by bells hearts and national flowers make up the design.

*672 Silhouette profiles of Andrew and Sarah are on one side of this porcelain mug (9.5cm) from *Caverswall*. A blue printed scroll design separates the other framed set of Arms.

*673 *Honiton Pottery* issued this interesting plate (23.5cm). The detailed design, printed overall in pale blue, is created from a wide variety of emblems reflecting Andrew's connections with the sea and his naval career. Hawser ropes and anchor chains hold together an anchor, ship's propeller, compass, helicopter blades and entwined initials.

*674 This pottery plate (26.5cm) has a bold design printed in black, depicting Andrew and Sarah in oval frames beneath which is the commemorative inscription. Details on the reverse state it was designed by the Hampshire artist Alan Roe on English fine bone china from Staffordshire.

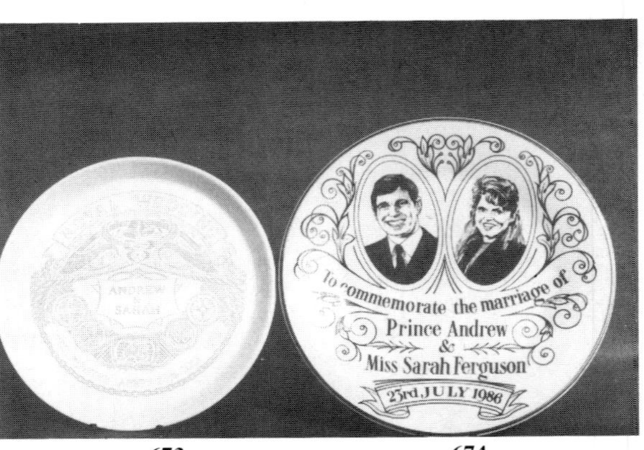

673 674

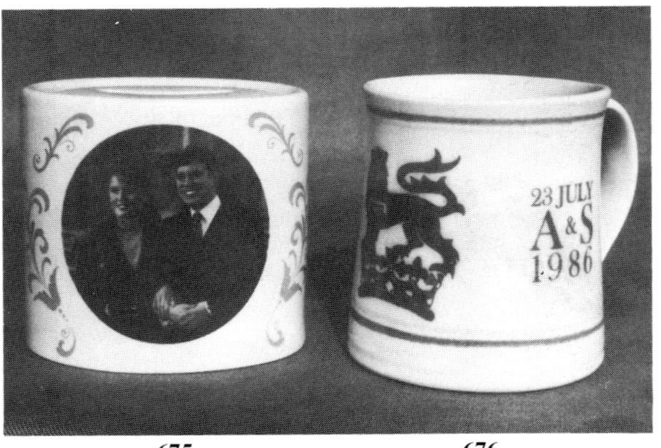

675 676

*675 Money boxes have always been a popular collector's item, and *Adams* produced this pottery example (6cm) to mark the wedding. Oval in shape it features a full colour "engagement" portrait of the couple on the front with commemorative inscription on the reverse.

*676 This cream coloured mug (8cm) comes from the *Rye Pottery*. An heraldic lion atop a crown are on the front whilst initials and date are on either side of this pretty piece. Another example of good pottery items yet to be fully appreciated.

*677 *678 A matching pair of porcelain thimbles from *Royal Crown Derby* (2cm) which depict the Arms of Prince Andrew and of Sarah Ferguson. Each has the same entwined initials and inscriptions. Typical Derby imari-style pattern and raised gold make these an attractive set.

*679 *681 *Sutherland China* issued these two porcelain thimbles (2cm). The one on the left marks the Engagement and has entwined crowned initials, doves and national flowers. That on the right, for the marriage, has Andrew's Arms, bells and flowers with inscription.

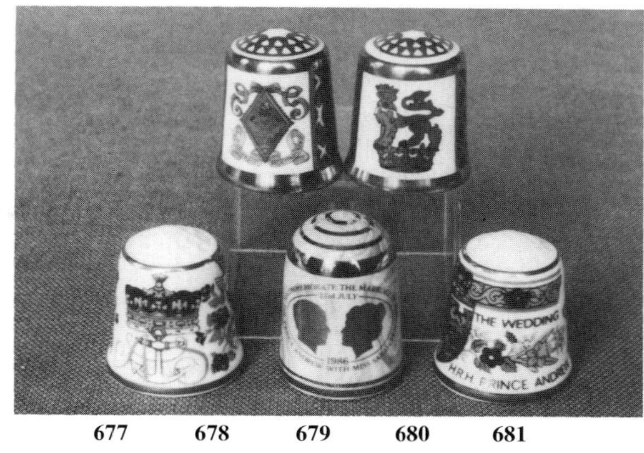

677 678 679 680 681

*680 Gold profile portraits on a light blue, pink and white body with inscription also in gold make this a very attractive product (2.5cm) from *Bouchet Agateware* in Jersey.

*682 *683 Another pair of "cheap and cheerful" pottery mugs (9cm) by *Kilncraft* to mark the engagement and wedding. Black printed portraits of the couple within circular frames are separated by the relevant inscriptions for betrothal and marriage. Decorative trim has an anchor and laurel for the former and wedding bells for the latter (see 653).

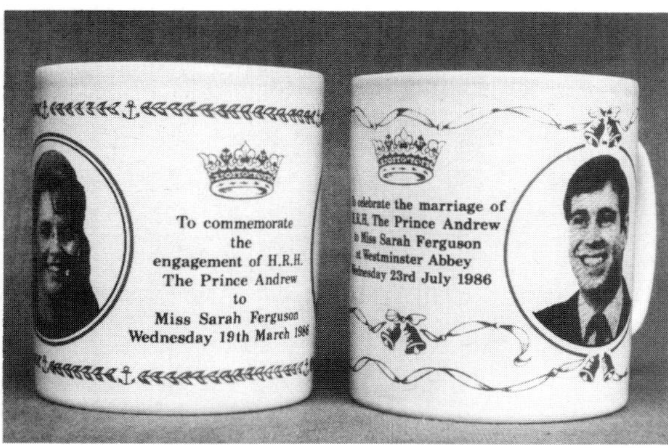

682 683

Wedgwood Pint Sized Mugs by Richard Guyatt

In 1937 Wedgwood commissioned Eric Ravilious, a talented artist, to design a pint-sized mug for the coronation of Edward VIII. It was made in two different colours and later adapted, again in two colours, for the coronation of George VI. Unfortunately, Eric Ravilious was killed on active service during the war but his basic designs were repeated, with modifications, by Wedgwood for the coronation of Queen Elizabeth in 1953.

At the same time Richard Guyatt was asked to submit his own design for coronation ware though keeping the successful pint-size shape. This was to become the first of what has proved to be a very popular series for collectors. Listed are the Richard Guyatt pint-sized mugs known to us which commemorate royal occasions.

Coronation of Elizabeth II 1953
Queensware with sepia,pink and gold decoration.
Queensware with black decoration.
Moonstone glaze with platinum decoration.
Royal blue ground with gold decoration.

Investiture of the Prince of Wales 1969
Black basalt with gold decoration.
Queensware with black and gold decoration.

Visit of Prince Philip, Duke of Edinburgh, to Wedgwood factory 1971
Black basalt with gold decoration.

Silver Wedding of Queen Elizabeth and the Duke of Edinburgh 1972
Drab ware with gold, white, black and grey decoration.
Black basalt with white and gold decoration. Limited to 500.

Marriage of Princess Anne to Captain Mark Phillips 1973
Queensware with multi-coloured decoration.

Silver Jubilee of Queen Elizabeth II 1977
Black basalt with 24c gold decoration. Limited to 500.
Queensware with black decoration and 24c gold decoration (Jubilee edition).
Queensware with black printed design with platinum decoration.

25th Anniversary of the Coronation of Queen Elizabeth II 1978
Queensware decorated with blue and gold coronation regalia. Limited to 5000.
Black Basalt with gold decoration. Limited to 500.

Marriage of Prince Charles to Lady Diana Spencer 1981
Black basalt. Limited to 250.
Queensware black, gold, blue and green decoration. Limited to 1500.
Queensware coloured with platinum. Limited to 3000.

Birth of Prince William 1982
Queensware with blue design and platinum trim. Limited to 1000.

Birth of Prince Henry 1984
Queensware mug. Limited to 1000.

Christening of Prince Henry 1984
Queensware mug. Limited to 1000

Marriage of Prince Andrew to Sarah Ferguson 1986
Queensware coloured decoration. Limited to 750.

Conferment of Dukedom of York 1986
Queensware blue decoration. Limited to 1000.

Queen Elizabeth II 60th birthday 1986
Queensware multi-coloured with gold. Limited to 500.
Queensware blue with green. Limited to 2000.

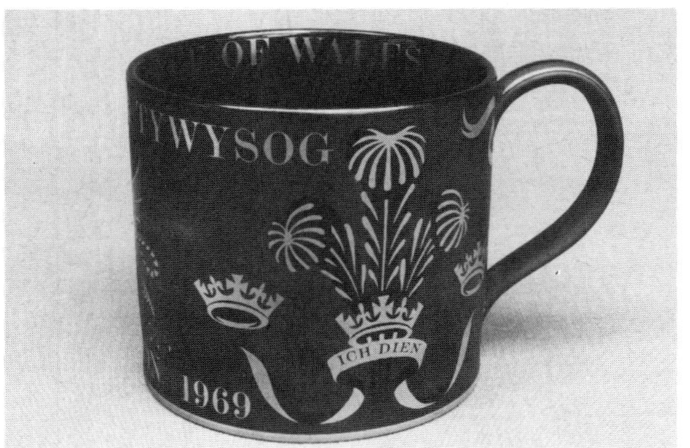

683A

*683A On 4 June 1971 the Duke of Edinburgh visited the Wedgwood factory at Barlaston. To commemorate the event a black basalt pint-size mug, to the Guyatt Investiture design, was presented to the Duke suitably inscribed on the base for the occasion. A similar mug is shown.

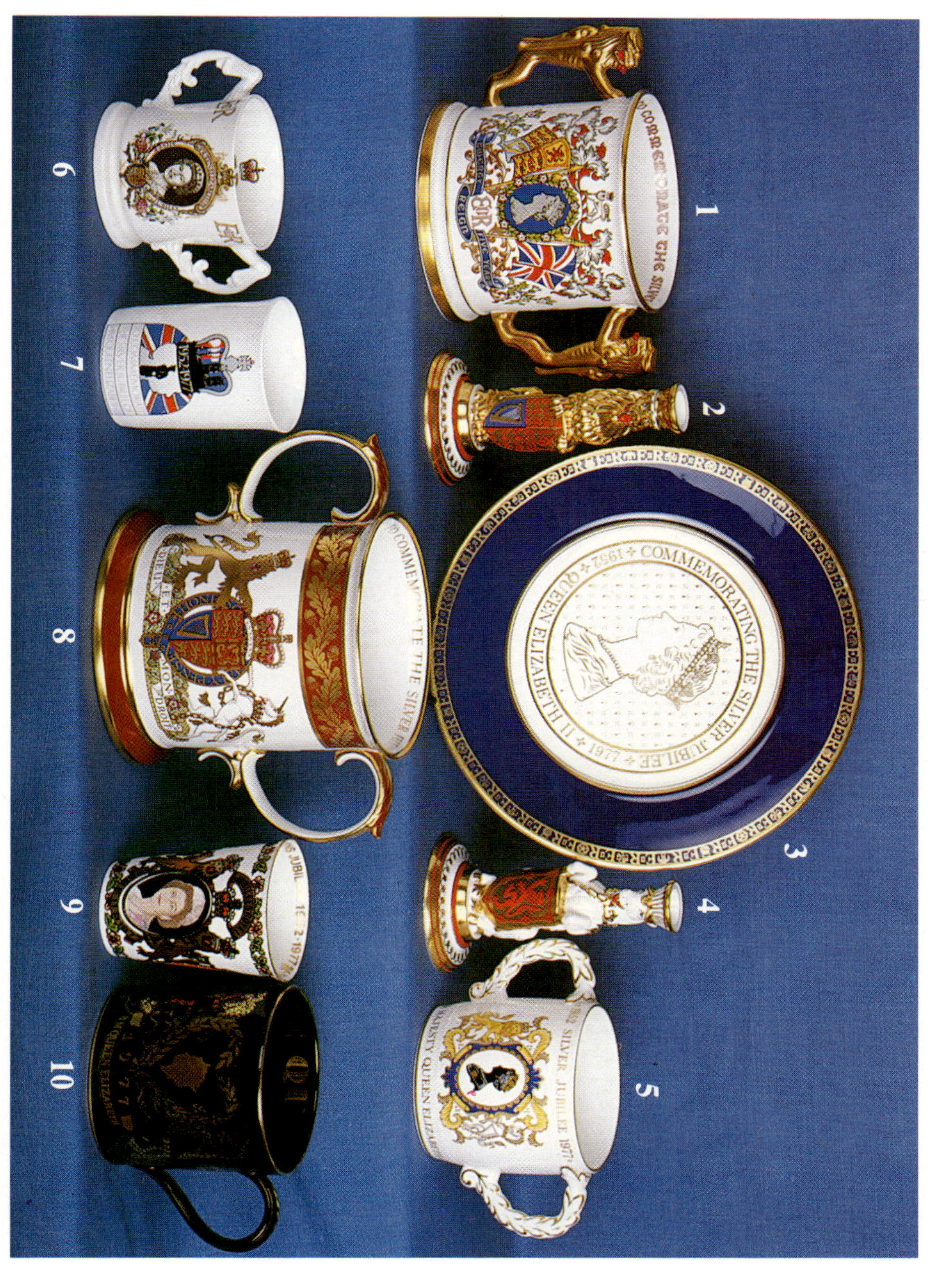

The Silver Jubilee of Elizabeth II • 1977 •

(see page 82) Plate JJ

Colour Plate JJ (page 81)

The Silver Jubilee of Elizabeth II • 1977

JJ1 An impressive loving cup (13cm) from the *Paragon* factory made in a small limited edition of 750. The Queen's profile, set against a blue background, is flanked by coloured flags with the reverse side showing the coat of arms supported by lion and unicorn. Gold lion handles in true Paragon tradition.

JJ2 and 4 William Harper designed these candlesticks (16cm) for *Minton* in the form of a lion and unicorn holding a shield showing the Royal Arms and Arms of Scotland respectively. The idea bears some resemblance to royal beasts made by Minton previously for the 1953 coronation **(GG7)**. Hand painting and extensive gilding maintain the superb quality of the work we have come to expect from this manufacturer. Made for Mulberry Hall, York, in a limited edition of 250 pairs.

JJ3 Imaginative use of repeated gold cyphers form the narrow border of this plate (27cm) from *Wedgwood*. A profile in gold within an inscribed border dominates the centre. Limited edition of 1000.

JJ5 *Coalport* made this attractive porcelain loving cup (10.5 cm) for the Royal General Theatrical Fund Association in a limited edition of 1000. A black and gold profile of the Queen framed in blue, with delicately coloured lion and unicorn are shown. Appropriately, a colourful picture of the Theatre Royal, Drury Lane, whose first patron was King Charles II 1663, is on the reverse.

JJ6 This shape was used on a variety of *Aynsley* loving cups (8.5cm). A framed facing portrait of the Queen is flanked by royal cyphers with the cypher repeated on the reverse.Unmarked.

JJ7 Items commissioned by *J. & J. May* have been made in very small editions and their innovative designs **(634) (747)** must make them very collectable in the future. This porcelain mug (10cm) shows a profile of the Queen against the union flag. Within the crown are silhouettes of the royal children and Westminster Abbey. A silver inscription is shown below the portrait. Clifford Richards was the designer.

JJ8 Made in a limited edition of 500 by *Spode*, this lavishly decorated loving cup (16cm) shows the Royal Arms with a panel of acorns and oak leaves to the top rim. A frame of gold Commonwealth flags containing stylized national emblems is shown on the reverse of the cup. An inside rim inscription records the Silver Jubilee of Queen Elizabeth II.

JJ9 Supporting crowned lions hold a framed portrait of the Queen against a black ground on this beaker (11cm). Additional framed portraits of George III, George V and Queen Victoria, all Jubilee monarchs, are shown round the remainder of the beaker. Made by *Mercian China Co.*

JJ10 A heart shaped leaf frame surrounds a crowned profile of the Queen together with supporting lion and unicorn. The overall design is in gold against a black ground and is boldly inscribed on the inside rim. The pottery mug (10.5cm) is made by *Wedgwood*, designed by Professor Richard Guyatt, in a limited edition of 500.

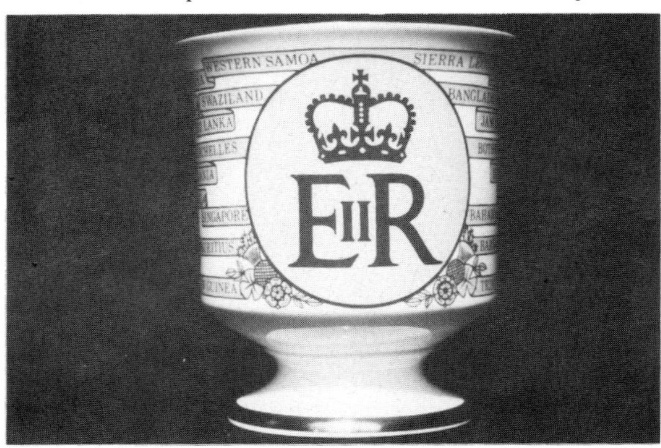

684

*684 Shown here is one of the three porcelain goblets (12cm) made by *Coalport* to mark the Silver Jubilee in 1977 **(572, 573)**. This one was produced in association with the Royal Commonwealth Society in an unlimited edition. The front has a crowned EIIR cypher within a circular frame and on each side are the names of the Commonwealth nations. A view of Marlborough House, home of the Commonwealth Secretariat is on the reverse. The whole design is printed in pale and deep blue.

Colour Plate KK (page 84)

The Wedding of Prince Charles and Lady Diana Spencer • 1981 •

*KK1 *Coalport* produced a series of these attractive china goblets (12cm) to mark major royal events, and this one in rich cobalt blue is typical of the range **(572, 573)**. A continuous decoration of Buckingham Palace, Caernarvon Castle and St Pauls Cathedral all in gold encircles the piece, with pennants above containing a variety of national emblems. Issued in a limited edition of 2000 each piece is numbered.

*KK2 This tall (12cm) waisted china mug comes from *Crown Staffordshire*, one in a series from this company **(575) (772)**. Portraits of Charles and Diana are within a cartouche of national flowers over which is the Prince of Wales feathers. The reverse has entwined arms of Prince Charles and the Spencer family.

*KK3 A framed sepia portrait of Princess Diana is shown on one side of this mug, with a similarly framed portrait of Prince Charles on the other (9.5cm). Made by *Royal Overhouse Pottery*.

*KK4 *Caverswall* produced this large, interesting porcelain tyg (15.5cm) in an edition limited to 500. Colour portraits of Charles and Diana, each in an oval frame, the arms of Charles and the Spencers, a view of Highgrove House are the main decorative features of each of the three "faces". Each is surrounded by intricate patterns of national flowers, wedding bells, and heraldic emblems. The handles are formed of three Welsh dragons peering over the rim. Three handled pieces are no longer often produced, but this is a fine example of these wares.

*KK5 Produced by *Carlton Ware* **(574) (608)**, this pottery mug (9cm) has a cartoon face of Charles drawn by Marc, an ear for a handle, and a light-hearted poem on the reverse. Published to celebrate the engagement and publication of Clive James' "Charles Charmings Challenges on the Pathway to the Throne".

*KK6 An unmistakable product of the *Paragon* factory. An entwined cypher, emblems, Welsh dragon and feathers dominate the front of the porcelain loving cup (8cm) with a coloured coat of arms on the reverse. An inscription on the outer rim records the occasion.

*KK7 *Spode Ltd* made this impressive covered chalice (31cm) in a limited edition of 500. The stem is predominantly in gold with a circle of gold decorated roses to the foot and cover. Coloured personal coats of arms are shown to the front, with a gold framed inscription to the back.

*KK8 *Coalport* issued this finely modelled group of Charles and Diana (11cm). Produced all in white the only colour being the gilded inscription and trim at the base. Limited to 250 numbered pieces.

*KK9 An example of the unusual commemorative is this framed pottery pot lid (10cm) made for the Clipper Tea & Produce Co Ltd in an edition of 5000. The very colourful design is well thought out, with the Royal Standard picking up the red of Charles' uniform, whilst Diana's blue dress is set off by the Union flag.

*KK10 Chinacraft commissioned this china mug (7.5cm) from *Coalport*. Portraits of Charles and Diana are in oval frames on a cobalt blue ground. Decoration is in gold with an inscription inside the rim. Limited to 5000.

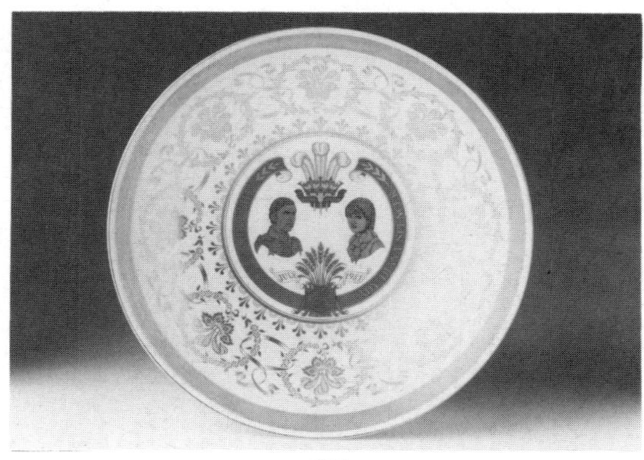

685

*685 This bowl (29cm) was made by *Minton* in a limited edition of 100 to commemorate the royal wedding of Prince Charles and Lady Diana. Prince of Wales feathers in gold dominate the design, with portraits framed in a blue and gold inscription.

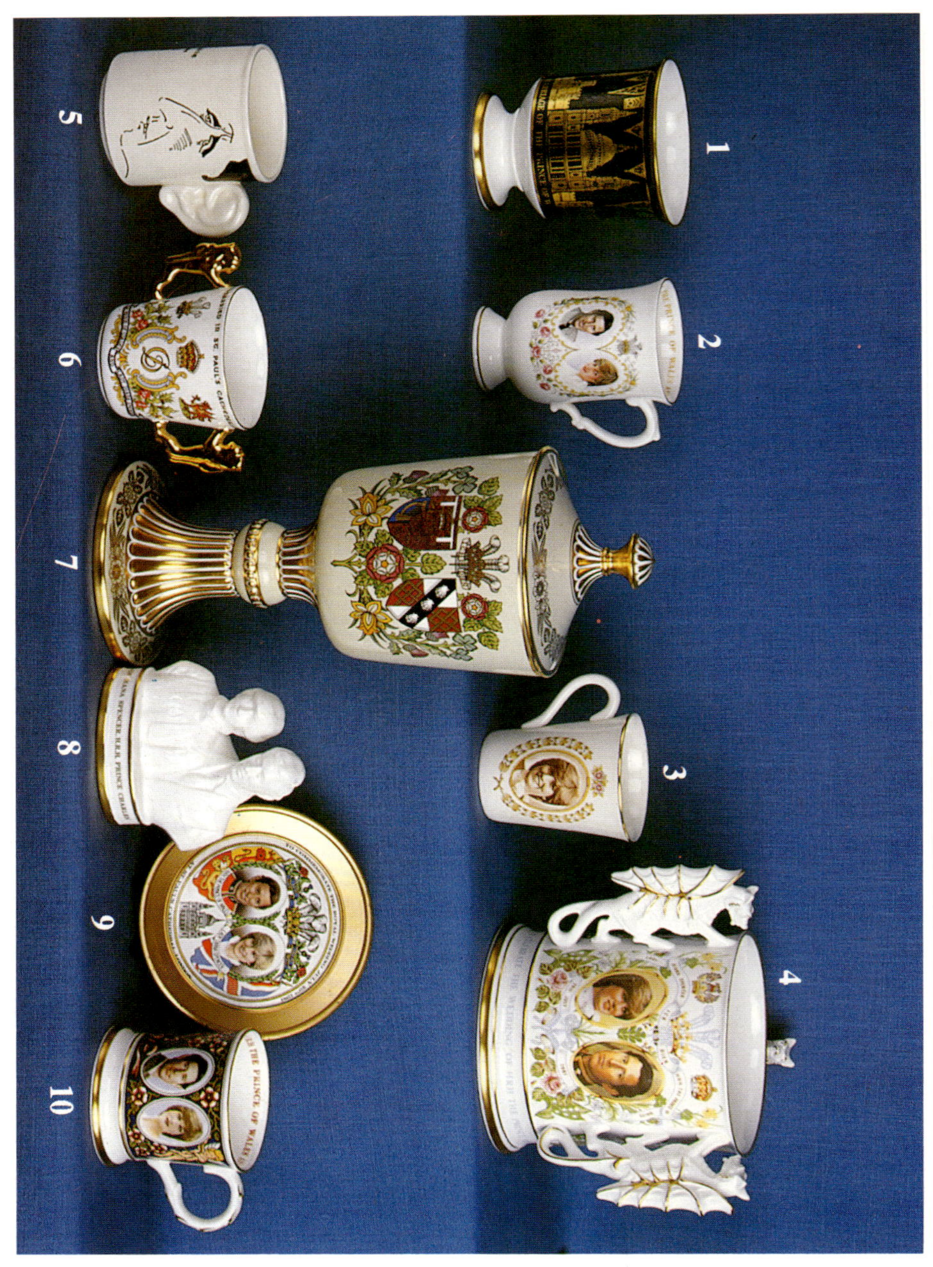

The Wedding of Prince Charles and Lady Diana Spencer • 1981 •

Plate KK (see page 83)

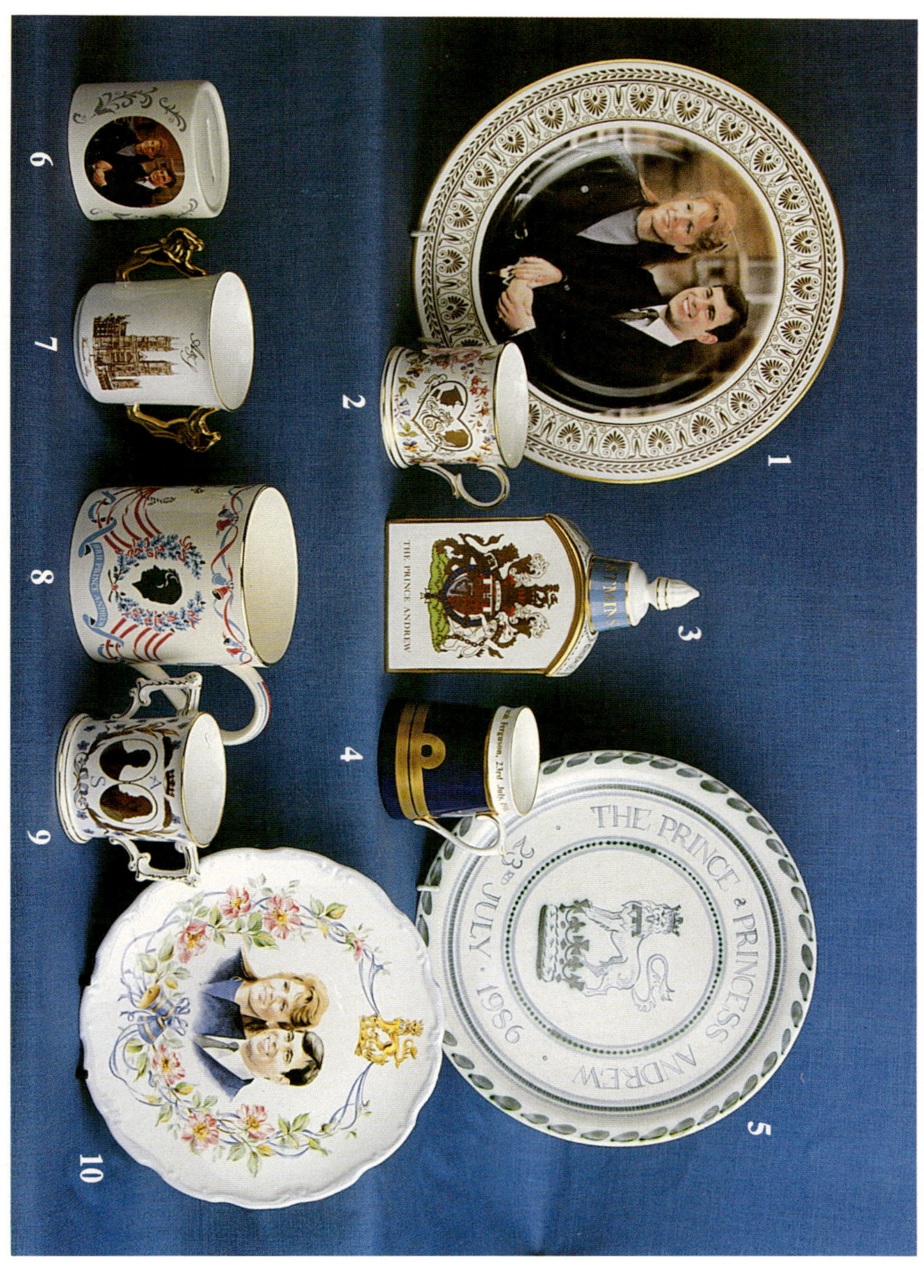

The Wedding of Prince Andrew and Miss Sarah Ferguson • 1986 •
(see page 86) Plate LL

Colour Plate LL (page 85)

The Wedding of Prince Andrew and Miss Sarah Ferguson • 1986 •

LL1 A large portrait of the happy couple with the ring in full prominence dominates this plate (27cm) from the *Coalport* factory. The reverse shows a family tree demonstrating the descent of them both from the 4th Duke of Devonshire 1720-1764. Made exclusively for Peter Jones, Wakefield, and limited to 1000.

LL2 One of the most attractive porcelain mugs (7.5cm) that we have come across for this occasion. Gold profiles of Prince Andrew and Miss Sarah Ferguson are framed within a heart, which in turn is surrounded by floral decoration. An inscription in gold on the reverse gives the betrothal date, 19th March 1986 and the wedding day. Commissioned by *Britannia* in a limited edition of 150.

LL3 Tea caddies are rarely chosen as commemorative items **(B4)** and *Minton* are to be congratulated on their imaginative choice. Coats of arms of Prince Andrew and Sarah Ferguson are shown on front and back respectively with extensive gold lining to the edges. The pale blue cover and neck are inscribed with "Westminster Abbey" and the date. Limited edition of 500. (19cm) high.

LL4 *J. & J. May* yet again demonstrate that an imaginative design **(QQ2)** does not need the support of portraits or coats of arms to capture the spirit of the occasion. The gold Lieutenant's stripes and inscription say it all. Made in a very limited edition though not marked as such.

LL5 Art pottery commemorative items continue to prove attractive to the collector **(430) (587)** since their designs frequently depart from the more conventional ideas we have come to expect from the large manufacturers. *Rye Pottery* made this plate (25cm) with a central design and bold inscription in pale Rye green.

LL6 Something different from *Adams* (Wedgwood). An oval shaped money box (7.5cm) showing the same portraits as **(LL1)** and inscribed with details of the wedding day on the reverse. Unlimited edition.

LL7 Gold lion handles are a feature of this porcelain loving cup (8.5cm) from *Royal Grafton*. A sepia picture of Westminster Abbey and script cypher are shown to the front. Inscribed with details on the reverse. Limited to 1000.

LL8. When *Wedgwood* issued this Richard Guyatt mug (10.5cm) in a limited edition of 750 they did not anticipate that the demand would be so great. Many potential customers were disappointed and it is now a very difficult item to find. Profiles of Andrew and Sarah are shown front and back with an anchor to the side giving the whole design a nautical flavour.

LL9 The same shape has been used by *Royal Crown Derby* for this loving cup (8cm) as for those for the Queen Mother's birthdays **(MM2 and MM4)**. Joined frames are repeated on the reverse in which are inscribed the details of the occasion. Limited to 1000.

LL10 This small plate (10.5cm) was made by *Royal Albert* and sold in an unlimited edition. The portrait used would appear to be the one taken at the time of their engagement and was a popular choice by other manufacturers **(667)**. Inscribed with the wedding date on the reverse.

Colour Plate MM (page 88)

Queen Elizabeth the Queen Mother

MM1 This plate (27cm) was made in a limited edition of 2000 by the *Coalport* factory for the Queen Mother's 85th birthday. The intricate pattern forming the border incorporates national emblems.

MM2 and 4 Both these loving cups (8cm) are quality items from *Royal Crown Derby* and commemorate the 85th and 90th birthdays of the Queen Mother. The shapes are the same and show gold profiles of Her Majesty against different framed backgrounds. Cypher and crown within these frames are repeated on the reverse of both pieces. Limited to 500 each.

MM3 Very few quality porcelain figures of royalty seem to have been produced over the years but this one (19cm) made by *Carlton* at the time of the 1937 coronation is the exception. Detail is superb, particularly of the hands and gloves and careful use of colours for the robe and insignia add to the delicate charm. The matching figure for King George VI can also be found **(BB3)**. Though there is no indication of the number made, it would have been expensive to produce and made in a very limited number.

MM5 A large "75" on this plate leaves no doubt about the occasion for which *Panorama* made this plate (21cm). The happy picture of the Queen Mother is accompanied by suitable inscriptions recording the day.

MM6 Since the Duke of York was not the immediate heir to the throne when he married Lady Elizabeth Bowes-Lyon in 1923 few commemorative pieces were made for this royal wedding. A similar pottery mug (9.5cm) was made showing the sepia portrait of the future King **(203)** and small ashtrays are to be found in the same vein. The portrait is signed Bassano Ltd but there is no maker's mark. A rare item.

MM7 *Coronet* made this porcelain mug (9cm) to celebrate the Queen Mother's 80th birthday. The reverse bears an inscription to this effect within a similar frame to the front.

MM8 An imposing large loving cup (13cm) in the unmistakable *Paragon* style. The framed profile is supported by royal beasts and extensive use has been made of gold lining to rim, foot and lion handles. A large inscription in gold circumscribes the inside rim. The reverse shows St Pauls Walden Bury, birthplace of the Queen Mother. Made in a limited edition of 750 for the Queen Mother's 80th birthday.

MM9 Another loving cup (7.5cm) with an imaginative design for the 90th birthday. The inside rim bears a loyal inscription and the dates in gold are on the reverse of the cup. Made by *Crown Duchy* with a reference to the Guild of English Master Potters on the backstamp.

MM10 Not a particularly imposing piece from *Coronet* showing a coloured portrait of the Queen Mother framed by the inscription. Royalists will immediately spot the error in the inscription which may make this a collector's piece of the future. Made for the 90th birthday.

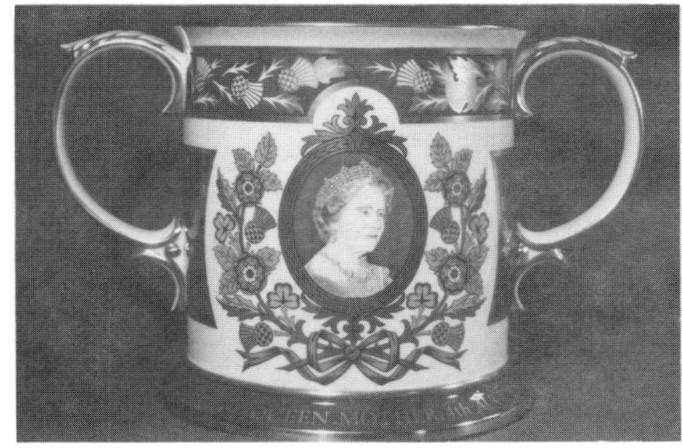

686

*686 Another impressive, porcelain loving cup from *Spode* (16cm). The front has a printed portrait of Queen Elizabeth in an oval frame surrounded by sprays of national flowers. The reverse depicts the Queen Mother's personal Coat of Arms. The decoration in white, maroon and gold makes for a luxurious appearance. The base has an inscription commemorating her 80th birthday printed in gold. There is some gilding on rim, foot and handles. A limited edition of 500.

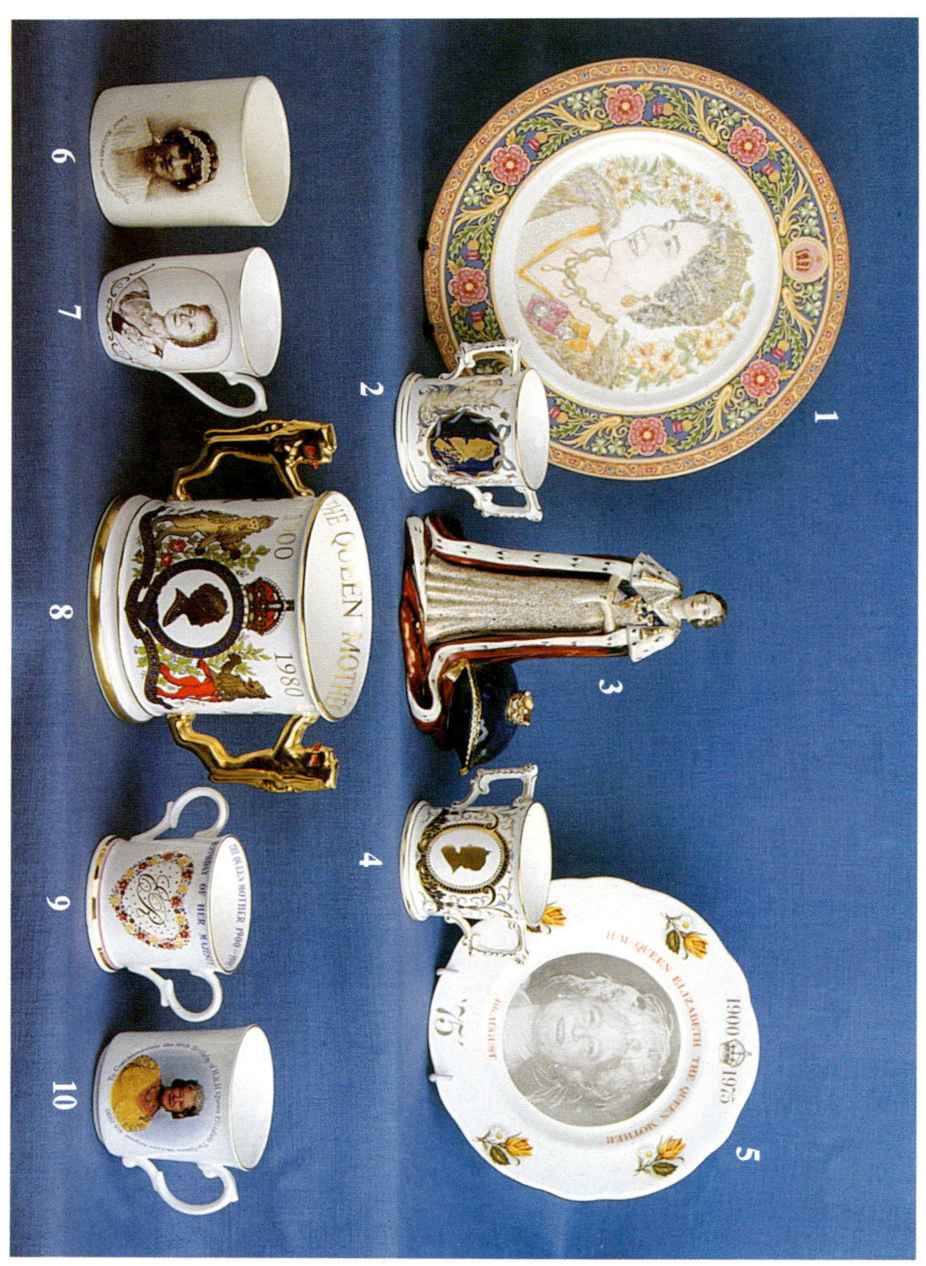

Queen Elizabeth the Queen Mother

Plate MM

(see page 87)

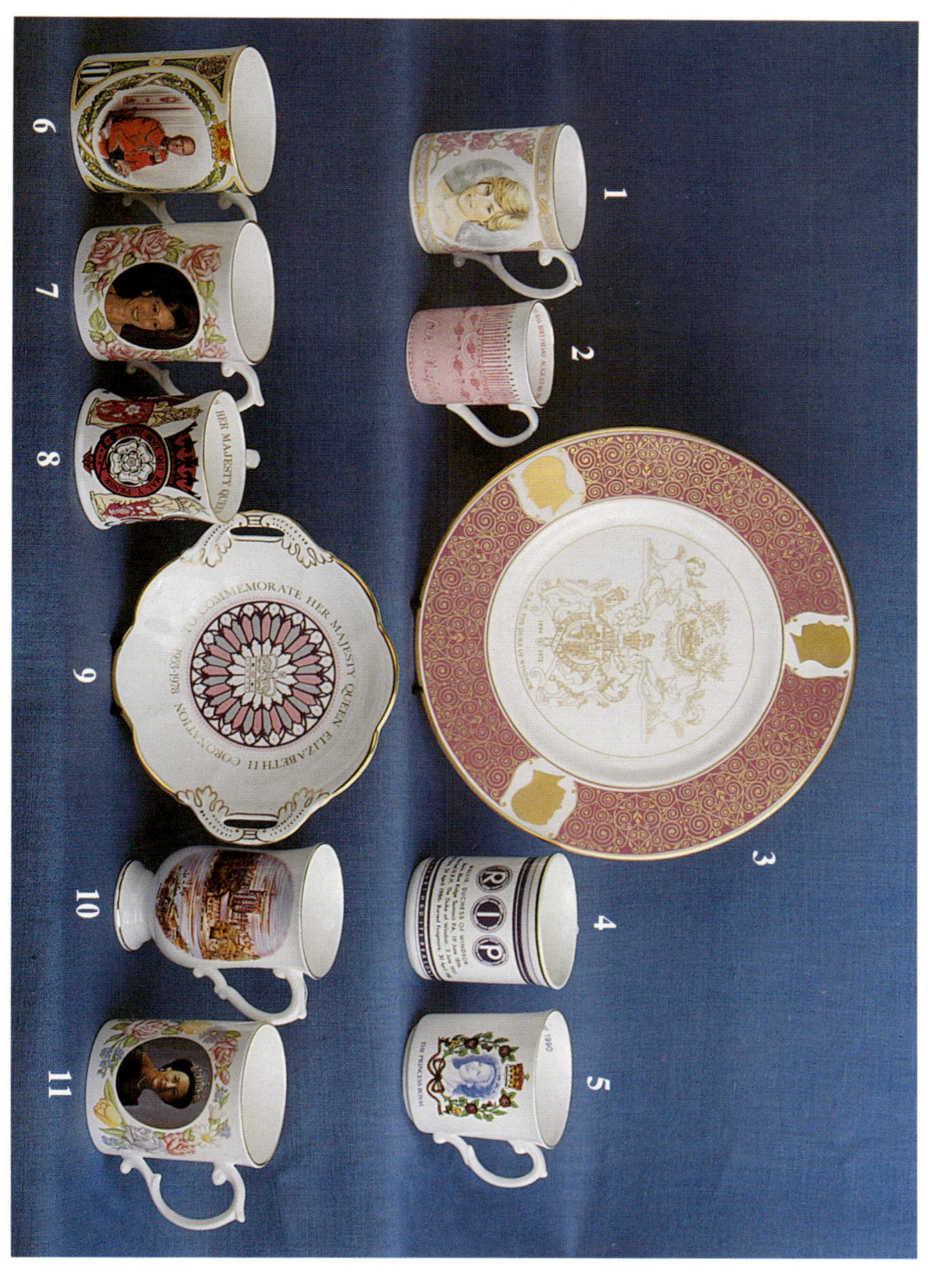

Royal Anniversaries and other Events

(see page 94) Plate QQ

Colour Plate QQ (page 93)

Royal Anniversaries and Other Events

QQ1 A portrait of the Princess of Wales reproduced from a painting by John Ball fills the front of this porcelain mug (9cm) from *Caverswall*. A rim inscription commemorates her 21st birthday.

QQ2 The sheer charm and innovative design makes this a favourite with collectors. 80 candles in pink and gold encompass this porcelain mug (8cm) from *J. & J. May*. An inside rim inscription records the date of the Queen Mother's birthday with "Happy Birthday your Majesty" in script against the pink ground.

QQ3 *Coalport* made this porcelain plate (27cm) to commemorate the death of the Duke of Windsor. Extensive use is made of gold to the central decoration and profiles. Inscribed with a quotation from Winston S. Churchill on the reverse. Limited edition of 1000.

QQ4 Details of the Duchess of Windsor's birth and marriage dates are tastefully presented in purple on the front of this pottery mug (9cm) commemorating her death. Made for *J. & J. May*.

QQ5 On 13th June 1987 Princess Anne was created Princess Royal and this was commemorated on a porcelain mug (9cm) from *A. & C. Dorincourt*. The design was later adapted to commemorate her 40th birthday in August 1990 and is thus inscribed on the inside rim. Made in a limited edition of 150.

QQ6 *Sutherland China* made this large mug (10cm) in porcelain to commemorate the 65th birthday of the Duke of Edinburgh. The portrait of the Duke in military uniform is accompanied by an inscription on the reverse of the mug with the birthday date, 10th June 1986. Made in a limited edition of 1000 exclusive to Peter Jones, Wakefield.

QQ7 and QQ11 Two matching porcelain mugs (9.5cm) which record the 40th and 60th birthdays of the Princess Royal and Princess Margaret respectively in August 1990. Personalised coats of arms are on the reverse. Exclusive to Peter Jones, Wakefield, from *Sutherland*.

QQ8 Royal beasts supporting a shield dominate the front of this *Coalport* mug (8cm) which celebrates in 1978 the 25th anniversary of the coronation. The event is recorded in an inscription on the inside rim.

QQ9 Attractive handles lined in gold decorate the shallow dish (19.5cm) also from the *Coalport* factory. Purple and pink stylized leaves fan out from the gold crown in the centre, which in turn is circled by the inscription recording the 25th anniversary of the coronation.

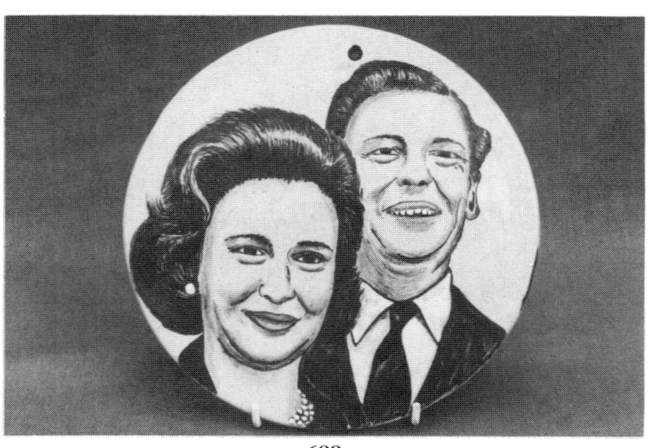

688

QQ10 This footed mug (12cm) in porcelain shows a framed coloured picture of Windsor Castle and records the 25th anniversary of the coronation on the reverse. Top and bottom rims are silver coloured. *Crown Staffordshire*.

*688 A most unusual, hand coloured plaque. It features the Earl and Countess of Harewood and may have been made at the time of their wedding in 1949 (although the portrait of Miss Marion Stein as she then was is none too flattering of a 22-year-old bride).

Colour Plate RR (page 96)

Royal Tours and Visits

RR1 This large porcelain tyg (15.5cm) was made by *Caverswall* to celebrate the 150th anniversary of the founding of the State of Western Australia in 1829. The celebrations were attended by the Prince of Wales. Three panels in sepia show the Prince and the first and present Prime Ministers against a rich blue and gold background. Made in a limited edition of not more than 500.

RR2 The Union Flag and the flag of Brunei are flanked by framed portraits of Queen Elizabeth and the Sultan of Brunei on this pottery mug (8cm). A reverse inscription reads "Brunei Tattoo 1977". Manufactured by *Sango China,* Japan.

RR3 A similar designed porcelain plate (25.5cm) with a portrait painted by Allen Hughes **(463)** was used for the coronation and has been here adapted to celebrate the visit of Queen Elizabeth and Prince Philip to the United States in 1957 and is thus recorded on the back. A patriotic inscription reads "Welcome to our friendly land, let's face the future hand in hand. Made in USA but no maker's mark.

RR4 Numerous examples are to be found of pieces commemorating the opening of the St Lawrence Seaway in 1959 by Queen Elizabeth II **(DD5)**. This particular pottery mug (7.5cm) was made by *Alfred Meakin* and shows a ship flanked by portraits of the Queen and the Duke of Edinburgh. The Great Lakes complex and seaway are outlined on the reverse in blue.

RR5 *Royal Crown Derby* were commissioned by Wm Plummer & Co, NY, to produce this exquisite porcelain vase (11.5cm) to celebrate the visit of King George VI and Queen Elizabeth to the United States in 1939. The sepia portraits are set against a pale blue ground, with extensive gilding decorating the foot, rim and eagle head handles. An inscription on the reverse against a gold shield and eagle reads "Friendship makes peace". Limited edition of 3000.

RR6 *Tuscan* used this bold sepia portrait to commemorate the visit of the Queen to Australia and New Zealand in 1953/54. The lower part of the plate (16cm) is inscribed with the details.

RR7 An attractive dish (11cm) from *Copeland Spode* showing a simple cypher bordered by national flora celebrating the Queen's visit to Australia in 1954. Inscription on the reverse.

RR8 Informal portraits of royalty are not often seen on commemorative china, but this mug (7cm) from the *Royal Winton* factory is the exception. The reverse records "In commemoration of the visit of Their Majesties to Australia, 1949". National emblems and gold lining decorate the upper rim.

RR9 *Minton* have made use of their 1937 coronation design **(279)** for this beaker commemorating the visit of the King and Queen to the United States in 1939. A scattering of gold stars has been added to the white ground, with a gold shield and eagle inscribed "Charity, tolerance and friendship makes peace" on the reverse side. Limited edition of 3000.

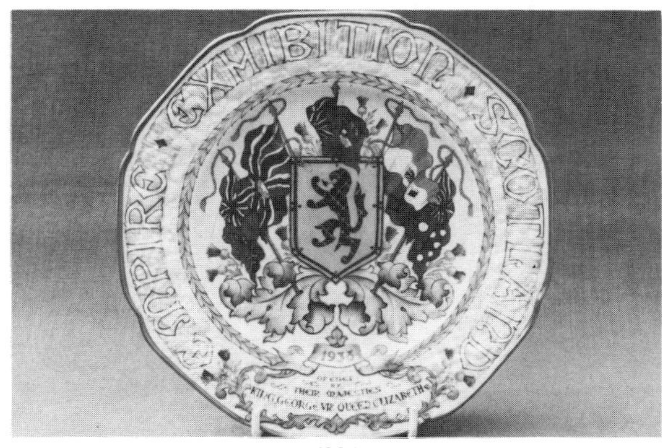

688A

RR10 A cypher and inscription is contained within an intricate design on this *Hammersley* mug (7cm) for the royal tour of Princess Elizabeth and the Duke of Edinburgh to Australia and New Zealand in 1952.

RR11 A *Paragon* dish (20cm) celebrates the royal visit to the USA and Canada in 1939. The enamelled shield and border inscription is accompanied by a floral border and maple leaves.

*688A This *Paragon* plate marks the opening of the 1938 Empire Exhibition in Glasgow by King George VI and Queen Elizabeth. The centre has a shield containing the Scottish Lion and flags of Empire. An inscription records the opening. Loving cup at **(HH3)**.

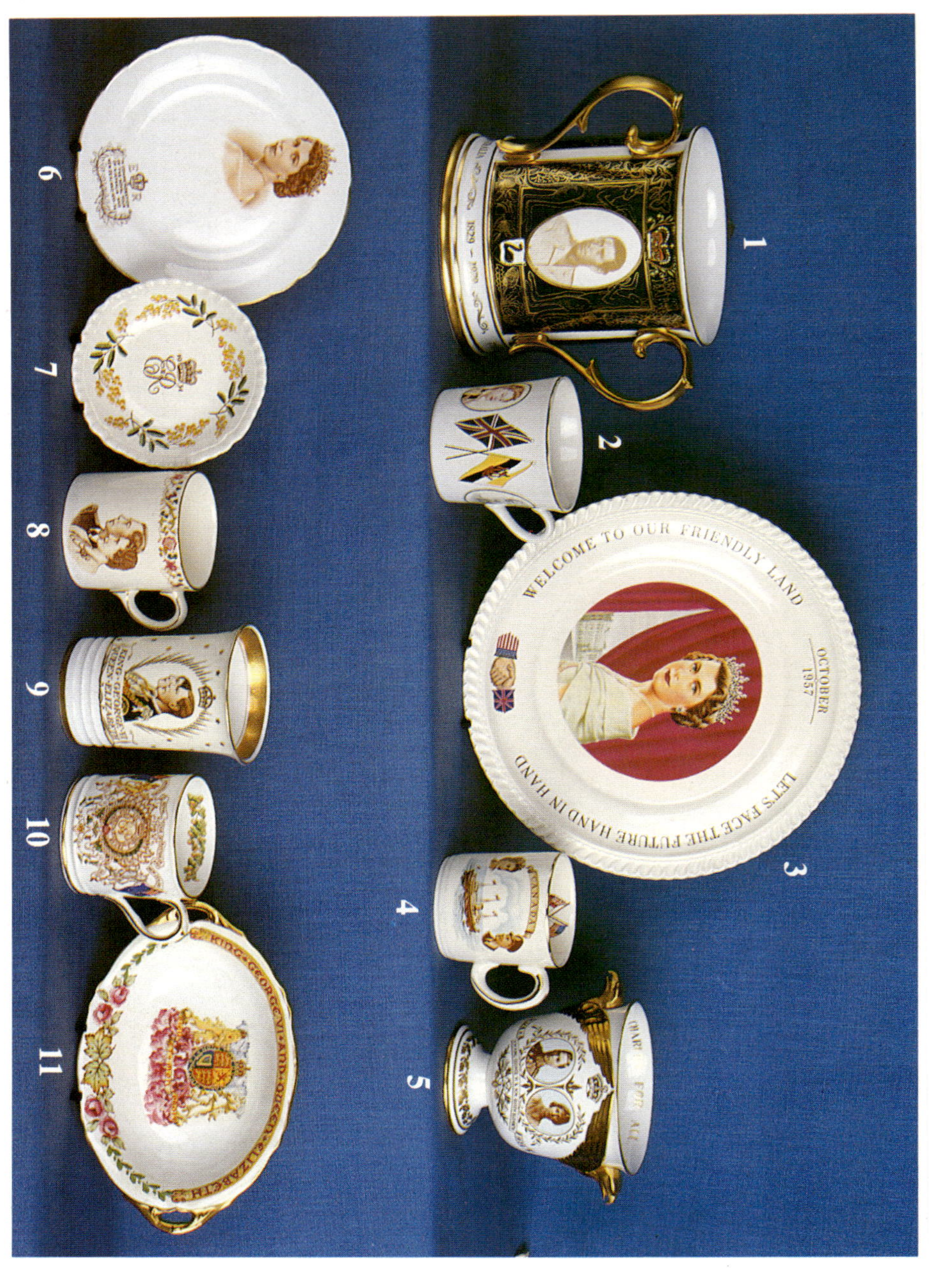

Royal Tours and Visits

Plate RR

(see page 95)

Royal Tours and Visits

The number and types of royal tours and visits increased as the 20th century progressed. By the time Edward VIII had come to the Throne it was reputed that he had covered over 300,000 miles on official duties – an incredible amount when one considers that air travel was still virtually unknown.

George VI had made several important visits before he came to the Throne, but none was more important politically than the visit to Canada and the USA in 1939 just prior to the outbreak of the Second World War. It is said that he helped substantially to persuade President Roosevelt to aid the Allies, and established a close personal relationship with the President which proved crucial during the War. The visit was a resounding success and was widely commemorated **(691)**.

On 1st February 1947 the Royal Family sailed in HMS Vanguard for a State visit to South Africa. This was the first major tour since the War **(699)**. Two years later a royal tour to Australia and New Zealand was cancelled due to the King's illness but many commemorative pieces had already been issued **(700, 701)**. King George VI, whose health was never robust, did not go on an overseas tour again. The burden of State Visits now fell mainly on Princess Elizabeth and Prince Philip who were to carry out the next major tour to Canada in 1951 **(703)**. It was in Kenya on 6th February 1952, en route to Australia **(706)**, that Elizabeth heard of the death of her father and of her succession to the Throne.

The increasing use of air travel has made visits overseas more frequent. As a result, and perhaps also due to a decrease in their political importance, we now pay less "ceremonial" attention to royal tours. Although many events are still celebrated, commemoratives are now often designed more for a collector market than as popular souvenirs.

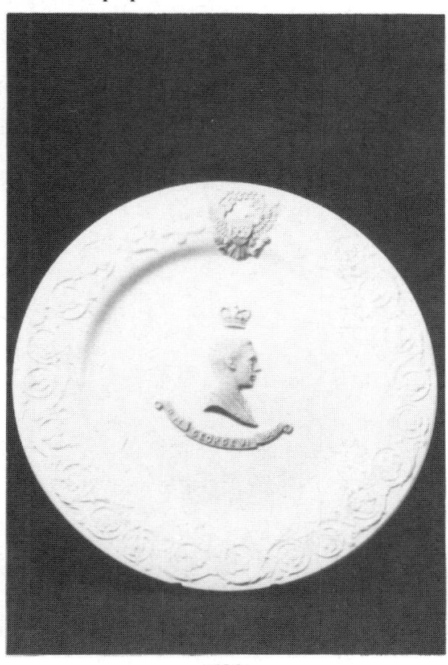

689

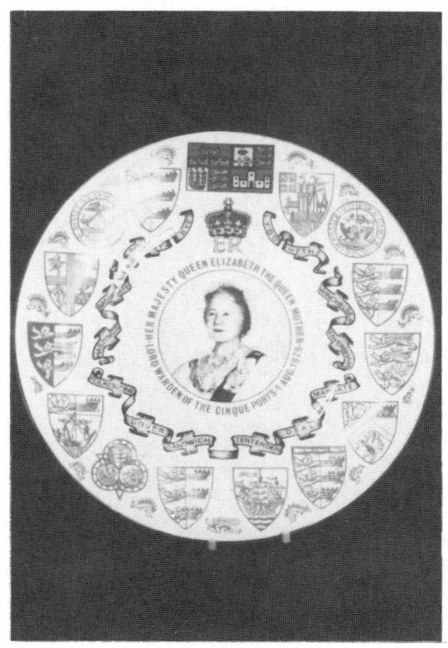

690

*689 This plate has a Queensware cream ground and commemorates the visit of George VI and Queen Elizabeth to the USA in 1939. A relief moulded border of shamrocks, harps, roses and thistles surrounds the central portrait of George VI which is in blue relief. Made in a limited edition of 3000 for W. Plummer & Co, New York, by *Wedgwood.*

*690 Forty years later Queen Elizabeth, now the Queen Mother, was installed as Lord Warden of the Cinque Ports at a ceremony in Dover Castle on 1st August 1979. This white, porcelain plate (24cm) from *Coronet Pottery* marks this auspicious occasion. A portrait of the Queen is in the centre, surrounded by shields of the fourteen towns which now constitute the "Cinque Ports" together with their names.

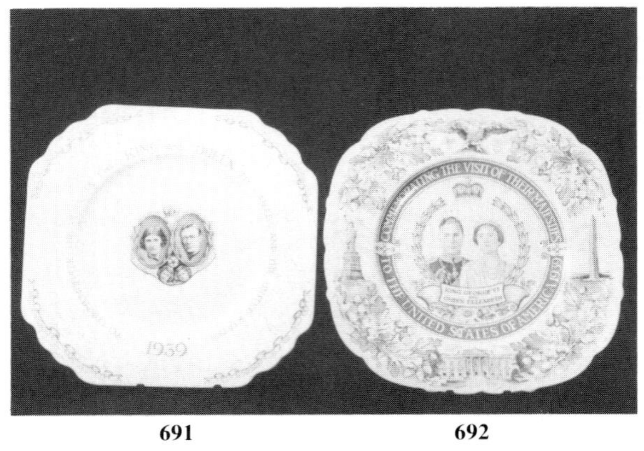

691 692

*691 The same transfer of the Royal Family decorates this pottery plate (23.5cm) from *Wedgwood & Co.* as was used on their Coronation pieces **(294)**. An additional inscription "To commemorate the visit of the King and Queen to Canada and the United States 1939" encircles the portraits.

*692 A similarly shaped pottery plate (22cm) made by *John Maddock & Sons* has an ornate "engraved" transfer in rose. Portraits of Their Majesties are framed by laurel and an inscription (which only mentions the USA). The rim has American views interspersed with acorns. A matching plate was produced for the Canadian part of the tour. See also **(434)**.

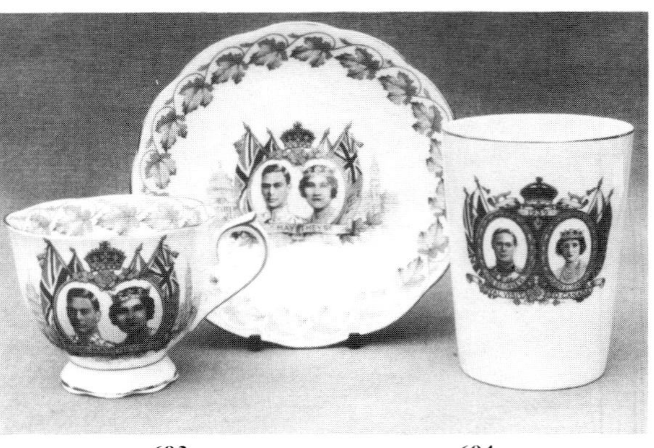

693 694

*693 *Royal Albert* produced this fine porcelain cup and saucer (6.5cm). Sepia portraits of Their Majesties, encaptioned "Long may they reign", are framed by coloured flags. In the background are The Capitol in Washington and the Parliament Buildings in Ottawa. Commemorative inscription is on the reverse and maple leaves decorate the inside.

*694 Sepia printed portraits (marked "copyright Vandyk") are surrounded by colourful flags and the caption "Royal visit to Canada 1939" on the front of this pottery beaker (10cm) from *Alfred Meakin.* The two young princesses are on the reverse.

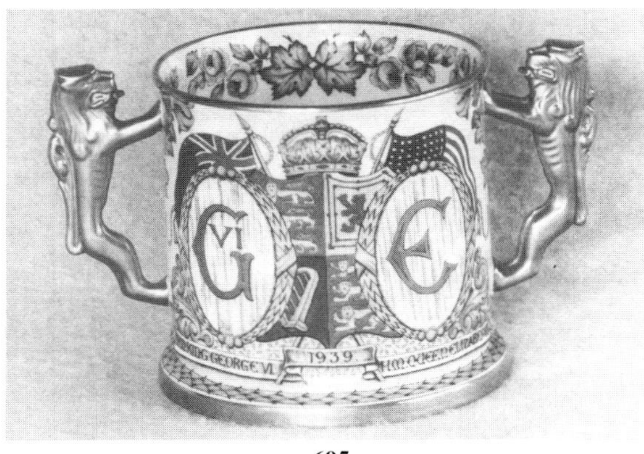

695

*695 This large porcelain loving cup comes from the *Paragon* factory and was issued to celebrate the State visit to Canada and The USA in 1939. A beautifully ornate design has the cyphers of George and Elizabeth in cartouches on either side of the Royal Arms. American and Canadian flags are above and the date 1939 below. National flowers and maple leaves are inside the rim. On the reverse are shields with Royal Arms and American flag beneath a crown all set within a pattern of laurel, maple leaves and acanthus. Limited to 350.

*696 The pottery ashtray (12.5cm) shown here was made in Canada by the *Sovereign* company. An interesting case of a royal commemorative piece being imported for a change! Colour printed medallion portraits of Their Majesties flanked by flags and surmounting the visit inscription is the decoration in the dish.

*697 Also from *Paragon* for the 1939 visit comes this porcelain mug (7.5cm). Interestingly it has the handle used on the 1935 Jubilee commemoratives **(204) (E2)**. The body is ivory coloured and the front features the Arms of Canada and the USA beneath a crown. National flowers are printed inside and outside the rim.

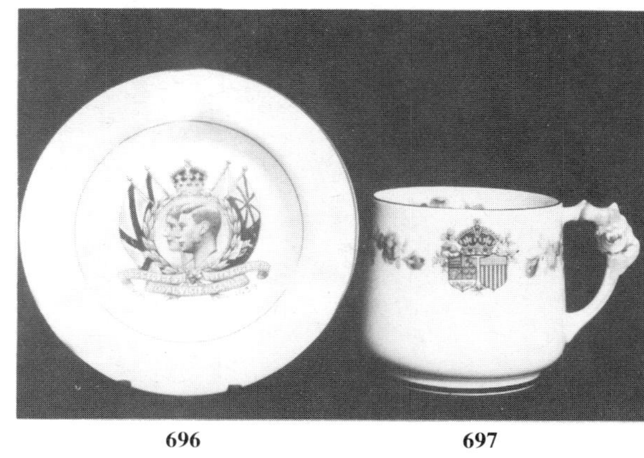

696 **697**

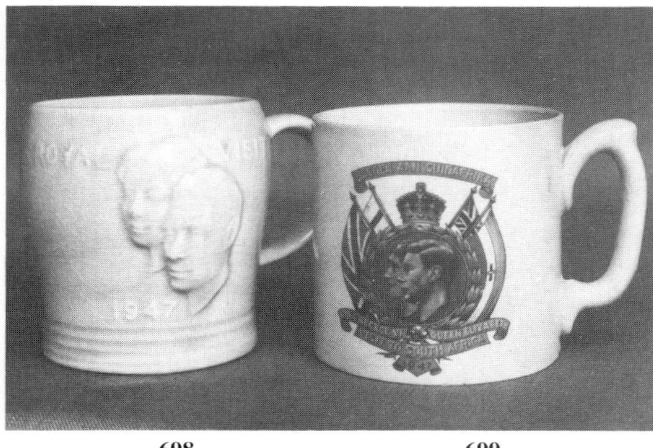

698 **699**

*698 *Crown Devon* made this ivory coloured pottery mug (8.5cm) to mark the 1947 visit to South Africa. Moulded heads of the King and Queen together with "Royal Visit 1947" are on the front with a springbok and "South Africa" on the reverse.

*699 This unmarked pottery mug (8cm) for the same visit is of particular interest because it was probably made in South Africa, having the inscription "Besoek aan Suid Afrika" in Afrikaans above the colour printed portraits of Their Majesties.

*700 This barrel shaped, pottery mug (7.5cm) was issued to mark the Australian visit of 1949 (which was cancelled due to the King's illness). It is of yellow ivory colour with moulded heads of Their Majesties within laurel on the front and GR cypher and national flowers on the reverse. At the top is "Royal Visit 1949". Marked *PPC*.

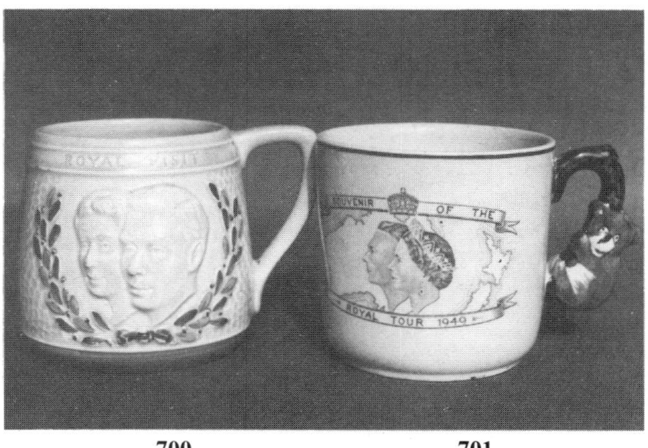

700 **701**

*701 Sepia printed medallion portraits of Their Majesties superimposed over Australia with the inscription "Souvenir of the Royal Tour 1949" decorate the front of this pottery mug (7.5cm) from *Brentleigh*. A friendly koala bear climbs up the handle.

*702, *703 Canadian maple leaves predominantly feature on both these items celebrating the visit to Canada in October 1951 of Queen Elizabeth and the Duke of Edinburgh. Collectors will quickly recognise both these as being from the *Paragon* factory **(475) (127A)**. The pin tray (11.5cm) shows an inscription within a narrow blue band surrounding the maple leaf, pink roses and a crown. Both cup (5.5cm) and saucer have the same basic design showing a cypher surrounded by maple leaves.

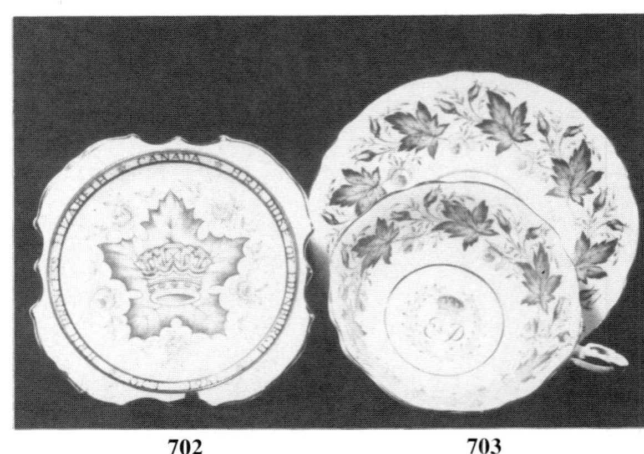

702 **703**

*704 For the royal visit to Australia and New Zealand in 1949 *Hammersley* produced this porcelain mug (7cm) which has a most elaborate printed design of medallion portraits within a circular frame of the Garter motto, acanthus scrolls and supporters carrying flags. The reverse has a cypher within a cartouche of laurel and acanthus with a crowned inscription "Long may they reign".

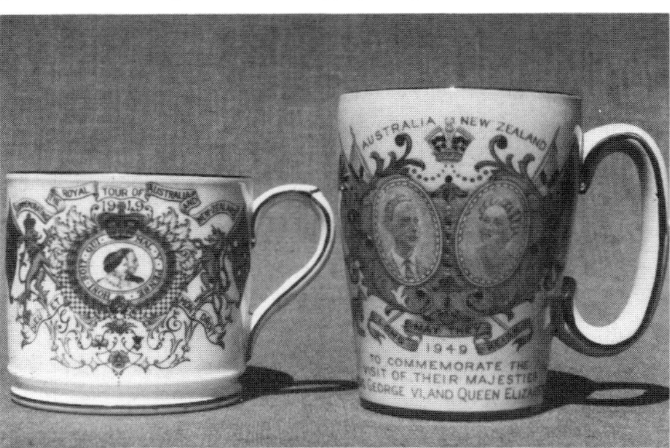

704 **705**

*705 In contrast, from *Sadler*, comes this pottery mug (10cm) which carries portraits of Their Majesties and (on the reverse) Princess Margaret. The portraits of the Queen and Princess are particularly naive. Printed in full colour with hand enamelling, the piece is both appealing and amusing.

*706 Another porcelain mug (7cm) from *Hammersley* marks the proposed visit of Princess Elizabeth and Prince Philip to Australia and New Zealand in 1952. The couple had progressed only as far as Kenya when the death of George Vl resulted in the Accession of Elizabeth to the throne and the cancellation of the rest of the tour. Similar in style to **(704)** with "E & P" replacing portraits of George and Elizabeth.

*707 This pottery dish (12cm) made by *Alfred Meakin* celebrates the 1959 opening of the St. Lawrence Seaway by Queen Elizabeth II. The Royal Yacht Britannia is depicted together with a map of the Great Lakes.

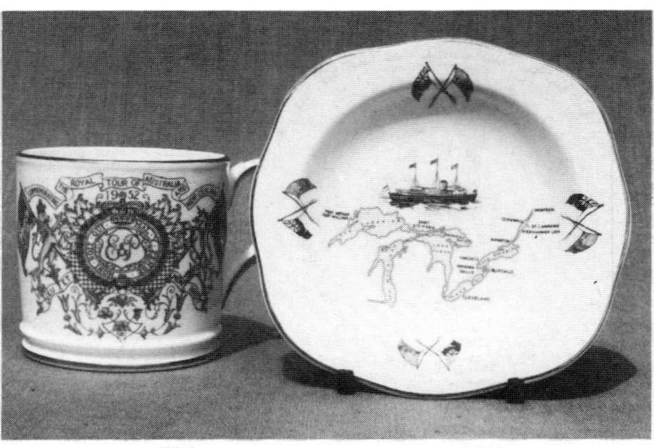

706 **707**

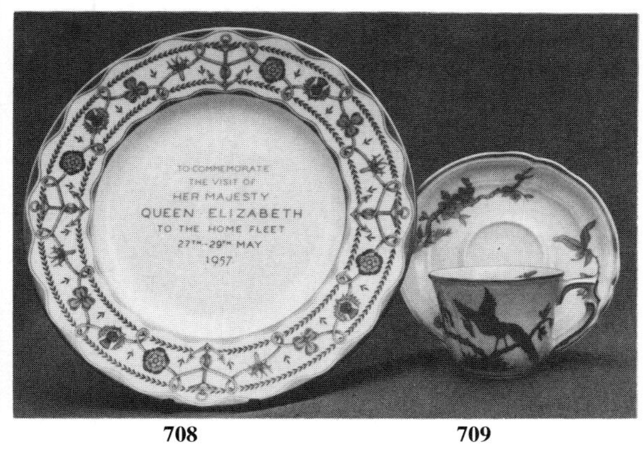

708 709

*708 To commemorate the visit of Queen Elizabeth to the home fleet in May 1957 *Minton* produced this porcelain plate (19.5cm). An inscription recording the event is in gold. The rim design incorporates an anchor, together with emblems representing the four home countries.

*709 By contrast, the dainty cup (5cm) and saucer bears no outward appearance of commemorating a royal event. Birds and trees are in gold, outlined in black. An inscription in French records the visit of Queen Elizabeth to France in April 1957. Made for *L. Bernard & Co, Limoges*.

*710 In October 1957 the Queen and Prince Philip went to Canada and the USA and these two porcelain tea ware pieces commemorate the visit. From *Paragon* a typical cup and saucer (5cm). A turquoise ground border with crowned E and P and ornamental filigree all in gold enclose a maple leaf with a superimposed crown. Commemoration on underside of the saucer.

*711 This tea cup and saucer (6.5cm) is from *Hammersley*. The black printed and hand enamelled Royal Arms is surrounded by national flowers including the maple leaf whilst lion and unicorn hold aloft flags of the USA and Canada. Designed by F.G. Clay.

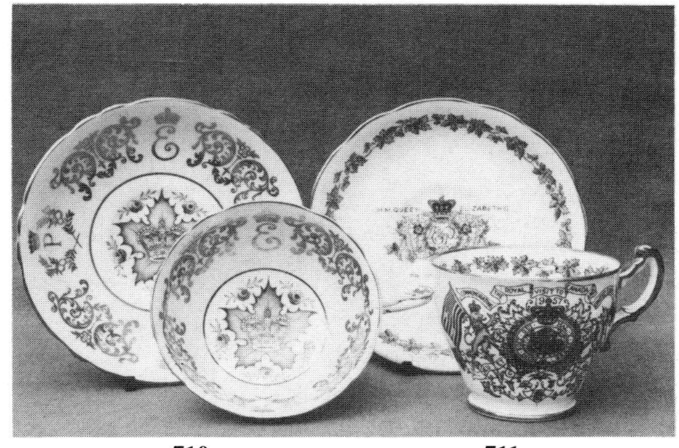

710 711

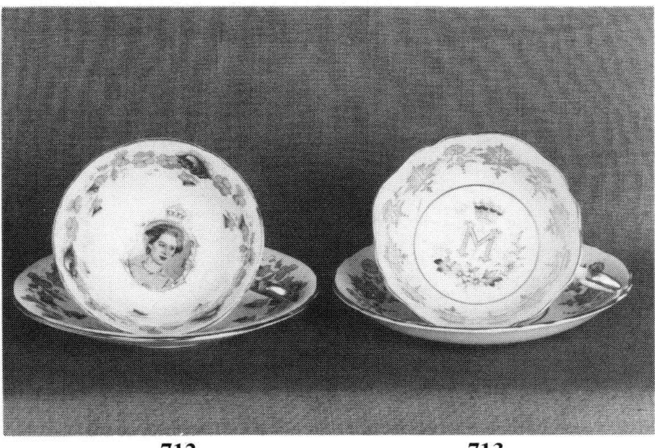

712 713

*712 Both cups (6cm) and saucers commemorate the visit of Princess Margaret to Canada in 1958 to coincide with the centenary celebrations in British Columbia. *Aynsley* made that showing a portrait of the Princess within the bowl of the cup, bordered with national emblems around the inside rim.

*713 The duck egg blue bowl of the *Paragon* cup shows a decorated initial within a narrow gold frame with appropriate maple leaves forming the broad border of the inside rim. This is repeated on the saucer with a reverse inscription detailing the occasion. Rims and handles are edged in gold.

*714 Two *Hammersley* mugs (8cm) bearing very intricate designs. Both commemorate overseas visits of Queen Elizabeth II and Prince Philip. Appropriately the crown against a maple leaf is used for their visit to Canada in 1959 to open the New St Lawrence Seaway and is thus inscribed on the reverse. Designed by F.G. Clay

*715 A more formal cypher within an inscribed frame has been used for the royal tour of Australia and New Zealand in 1953/54. Entwined coloured national emblems frame the initials E and P on the reverse, together with brief details of the occasion.

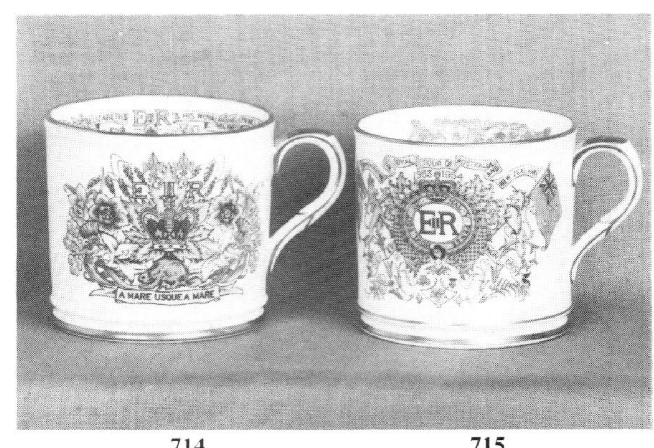

714 715

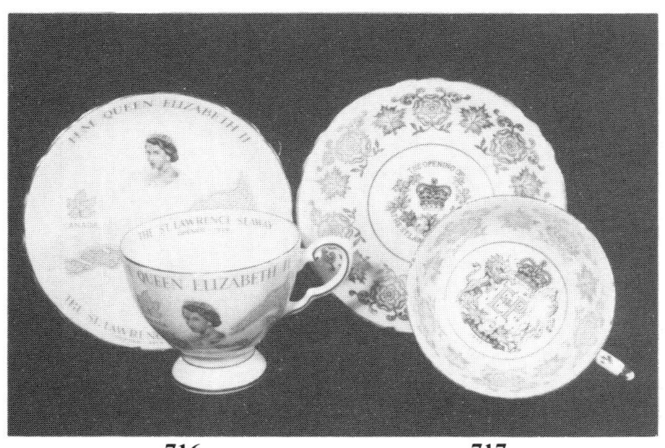

716 717

*716 Both these porcelain cups and saucers commemorate the visit of Queen Elizabeth II to Canada in 1959 to open the St Lawrence Seaway. That on the left (7.5cm) was made by *Tuscan* and shows sepia portraits, maple leaves and a map of the seaway on both cup and saucer. There is some gold lining to handle and rims.

*717 *Paragon* produced the other (5.5cm) which has a broad gold decoration of roses and maple leaves to both cup and saucer. Handle and rims are decorated with gold and the base of the saucer details the event.

*718 Made by *Hudson & Middleton*, this porcelain cup and saucer (7cm) has a colour printed design of a maple leaf enclosing sepia portraits of the Queen and Prince Philip. "Royal Visit to Canada June 1959" sits above the portraits. Reverse has a crowned EIIR cypher within laurel.

*719 This porcelain set (7cm) from *Jason China* features printed medallion portraits of the Queen and Prince Philip surrounded by flags and maple leaves. Interestingly the Queen is entitled "HM Queen Elizabeth II of Canada". Inscriptions record the opening of St Lawrence Seaway and State visit to Canada.

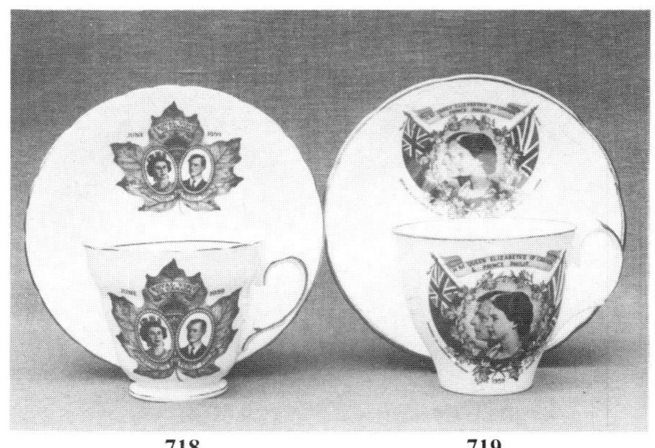

718 719

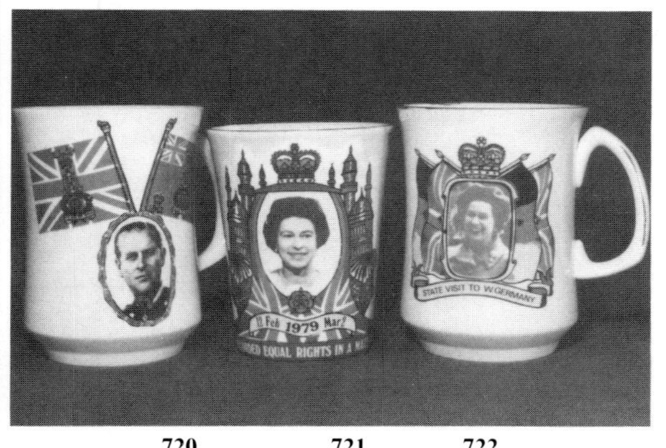

720 721 722

*720 *Panorama Studios* issued this porcelain mug (11cm) to commemorate the presentation of new colours to 40 Commando Royal Marines by Prince Philip on Plymouth Hoe, 1st July 1976. The front has a portrait of the Prince with Flags of the Royal Marines. Inscription on the rear.

*721 In 1979 the Queen visited the Middle East. This porcelain mug (11cm) from *Panorama* marks the event. A very colourful design with flags of six Gulf states and gilt mosques surrounding a portrait of the Queen. "The first woman to be accorded equal rights in a male-dominated society". 500 edition.

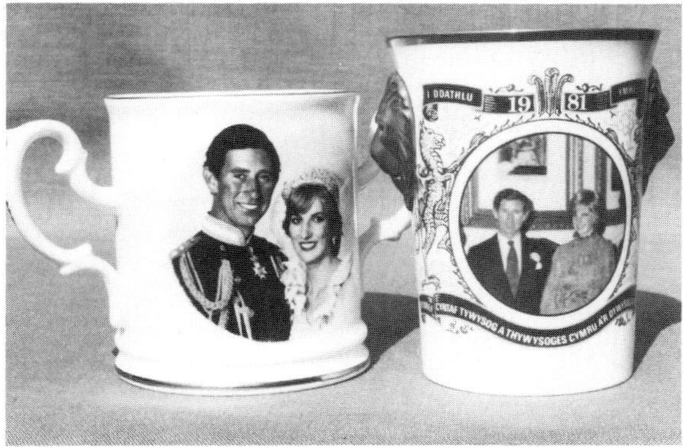

723 724

*722 A porcelain mug (11cm), also *Panorama*, marks the State visit of the Queen to West Germany between 22nd and 26th May 1978. On the front, a photograph of the Queen, and cities visited on the reverse.

*723 "To celebrate the first visit of the Prince and Princess of Wales to the Principality 27th-29th October 1981" in English and Welsh is on the reverse of this porcelain loving cup (9.5cm) by *Coronet Pottery*. There is a very attractive wedding day picture of the couple on the front. Limited to 250.

*724 For the same occasion, Peter Jones commissioned a porcelain, lion head beaker (11cm) from *Caverswall* in a limited edition of 250. An informal portrait of Charles and Diana supported by gilt dragons with an inscription in Welsh above and below is on the front. Welsh flags, Prince of Wales Feathers and daffodils are on the reverse.

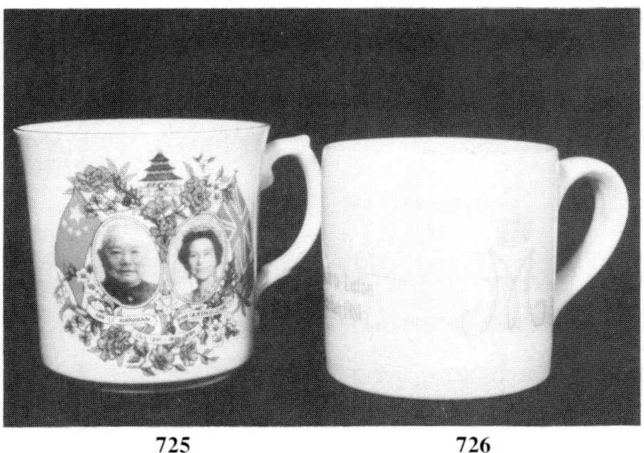

725 726

*725 A colourful porcelain mug (8.5cm) produced by *Dorincourt* commemorates the first State visit of a British reigning sovereign to China in 1986. Coloured portraits are surrounded by flowers, foliage and flags of both nations. An inscription records the unique event.

*726 Though the practice of commemorating royal visits to the provinces has steadily declined over the years, nevertheless this simple mug (8cm) in pottery by *Burleigh Ironstone* was produced to commemorate Princess Margaret's visit to Luton. The letter M and crown are in yellow and the mug is inscribed "NSPCC Young League; 21st October 1981".

Royal Births

During the period covered by this book four children were born to the Queen and Prince Philip, two to Princess Margaret and Lord Snowdon,two to the Prince and Princess of Wales (Prince Charles and Princess Diana), two to Princess Anne and Captain Mark Phillips,and two to the Duke and Duchess of York (formerly Prince Andrew and Miss Sarah Ferguson). Indeed the Queen has moved on from the "Empire's little Princess" at the time of her parents' Coronation in 1937 to being a grandmother six times over by 1990!

HRH Prince Charles of Edinburgh was born on 14th November 1948 at Buckingham Palace. King George Vl had, just prior to his grandson's birth, decreed that the children of his eldest daughter should hold the style, title or attribute of Royal Highness which would automatically have been accorded to the children of his sons had there been any. No known ceramic pieces exist to mark the birth of Prince Charles.

Similarly Princess Anne's birth, on 15th August 1950, at Clarence House has gone unrecorded by the potteries. In retrospect it does seem strange that neither of these important Royal events was commemorated. Not until 1951 with the Festival of Britain celebrations did the country shake off its wartime austerity to produce commemorative china in any quantity. Even so no pieces were produced for the births of Prince Andrew in 1960 or Prince Edward in 1964. The birth of the two children of Princess Margaret and the Earl of Snowdon, Viscount Linley, born 3 November 1961, and Miss Sarah Armstong Jones born in 1961, have not been marked by commemoratives either.

In 1977, however, the first of Princess Anne's children Peter Phillips, did receive a little recognition and three known pieces are included **(728 729 PP10)** together with the sole item we have discovered for Zara by Panorama studios **(PP9)**.

The flood gates were opened, commemoratively speaking, in 1982 for the birth of Prince William of Wales and this marks the beginning of a wealth of commemoratives celebrating the births of Prince Henry, Princesses Beatrice and Eugenie.

*727 A charming, informal, colour portrait of the Princess of Wales holding the new born Prince William is on the front of this porcelain mug (8cm) from *Coronet Pottery.* The reverse has an inscription, printed in blue, giving the prince's full name and date of birth.

*727A This porcelain beaker (11.5cm) with lion handles, in a 1000 edition, from *Caverswall* marks the birth of Prince William. A coronet surmounted by Welsh dragon with flags and National emblems is on the front with full names on the reverse.

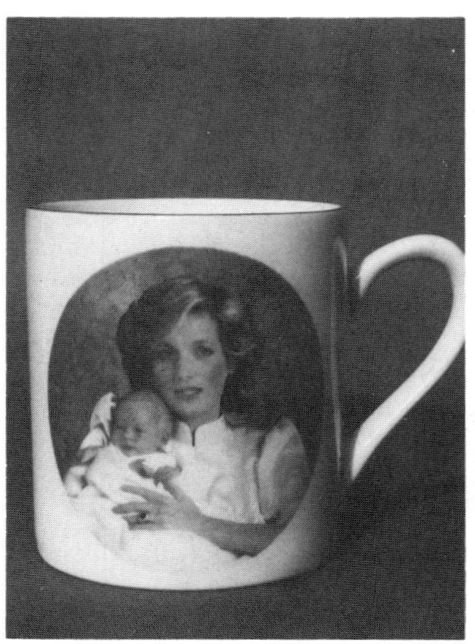

727

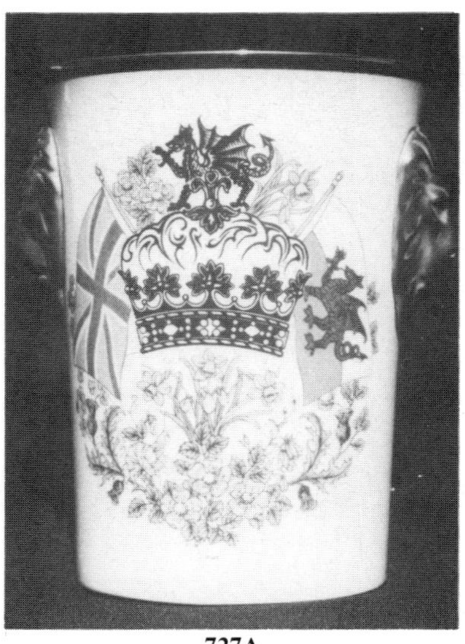

727A

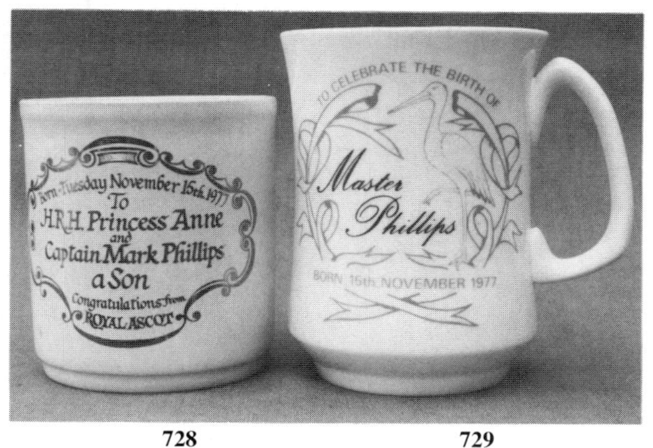

728 729

*728 West Country potters have made interesting contributions to royal commemoratives over the years but there has been a decline in the number of factories and, consequently, their contribution. *Honiton* made this pottery mug (9 cm) which simply records, in gold, the birth of a son to Princess Anne and Captain Mark Phillips.

*729 Princess Anne declined a title for her son. This porcelain mug (11 cm) celebrates the birth of Master Phillips and is thus inscribed in red with further decoration in blue. The reverse records that this is the first grandchild of Queen Elizabeth II and Prince Philip Duke of Edinburgh. *Panorama.*

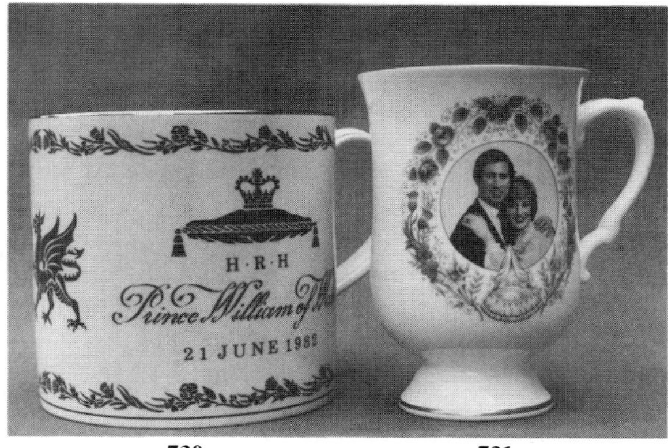

730 731

*730 Richard Guyatt designed this pottery mug (10.5 cm) for *Wedgwood* in a limited edition of 1000 to celebrate the birth of Prince William. A design similar in some respects was produced for the birth of Prince Henry (**PP11**). The front decoration in royal blue is repeated on the back.

*731 *Crown Staffordshire* made this modern style tall porcelain beaker (12cm). An informal coloured portrait of the happy parents framed by national emblems is complemented by a small pink crib. The reverse has a suitable inscription.

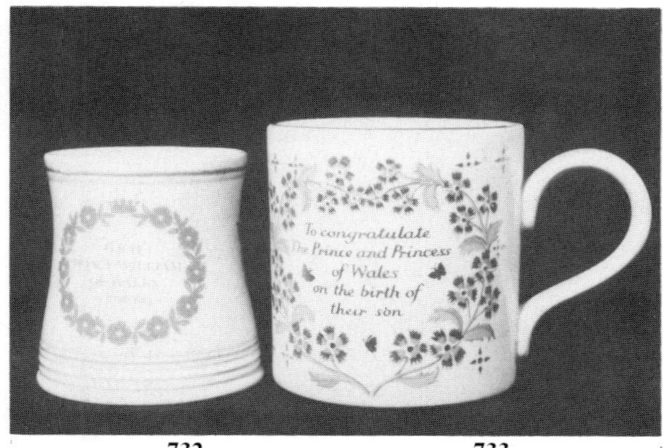

732 733

*732 Printed inscriptions within a rose decorated border in blue record the birth of Prince William of Wales on 21st June 1982 on the front of this pottery mug (7.5cm). Crowns and date are .shown either side of the handle with narrow blue lines outlining the base and rim. *Rye Pottery.*

*733 Another pottery mug (8.5 cm) commemorates the birth of Prince William – this time from *Cardigan Pottery* and specially commissioned by the National Trust. Cherubs and inscriptions are in gold with foliage and flowers in greens and blues. The front design has been repeated on the back.

*734 Loving cups continue to be popular with collectors. *Aynsley* produced this one (6cm) in porcelain to commemorate the birth of Prince William. The front shows a framed coloured picture of Windsor Castle with an inscription recording the event on the reverse.

*735 An all gold decoration is favoured by *Wedgwood* who manufactured this fine porcelain mug (7.5cm) for the proclamation of the birth of Prince William. National emblems shaped in a fashion similar to that of the Prince of Wales feathers are cleverly used with cypher and date either side of the handle. Designed by Richard Guyatt.

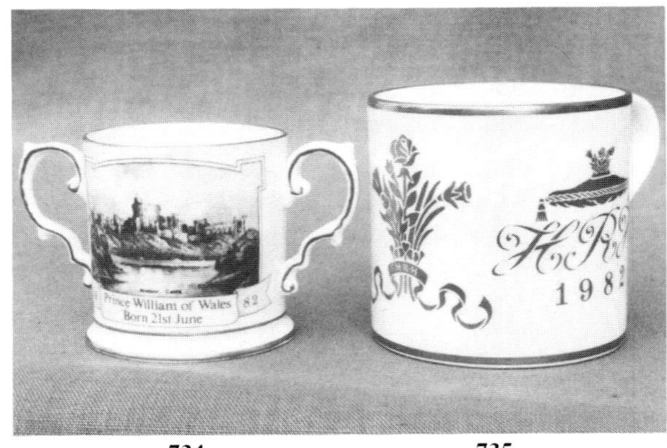

734 **735**

*736 Another porcelain goblet (12cm) in the series produced by *Coalport*. This example in cobalt blue and gold has a continuous decoration of royal residences including Windsor, Highgrove House, Caernarvon and Kensington Palace. Pennants contain national symbols, and an inscription commemorates the birth of the first child. Limited to 2000.

*737 A complete contrast is this studio pottery tankard (14cm) from the *Chelsea Pottery*. The glazed body is in blue/grey with "Happy Birthday Prince William of Wales 21st June 1982" in brown. On each side an angel looks on over coloured sprigs of flowers.

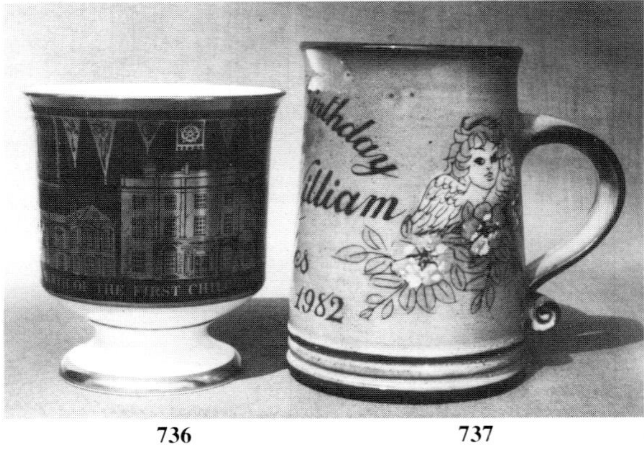

736 **737**

*738 Miniatures have always had a special appeal and many of today's collections include a selection of these delicate pieces. On the left this porcelain (2cm) set from *Caverswall* was issued to celebrate the birth of Princess Beatrice of York in 1988. A very delicate design of a baby in a cradle within a frame of roses with the Princess' names and birth date are printed in pink and sepia.

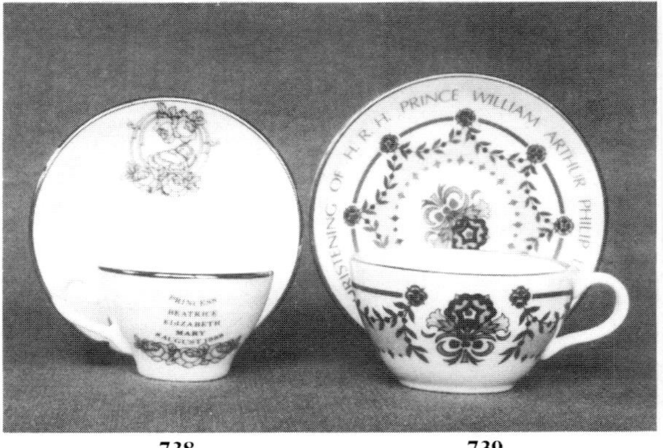

738 **739**

*739 This porcelain cup and saucer (2.cm) made by *Spode* marks the birth and christening of Prince William. A colourful frieze of roses and daffodils with the Prince's full names in gold make up the design.

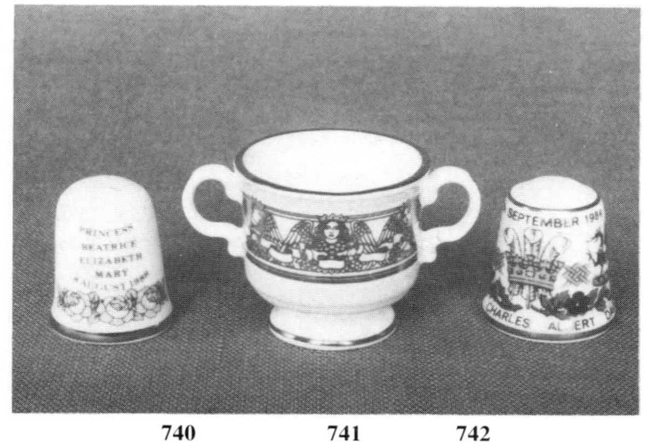

740 741 742

*740 This group of miniatures includes on the left a porcelain thimble (2cm) from *Caverswall* for the birth of Princess Beatrice which has the same design as (738).

*741 A porcelain loving cup from *Spode* (3cm) to celebrate the christening of Prince William on 4th August 1982. A group of angels printed in gold with a frame containing details of the christening make up the design.

*742 This porcelain thimble (2cm) commemorating the birth of Prince Henry of Wales in 1984 was produced by *Sutherland China*. Prince of Wales Feathers and Welsh dragons together with full commemorative details make this a colourful design.

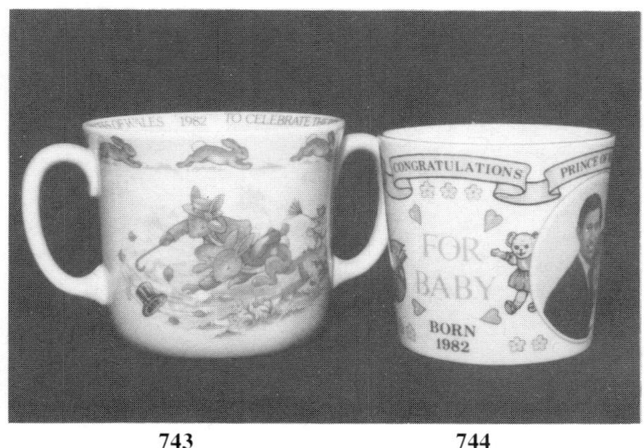

743 744

*743 This pottery loving cup (7.5cm) is one of the popular "Bunnykins" series from *Royal Doulton*. This example (a number of different designs were produced) has windswept scenes on front and reverse. "To celebrate the birth of the first child of TRH The Prince and Princess of Wales 1982" is inside.

*744 Another entirely appropriate children's design decorates a porcelain mug (7cm) by *Coalport*. Colourful nursery toys and "For Baby" surround a portrait of Charles and Diana. A very pretty memento for the birth of Prince William.

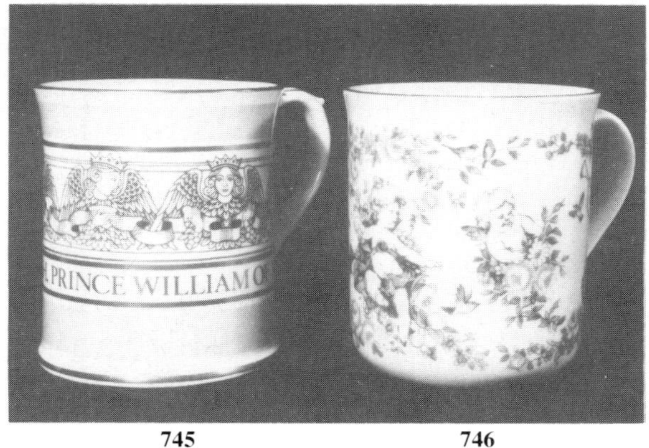

745 746

*745 Prince William was christened on 4th August 1982 and *Spode* commemorated the occasion with this fine porcelain mug (9cm). Two broad blue bands frame the gold inscription and angel-like figures **(741)**. Gold lining to the base, rim and handles enhance the quality.

*746 *Royal Worcester* produced this porcelain mug (9cm) to celebrate the birth of Prince William of Wales on 21st June 1982 and it is inscribed as such on the base. Four cherubs amongst garlands of flowers and leaves completely cover the piece. Colours are mainly in pink, yellow, green and blue. A pretty piece.

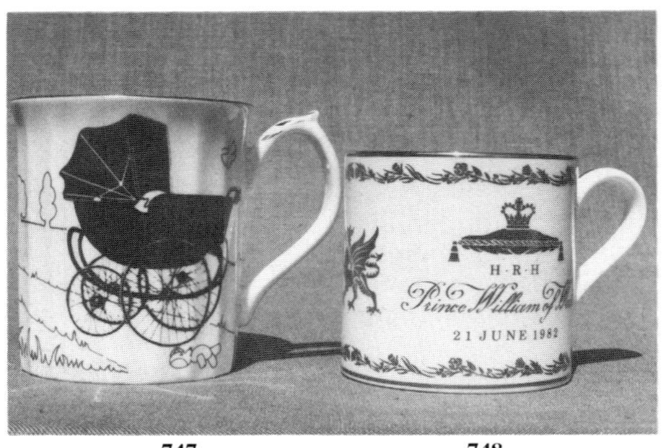

747 **748**

*747 A further example of the *J & J May* series of commemoratives is this porcelain mug (9cm) marking Prince William's birth. An elegant Victorian pram, coloured royal purple, with gilt monogram C and D is shown in a parkland scene coloured gold. A discarded teddy lies on the path. A commemorative inscription is inside the rim.

*748 This porcelain mug (7.5cm) from *Wedgwood* matches **(735)**. Here the dragon of Wales is on the front. On either side a cushion with crown, the Prince's full name and date of birth. All is printed in gold. Designed by Richard Guyatt

*749 This small porcelain coffee cup and saucer (6cm) from *Royal Worcester* was commissioned by Atelier Art Editions. A gold printed silhouette of Diana and the baby is the only decoration on the cup with "1982 the Princess of Wales" on the saucer.

*750 Ringtons of Newcastle commissioned this tulip-shaped, porcelain mug (9cm) from *Elizabethan China*. A cupid rests against an elaborate design of purple cloth with entwined C and D, crowned Prince of Wales feathers, and celebratory inscriptions.

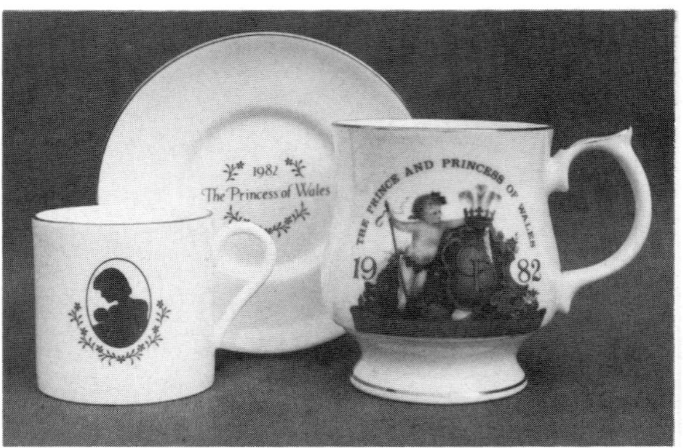

749 **750**

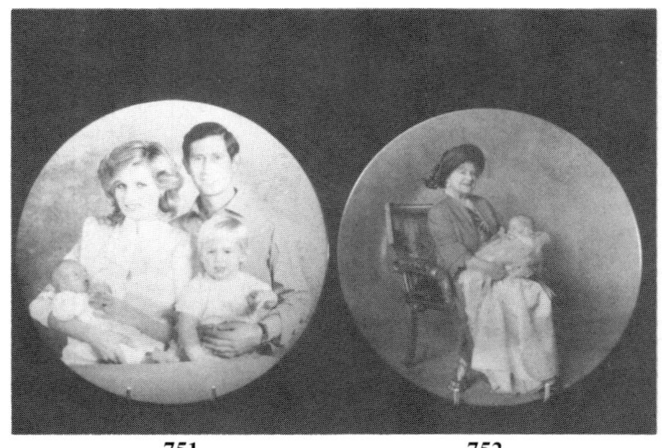

751 **752**

*751, *752 These two porcelain plates, (both 27cm) were produced to mark the birth of Prince Henry. On the left a fine portrait of Charles and Diana with their two children on a pale blue ground fill this plate made by *Royal Albert*.

On the right, The Queen Mother dressed in a typical purple outfit holds Prince Henry in this charming study on a plate from *Pall Mall ware*.

*753 *Royal Crown Derby* issued this porcelain loving cup (7.5cm) in an edition of 750 to mark the birth of Prince Henry. On the side not illustrated is a putto surrounded by flowers in a gold frame. Blue swags form a continuous design linking front and rear. Gold coronets surmount each frame.

*754 Richard Guyatt designed this porcelain mug (7.5cm) for *Wedgwood*. On either side of the armorial design on the front are inscriptions "HRH Prince Henry 15 September 1984" beneath a crown resting on a cushion. The complete design is printed in gold.

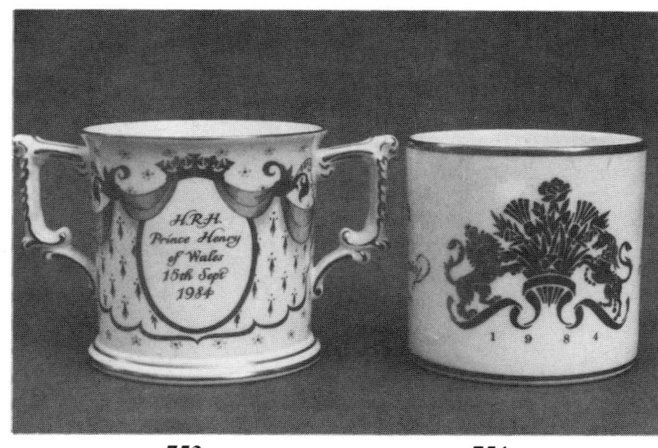

753 **754**

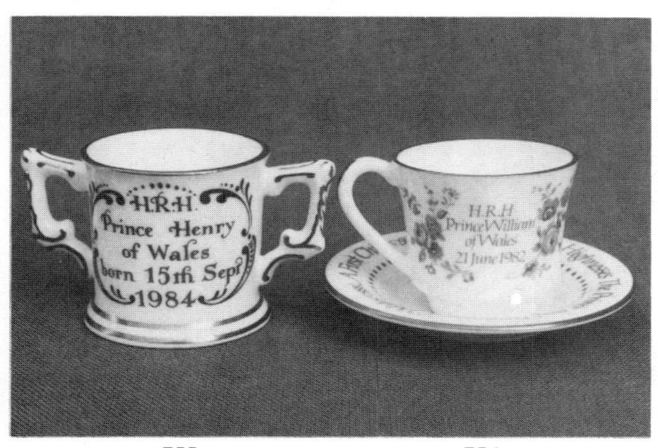

755 **756**

*755 From *Royal Crown Derby* comes this exquisite, miniature porcelain loving cup (3cm) to mark the birth of Prince Henry. On the reverse are Royal Pinxton roses printed in full colour with touches of gold highlights. The inscription shown is also in gold within a rose frame. A similar miniature was issued for Prince William's birth.

*756 Another porcelain miniature piece, this time from *Royal Worcester*, to mark the birth of Prince William. The cup (3cm) has a gold silhouette of a baby's head within sprays of flowers printed in blue. On the reverse a full inscription. The saucer has "A first child to their Royal Highnesses the Prince and Princess of Wales".

*757 This delightfully cheerful pottery mug (9cm) was designed by Benjamin Tonks, aged 8, of Hornsea Primary School for *Hornsea Pottery*. It has "a loyal message...I hope the baby will not be too noisy". The colourful scene depicts baby William in a yellow pram pushed by proud parents with the Queen looking on and Guards in attendance.

*758 *Honiton Pottery* produced this sand coloured mug (9cm) for the birth of "Prince Harry". All the decorative inscription is printed in brown.

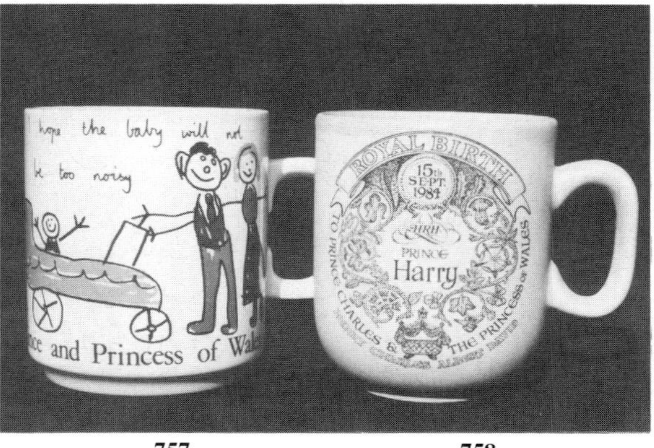

757 **758**

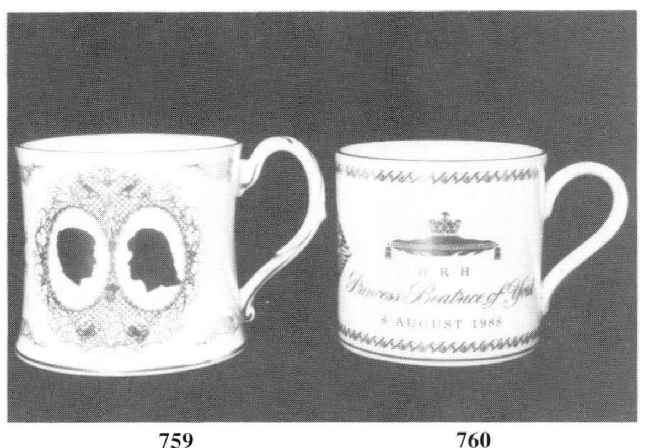

759 **760**

*759 Facing profile portraits in gold framed in an intricate design of national emblems, also in gold, feature on this porcelain mug (7.5cm) by *Coalport*. An inscription reads "To celebrate the birth of the first child Beatrice Elizabeth Mary daughter of the Duke and Duchess of York 8.8.1988". Issued in a limited edition of 2500.

*760 Richard Guyatt designed this porcelain mug (7.5cm) for the *Wedgwood* factory and it is somewhat similar to that produced for the birth of William in 1982 **(748)**. The complete design is in gold with a top and bottom frieze similar to **(660)** and has a suitable inscription to the base recording the event. Limited to 2000.

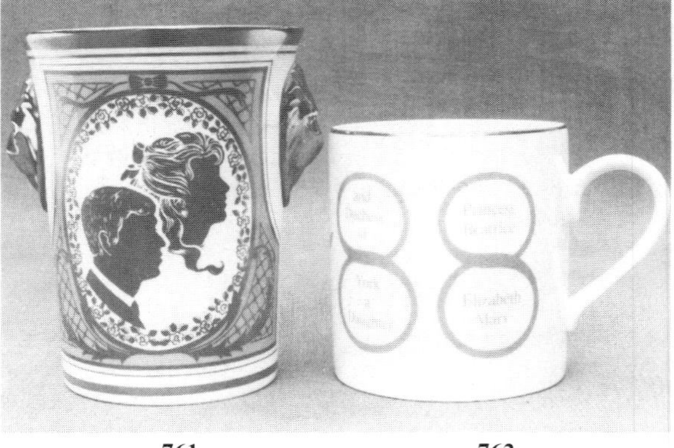

761 **762**

*761 Gilt profile portraits of the Duke and Duchess of York framed within a turquoise ground are on the front of this porcelain, lion head beaker (11.5cm), designed by Stephen Barnsley for *Caverswall China*. On the reverse a commemorative inscription recording the date and time of Princess Beatrice's birth. Limited to 250.

*762 A simple but effective design distinguishes this porcelain mug (8cm) from *J & J May*. The numbers 8-8-88 in pink contain the words "On this happiest of happy days to their Royal Highnesses the Duke and Duchess of York a daughter Princess Beatrice Elizabeth Mary".

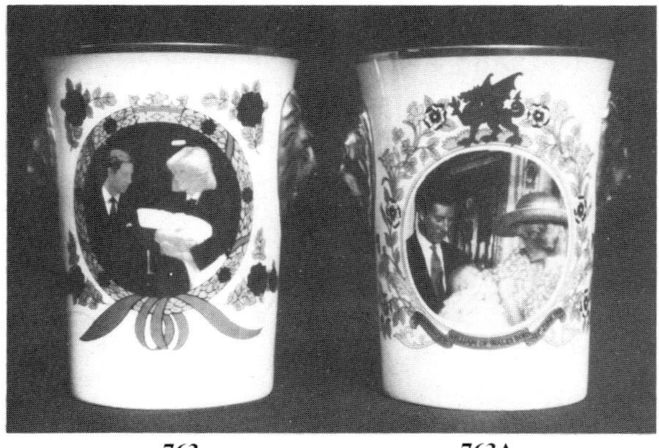

763 **763A**

*763 Two of the popular "lion head" porcelain beakers (11.5cm) made by *Caverswall* to mark the births of the two children of the Prince and Princess of Wales. The one on the left, commissioned by Peter Jones, has a picture of the happy parents holding Prince Henry. The reverse has Henry's full names framed by coloured roses. Edition of 250.

*763A On the right a photograph of Their Royal Highnesses holding baby Prince William surrounded by flowers and a Welsh dragon is on the front of the beaker celebrating the birth of William. On the reverse flags, lion, unicorn and flowers surround William's full names. 500 edition.

Royal Anniversaries

This chapter which illustrates a selection of wares produced to celebrate birthday anniversaries of members of the Royal Family is dominated by the birthdays of Queen Elizabeth the Queen Mother. Items were produced. albeit in small quantities for her 75th, then in greater numbers for her 80th and 85th. Somewhat surprisingly it appears that much less has been issued to mark her 90th birthday. Many of us had expected a flood of commemoratives for this most significant occasion bearing in mind the Queen Mother's widespread popularity.

Not until the 80's did the production of large quantities of these anniversary pieces get underway. Before 1980 we have only come across items for the Queen Mother's 75th birthday **(764, 765)**, Princess Alice's 95th **(766)** and Prince Charles' 30th **(767)**. With the celebration of the Queen Mother's 80th birthday the potters really went to town and have continued to produce a wide range of anniversary commemoratives ever since.

Whilst many of the designs, predictably, rely on portraits one or two have attempted something a little different. The Sutherland China mug **(795)** for the Queen's 60th birthday is very colourful, using the Trooping of the Colour to great effect. Similarly the Caverswall mug **(778)** for the Queen Mother's 80th has a charming illustration of the Queen in her coach. And perhaps Panorama's mug **(773)** for the same occasion captures a popular feeling with its inscription "To celebrate the 80th birthday of a great grand Queen and mother".

Princess Anne seems to have "missed out" in this area. Nothing was issued for her birthdays until her 40th in 1990, whereas Andrew and Edward both have pieces for their 21st and 18th respectively and Charles for his 30th and 40th. Inevitably, in the absence of a coronation or wedding, the potters will look more and more to birthdays as reasons for celebration. It is to be hoped they will do so in an interesting way.

*764 Illustrated are two of the relatively few pieces issued to mark the Queen Mother's 75th birthday. This cone shaped pottery mug (8.5cm) has a gold printed transfer of the Queen Mother on the front with crowned cypher, 1900-1975, August 4th on the rear. Around the foot "To celebrate the 75th Birthday of HM Queen Elizabeth the Queen Mother". *Dartington Pottery.*

*765 On the right is a porcelain mug (10.5cm) of waisted form produced by *Panorama Studios*. The only decoration is a black printed portrait of a smiling Queen with a commemorative inscription in blue on the front of the mug. A similar plate was made **(MM5)**.

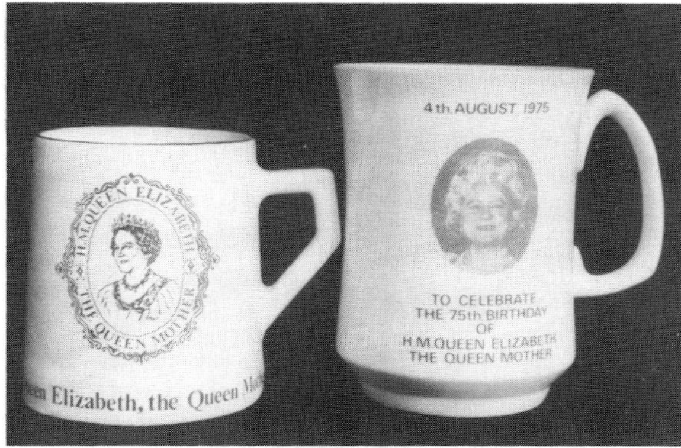

764 **765**

*766 Two birthday porcelain mugs (10.5cm) by *Panorama Studios*, Ashburton, issued in limited editions of 500. That on the left celebrates the 95th birthday of Princess Alice Countess of Athlone, a granddaughter of Queen Victoria. A sepia portrait is contained within a garland of yellow roses and green foliage. The reverse lists her titles and records that she was born at Windsor Castle on 25th February 1883.

*767 Prince Charles's portrait is also in sepia flanked by two red dragons. On the reverse is recorded that he is the 21st Prince of Wales together with a number of his titles. Made for his 30th birthday.

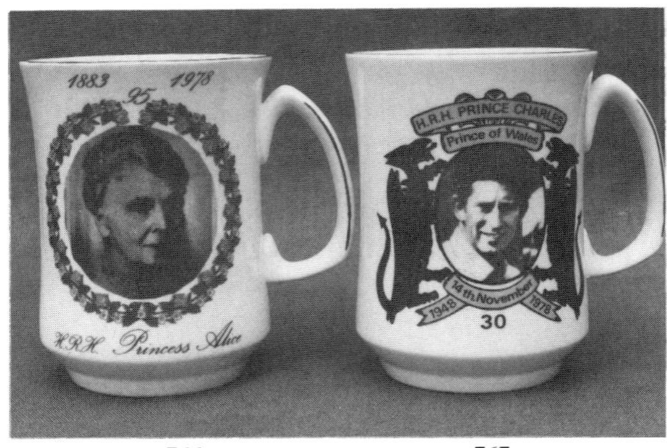

766 767

*768 Two porcelain mugs (10cm) recording the 50th birthday of Princess Margaret. *Panorama* made the one on the left to a design to be repeated in 1982 for Princess Diana's 21st birthday **(785)**. An inscription records that she was born at Glamis Castle on August 21st 1930. Gold coloured rose and "50" are printed on the inside rim. Limited edition of 250.

*769 *Caverswall* made the second mug (9cm) showing a more formal sepia portrait in an oval frame. Stylized flowers either side are in gold, yellow and green. The base is suitably inscribed.

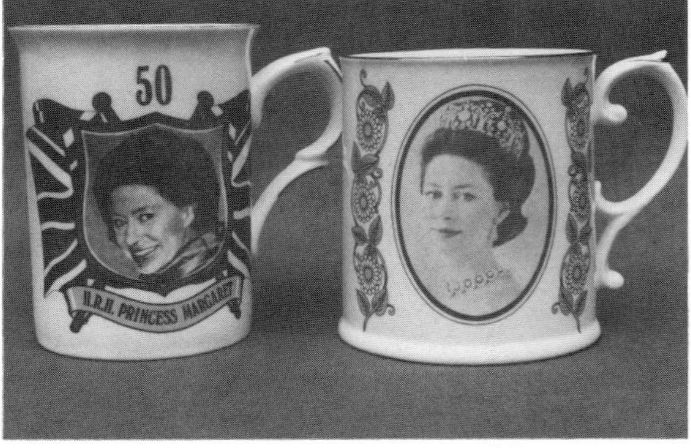

768 769

*770 This porcelain plate (22.5cm) was produced by *Royal Crown Derby* to mark the Queen Mother's 85th birthday. It has a splendid bouquet of flowers in the centre with a green scroll border. "E" in a shield at the top and small stars round the rim are in gold.

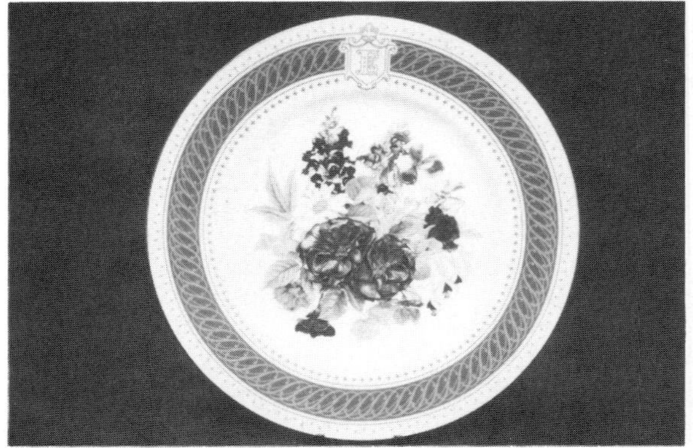

770

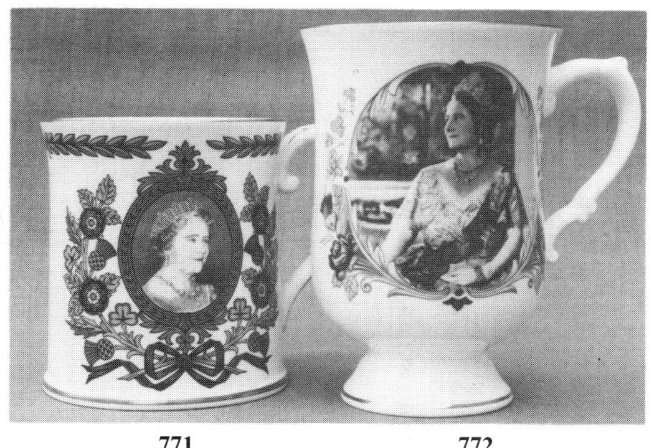

771 772

*771 Both these porcelain mugs use formal portraits of the Queen Mother to commemorate her 80th birthday. That on the left (9cm) is by *Spode* and shows a sepia portrait within a frame of coloured emblems. The reverse records the occasion inside a gold coloured frame.

*772 The other is a tall, shaped mug (12cm) and shows a coloured three quarter length study of the Queen Mother, with a garland of national emblems. An inscription in yellow is shown on the inside rim. Made by *Crown Staffordshire*.

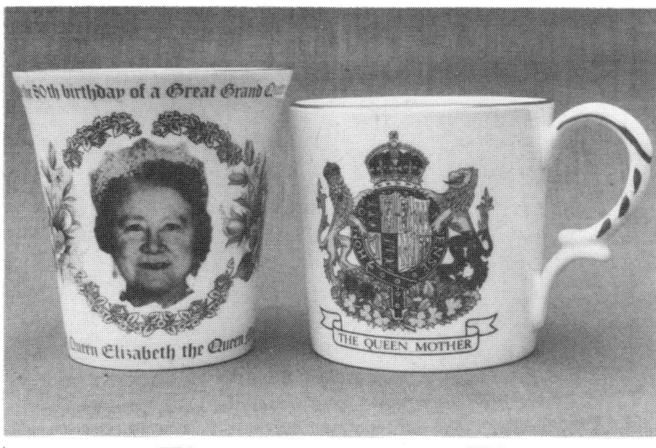

773 774

*773 This tall flared mug (9.5cm) with a rear handle was produced by *Panorama,* for the Queen Mother's 80th birthday, in a limited edition of 500. The sepia portrait of the Queen Mother is framed with blue foliage with inscription circumscribing top and bottom rims.

*774 *Aynsley* made this 80th birthday mug (8.5cm) showing a coloured coat of arms. In true Aynsley tradition of more recent years a family tree is shown on the reverse, in this case of the Bowes-Lyon family. The inside rim is inscribed and gold decoration applied to the rim and moulded handle.

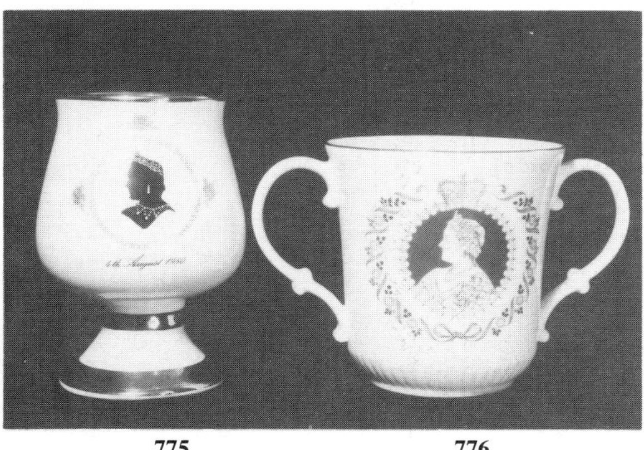

775 776

*775 *Prinknash Pottery,* Gloucester, commemorated the Queen Mother's 80th birthday with this cream ground porcelain goblet (12cm). A black profile is circled with an inscription in gold. The complete inside is gold as are bands around the foot, waist and rim. Dated 4th August 1980. See also **(630)**.

*776 A porcelain loving cup (10cm) produced for the Queen Mother's 80th birthday in an unlimited edition by the *Royal Doulton* factory. The sepia portrait of the Queen Mother is framed by a garland of coloured flowers surmounted by a gold crown. An inscription replaces the portrait in an otherwise similar back decoration.

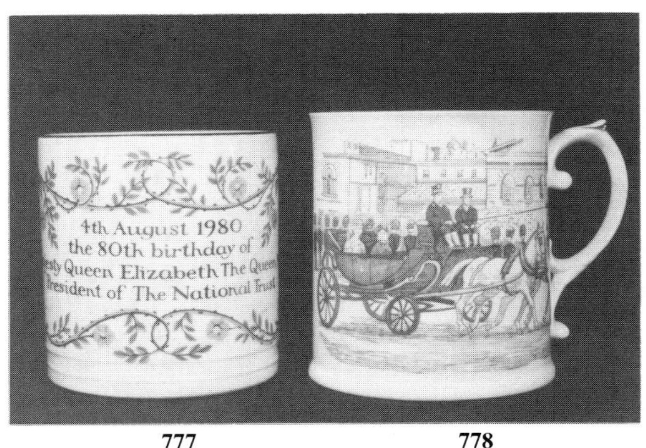

777 **778**

*777 The National Trust commissioned this pottery mug (8.5cm) from *Boncath Pottery* and it would have been sold to members and visitors through their various retail outlets. A simple but attractive design shows a silver coloured inscription decorated with flowers and leaves. The rim is outlined in silver.

*778 A coloured drawing of an open landau with two occupants is shown on the porcelain mug (9cm) made by *Caverswall*, for the Queen Mother's 80th birthday, in a limited edition of 2500. Vignettes of the Queen Mother's residences of Mey, Walden Bury and Glamis are featured on the reverse, together with a sepia coat of arms.

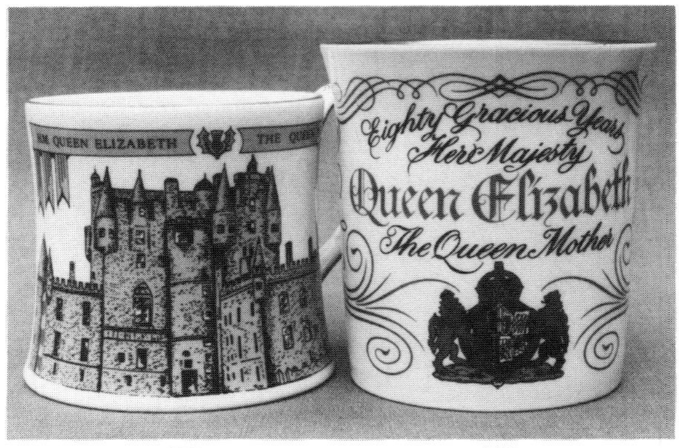

779 **780**

*779 A detailed print of Glamis Castle is on the front of this porcelain waisted mug (7.5cm) from *Coalport*. On the reverse the Queen Mother's Coat of Arms. Inside the rim "The 80th Year of HM Queen Elizabeth The Queen Mother 1900-1980". The whole is printed in rose. Limited to 2500.

*780 "Eighty gracious Years" is the title given to this porcelain mug (9cm) from *Elizabethan China*. The design is all colour printed and has as its main element the inscription shown. On either side are birth and anniversary dates.

781 **782**

*781 To celebrate Prince Philip's 60th birthday, *Royal Crown Derby* issued another in their series of porcelain loving cups (7.5cm). The front bears a gilt profile of the Prince against a background of naval symbols printed in blue and the date 10.V1.1981. On the reverse a view of the Maritime museum at Greenwich. There is lavish gilding. Limited to 500.

*782 For the same event, *Caverswall* produced this porcelain mug (9cm). The front has a sepia portrait of the Duke whilst his personal Arms are on the reverse. On the base are listed some of Prince Philip's achievements including his love of sports.

*783 These two porcelain mugs, issued in 1982, mark the 18th birthday of members of the Royal Family. This small mug (5cm) from *Coronet* has a sepia portrait of Prince Edward on the front with an inscription in blue on the reverse.

*784 The flared china mug (10cm) issued by *Panorama Studios* celebrates the birthdays of Prince Edward, Lady Sarah Armstrong-Jones, Lady Helen Windsor and James Ogilvy. Portraits of each is on the front with birthday details on the back. Edition of 250.

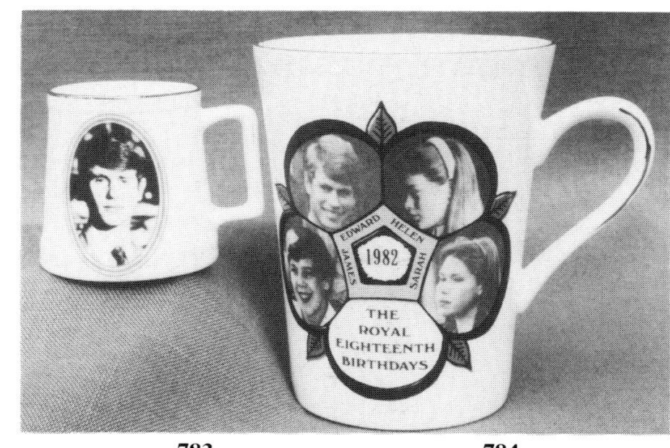

783 784

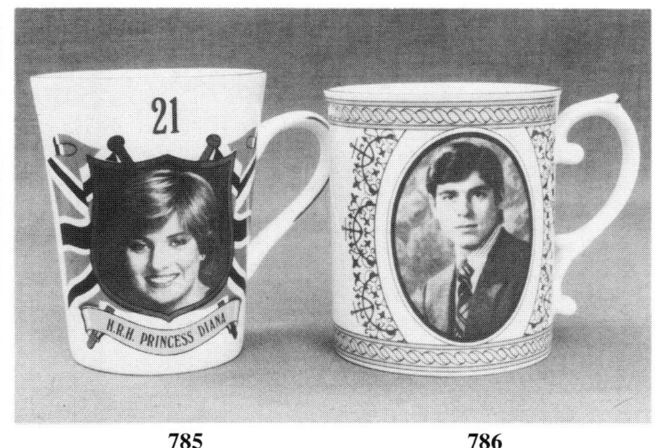

785 786

*785 Two interesting porcelain mugs record 21st birthdays. *Panorama Studios* made that on the left (10cm) in a limited edition of 250. A black and white portrait of the Princess against a gold coloured shield is flanked by coloured flags. Inside rim shows a shield and the figures "21" in gold.

*786 A head and shoulders sepia portrait of Prince Andrew is framed against an intricate anchor design. The reverse shows a pink, yellow and blue coat of arms incorporating a small anchor. On the base is an inscription recording details of the event. Made by *Caverswall*.

*787 A single candle in blue and gold signifies the first birthday of William, with a black and white portrait within a blue ribbon and an inscription completing the design. This attractive mug (6.5cm) was commissioned in a limited edition of 200 by *A. & C. Dorincourt*.

*788 *Coronet Pottery* produced this charming porcelain loving cup (7cm) recording the first birthday of Prince William. A coloured portrait of Prince William takes up most of the front whilst the back is inscribed "To celebrate the first birthday of Prince William Arthur Philip Louis of Wales 21st June 1983". Ornate handles have some gold lining.

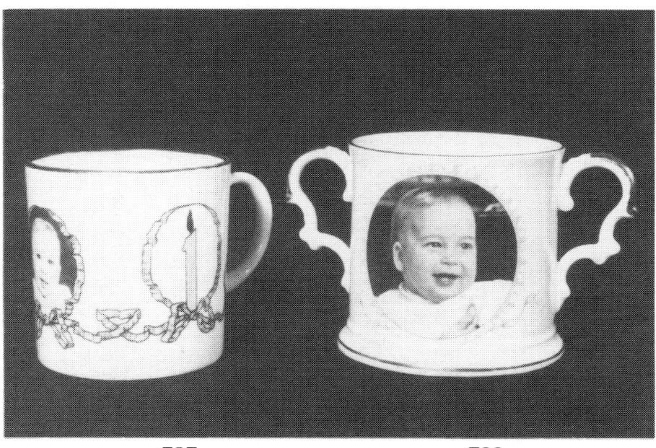

787 788

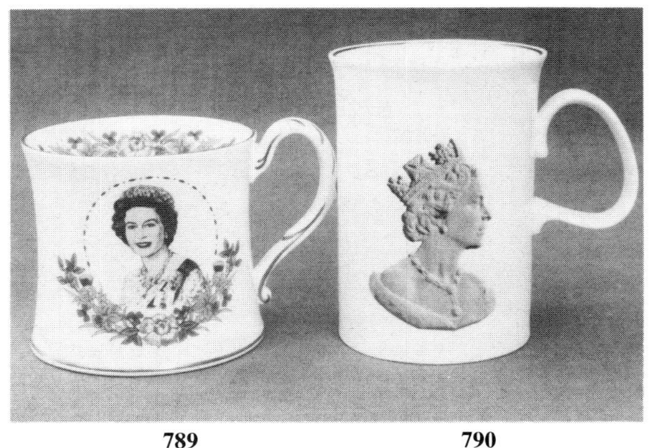

789 **790**

*789 A colour printed portrait of the Queen, with national flowers beneath, decorates the front of this waisted, porcelain mug (7.5cm) from *Coalport* for the Queen's 60th birthday. A commemoration is printed on the reverse and there is a colourful row of flowers inside the rim.

*790 A most striking use is made here of the Arnold Machin profile bust of HM the Queen. It is printed in silver on a straight sided, porcelain mug (10.5cm) designed by *Dunoon Ceramics* for a retailer called Anvil. The reverse carries a simple 60th birthday inscription.

*791 *Royal Crown Derby* produced this fine porcelain loving cup (7.5cm) commemorating the Queen Mother's 85th birthday in a limited edition of 500. Similar decorated frames in blue and gold are used for the front and back showing a gold silhouette and cypher with crown respectively. Moulded handles are outlined in gold.

*792 Lions supporting a crown and rose are contained within two broad blue bands on this porcelain mug (8.5cm) produced by *Sutherland* in an unlimited edition. The bold inscription is in gold with further gold lining to top and bottom rims.

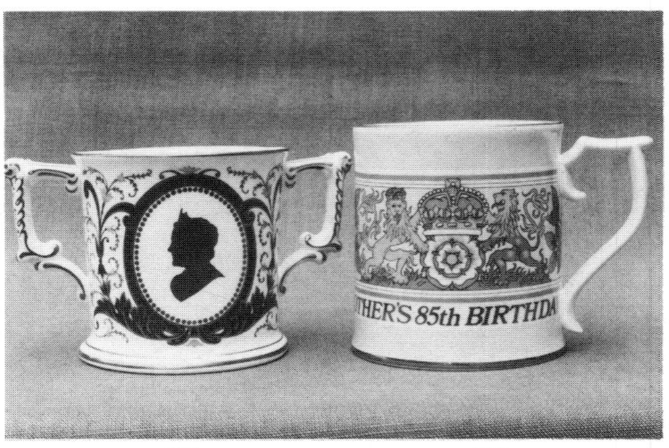

791 **792**

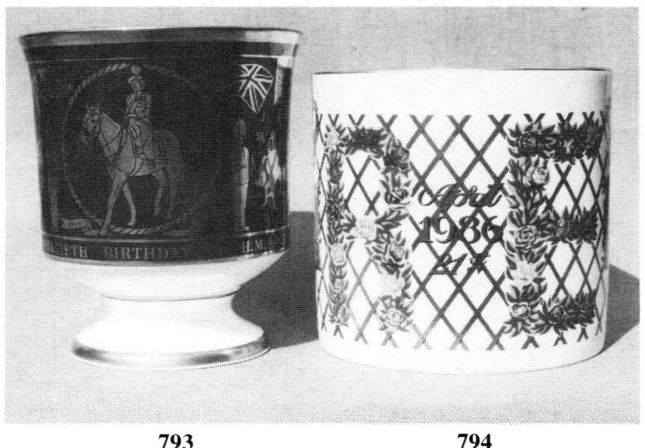

793 **794**

*793 Scenes from the Trooping of the Colour printed in gold on a cobalt blue ground provide the decorative inspiration for this porcelain goblet (12cm) from *Coalport*. "To celebrate the sixtieth Birthday of HM Queen Elizabeth II" captions the scenes. Limited to 2000.

*794 This pottery mug (10cm) was designed by Richard Guyatt for *Wedgwood*. "April 21st 1986" is printed in gold on the front with EIIR created in full colour roses on a gold trellis on either side. An inscription "Loyal birthday greetings" is printed twice inside the mug. This edition was limited to 500, whilst a similar piece in blue and "gold colour" was issued in an edition of 2000.

Both of these porcelain mugs call upon the Trooping of the Colour for their designs commemorating the Queen's 60th birthday.

*795 The example (8.5cm) from *Sutherland China* has a very colourful print and shows the Queen on horseback saluting the Guards as they march past. On the reverse a splendid picture of a field gun from the King's Troop being fired in Hyde Park.

*796 *Aynsley* made this mug (9.5cm) on which the Queen is again seen on horseback at the Trooping of the Colour. On the reverse are two verses of the National Anthem with a commemoration inside the rim.

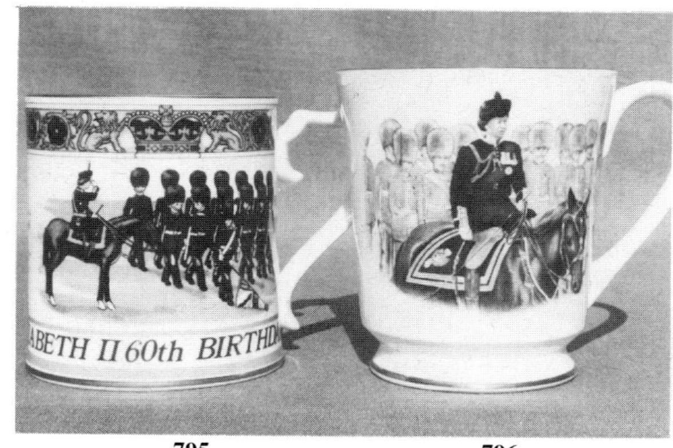

795 **796**

*797 The Queen and Prince Philip's Ruby Wedding in 1987 is commemorated by another *Caverswall* lion head porcelain beaker (11.5cm). This one has gold profile portraits framed in white ovals set on a deep maroon ground. On the rear is a commemorative statement. Fine gilt tracery, gold lion heads and rim make this an attractive piece. Limited to 250.

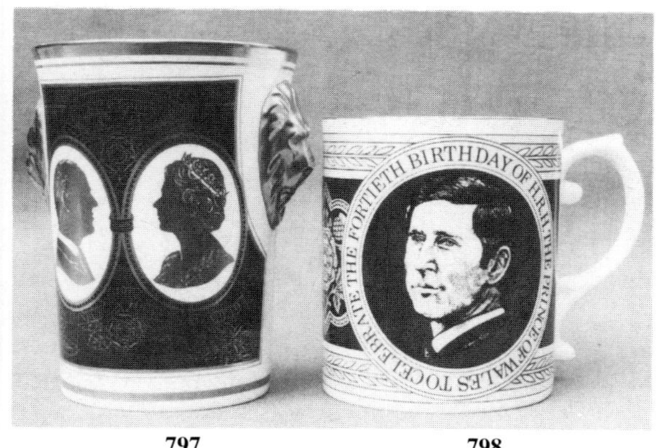

797 **798**

*798 For Prince Charles' 40th Birthday, in 1988, *Caverswall* produced, for Peter Jones of Wakefield, this distinctive porcelain mug (9cm). An "engraved" portrait in black is on both front and rear. The ground colour is a bright red. Designed by Stephen Barnsley.

*799 This porcelain mug (7.5cm) was commissioned by Govier's of Sidmouth from *Royal Crown Derby* to commemorate the Queen Mother's 90th birthday. A gold profile of Her Majesty on a white ground is within a circular frame. On the reverse a crowned cypher. The body is cobalt blue on which the decoration is of gold floral emblems. Limited to 500.

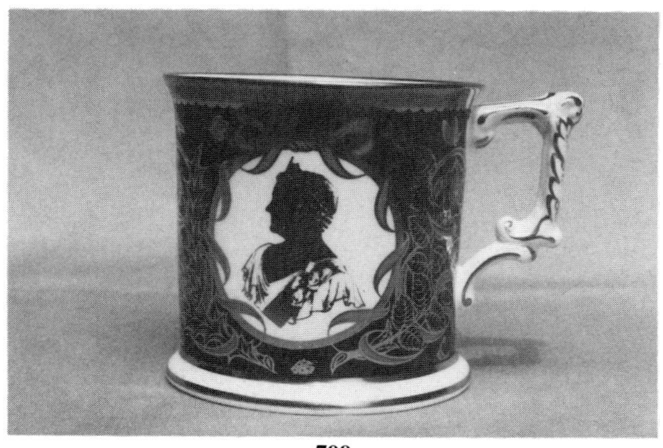

799

Other Royal Events

The following pages illustrate some of the commemorative wares which were issued to mark a variety of royal occasions. Events include the wedding of Princess Margaret in 1960, pieces for which event are very scarce **(801)**, her divorce in 1978 **(805)**, the deaths of Princess Alice **(817)**, Lord Mountbatten **(815)** and the Duke and Duchess of Windsor **(802, 819)**. For each of these occasions relatively few pieces were issued.

In contrast, however, the Jubilee of the Coronation in 1978 was commemorated by a large number of manufacturers. It appears to have found relatively little favour with collectors who were possibly sated with Silver Jubilee items the previous year. To some extent the 1978 occasion is perhaps a "secondary" event.

Nonetheless there are some very interesting items to be found for events ranging from "in memoriams" to the Queen's ruby wedding, and many people find these "non coronation" pieces have a fascination all of their own.

*800 Commemoratives for the Wedding of Princess Margaret to Anthony Armstrong-Jones in 1960 are rare. Only these two items are known to the authors. On the left a porcelain hand-painted plate (25.5cm) from the *Ancienne Fabrique Royale* in Limoges. The front has a traditional Limoges design, painted and gilded signed d'Artois. On the reverse, in French, an inscription reveals that this service was presented on the occasion of the Wedding of Her Royal Highness Princess Margaret, May 1960.

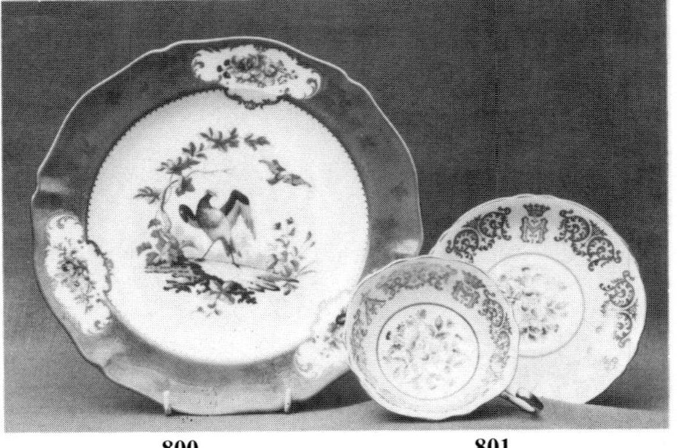

800 **801**

*801 Whilst the *Paragon* china cup and saucer (5.5cm) has the same basic decoration including turquoise and gilt rim as used for one of their 1953 pieces **(476)** the crowned M and A indicate its special royal wedding significance. Inscription is on reverse of the saucer. A mug with similar decoration has also been recorded.

*802 Two in memoriam items for the death of the Duke of Windsor on 28th May 1972. That on the left is a plate (25cm) by *Panorama* showing a black and white portrait within a broad band of laurel leaves with inscription in gold. On the reverse are detailed references to his investiture, accession and abdication.

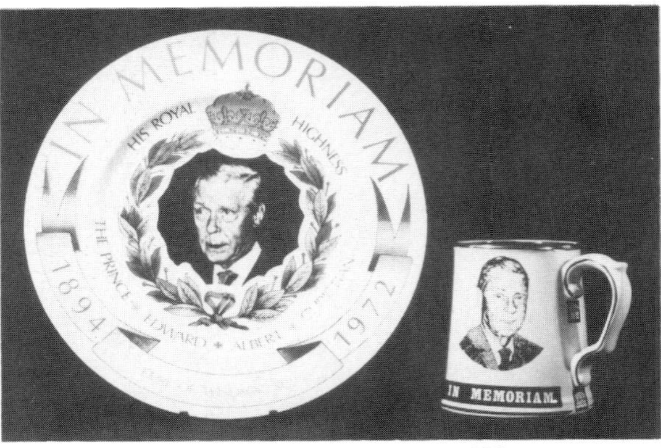

802 **803**

*803 The mug (11cm) shows black and white portraits of both the Duke and Duchess either side of the handle together with a quotation from Richard the Second. Made by *Mercian China*.

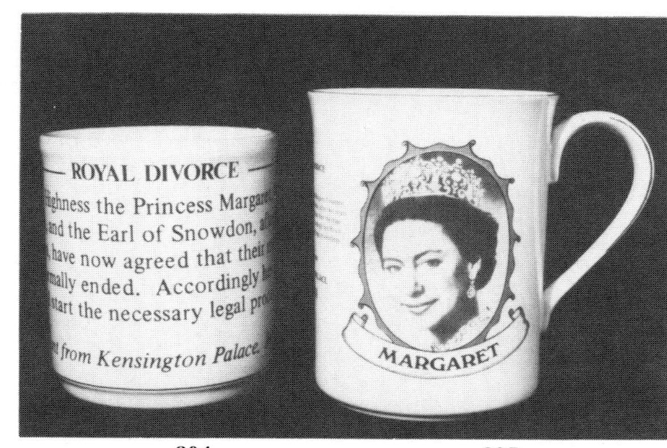

804 805

*804 Not a happy occasion but nevertheless Princess Margaret's divorce was commemorated by two pottery mugs. The first (9cm) simply details the statement issued from Kensington Palace on May 10th 1978. Potters mark *C & E*.

*805 *Panorama* produced the other mug (10cm) and shows black and white portraits of Princess Margaret on one side and the Earl of Snowdon on the other. The official statement from Kensington Palace is also inscribed in full. Commemorative items for Princess Margaret are not very numerous and are now being keenly sought after by collectors.

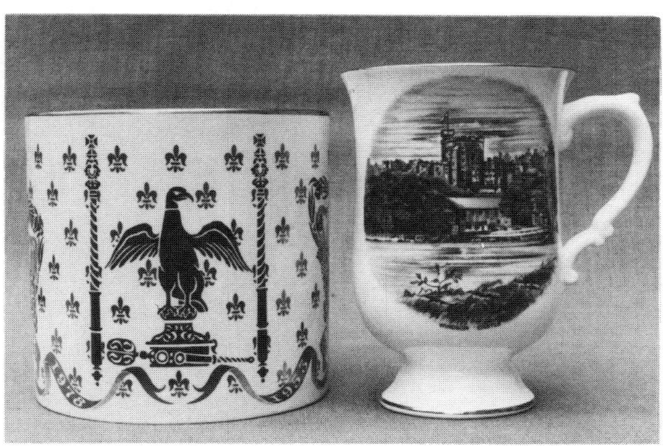
806 807

*806 Richard Guyatt designed this *Wedgwood* pint size pottery mug, thus continuing the series of commemoratives so popular with collectors. Front decoration is predominantly blue with gold fleurs-de-lis against an overall cream ground. An inscription "Long may she reign" is fashioned from sprigs of leaves. Produced for the 25th anniversary of the coronation in a limited edition of 5000.

*807 The taller porcelain mug (12cm) by *Crown Staffordshire* shows a large coloured picture of Windsor Castle. An inscription on the reverse records the 25th anniversary of the coronation. Silver lines are added to base and rim. This shape was used by Crown Staffordshire for other events **(772)**.

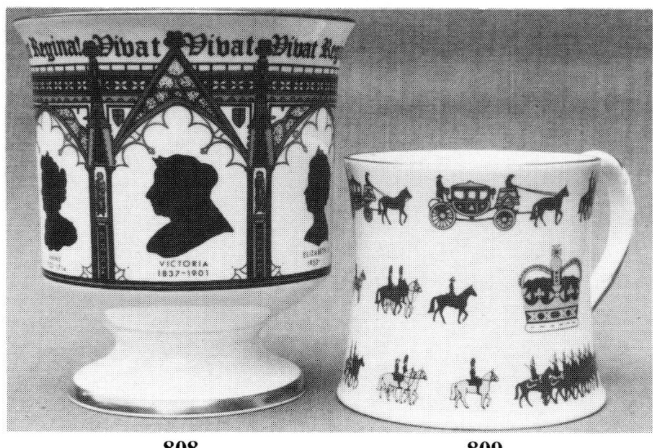

808 809

*808 Two attractive porcelain pieces from *Coalport* to celebrate the 25th anniversary of the coronation. A goblet (12cm) in a limited edition of 2000 shows black silhouettes of the six Queens of England against decorated panels of pink, purple and gold. The inside rim is suitably inscribed.

*809 By contrast, the mug (9.5cm) shows a stylized coronation procession, mostly in blue, surrounding a coloured crown. A moulded handle is picked out in gold. This charming item was limited to 2500.

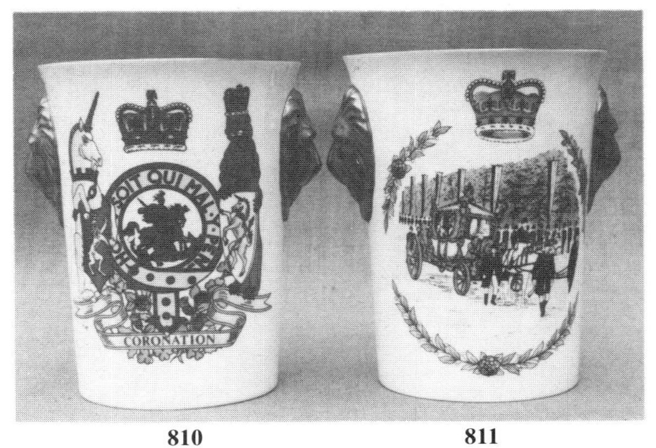

810 **811**

*810, *811 *Caverswall* produced both these porcelain beakers (11.5cm) with the familiar gold lion handles to commemorate the 25th anniversary of the coronation. That on the left was made in a limited edition of 1500 and shows an enamelled gold and blue shield flanked by royal beasts with a gold inscription on the reverse. The other produced in an edition of 2000 shows the coronation coach in colour on the front with a sepia inscription on the back. Rims are lined in gold.

*812 *Royal Doulton* made this loving cup (10cm) in porcelain to commemorate the 25th anniversary of the Coronation in 1978. The shape was used again in 1980 for the Queen Mother's birthday **(776)**. Westminster Abbey is shown in gold and the reverse details the event also in gold.

*813 Another shape used again **(758)** is this porcelain loving cup (8cm) by *Paragon*. A coronation coach in black and gold is accompanied by an inscription in red. A further inscription on the back refers to the coronation. "My life devoted to your service" is printed on the inside rim.

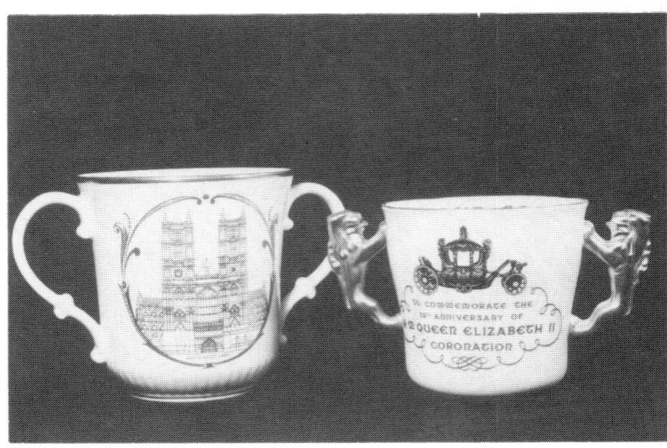

812 **813**

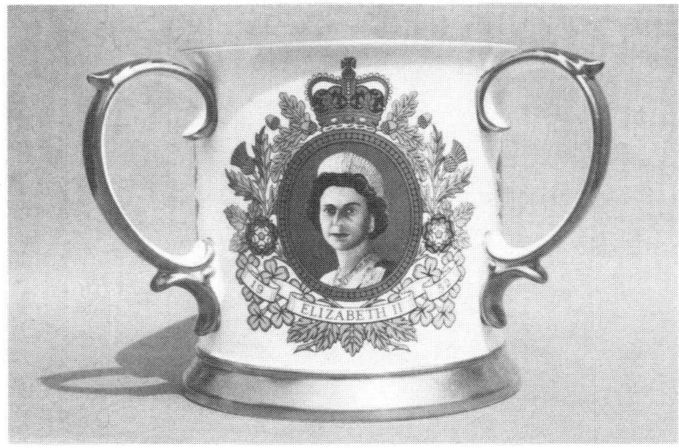

814

*814 In 1917 King George V had decreed that thenceforward the Royal Family would bear the name of House of Windsor, and would abandon all German titles and honours. To mark the diamond jubilee of this event *Spode* issued a three handled porcelain loving cup (17cm). All four monarchs of the Windsor line are illustrated (George V, Edward VIII, George VI and Elizabeth II), together with dates of their reigns. Issued in an edition of 250, and exclusive to Thomas Goode, this is the last (so far) three handled royal loving cup made by Spode.

*815 At the age of 79 Earl Mountbatten of Burma was killed by a terrorist bomb and his death was commemorated on two porcelain mugs. *J. & J. May* commissioned the first (8.5cm) which shows the funeral gun carriage draped with a coloured Union Flag. Inscriptions are in black and gold.

*816 The other taller mug (10cm) shows a black and white portrait of Earl Mountbatten within a wreath of laurel leaves. Inscriptions record in some detail the circumstances of his death. Made by *Panorama* in a limited edition of 500.

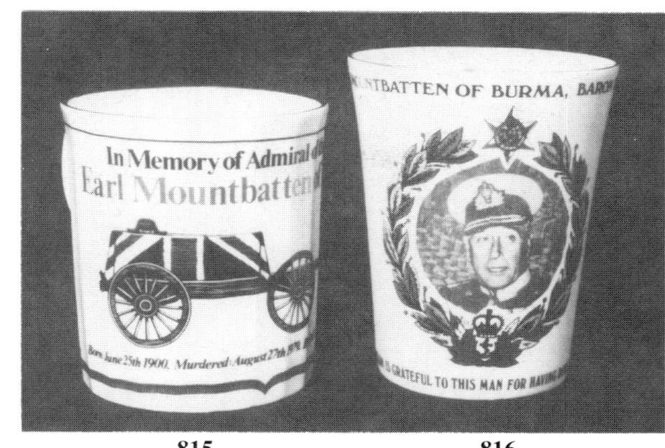

815 816

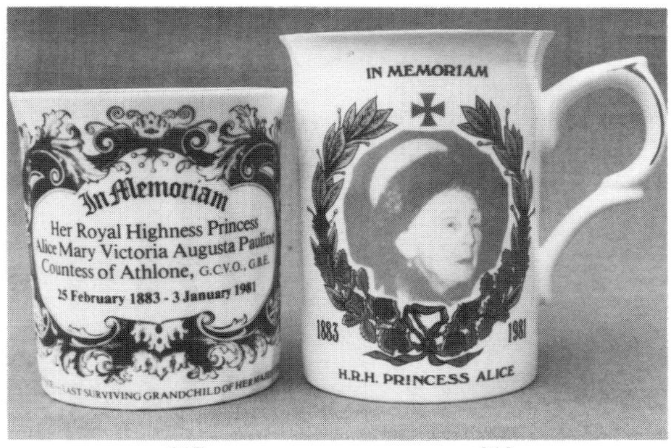

817 818

*817 Both mugs record the death of Princess Alice, Countess of Athlone, the last surviving grandchild of Queen Victoria. The first by *J. & J. May* is 8.5cm tall, in porcelain, with principal decoration in purple and an inscription in black.

*818 The second is taller (10.5cm), also in porcelain and made by *Panorama* in a limited edition of 250. A sepia portrait of Princess Alice is framed within a green wreath, with inscription in black. Her numerous titles and birth date are detailed on the reverse.

*819 These porcelain mugs commemorate the death of the Duchess of Windsor on 24th April 1986. The first (9cm) by *A. & C.* shows black and white portraits of the Duke and Duchess within a decorated purple frame. Side inscription records their birth and marriage dates.

*820 *Magpie Collectables* produced the second (8.5cm) in a limited edition of 250 and this also shows portraits of the Duke and Duchess flanked by coloured flags. On the reverse an inscription refers to the marriage of Edward VIII to Mrs Wallis Simpson.

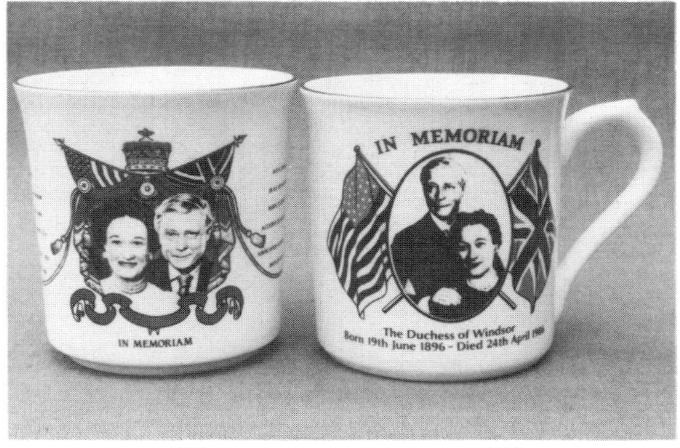

819 820

*821 Hope and Glory commissioned this porcelain mug (9cm) by *Caverswall* in an edition of 200 to commemorate "Princess Anne being granted the style and title of Princess Royal by HM the Queen 13th June 1987". The front shows a brown silhouette of the Princess Royal against a white ground and coloured decoration. The reverse bears the inscription.

*822 An exclusive design for Peter Jones of Wakefield made by *Coalport* and limited to 2000 shows an informal coloured portrait of the Princess with supporting decoration in predominantly yellow and mauve. On the reverse an orange coloured cypher is contained within a diamond shaped shield.

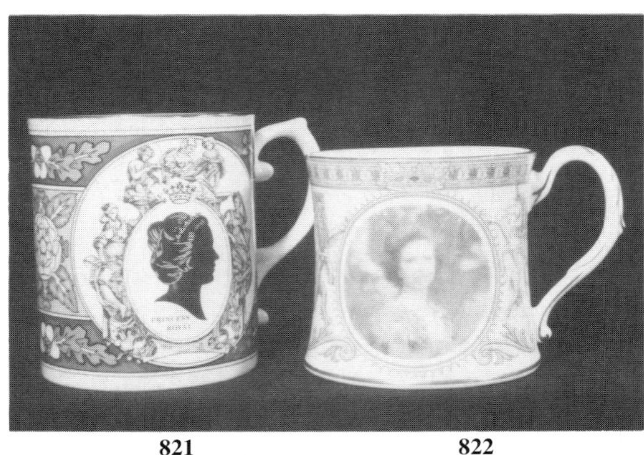

821 **822**

*823 This porcelain mug (6.5cm) issued in 1985 marks the first and third birthdays of Prince Henry and Prince William respectively. Black printed portraits within a blue ribbon enclose one and three candles on each side of the mug. Commissioned by A and C in an edition of 150 from *Dorincourt.*

*824 *Panorama* produced this flared porcelain mug (10cm) to celebrate the 60th birthday of Prince Philip in 1981. A portrait of the Queen and Prince Philip is surrounded by portraits of their four children. On the reverse an inscription includes the information that he was born in Corfu. Limited to 150.

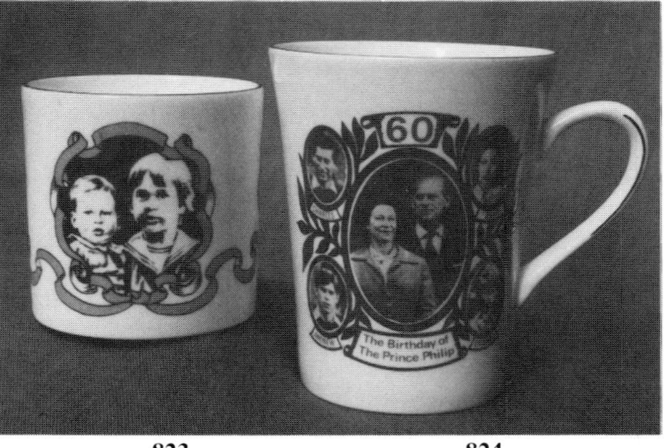

823 **824**

*825 An example of one of the more "tenuous" commemoratives is this porcelain mug (9cm) from *Caverswall.* Issued in 1988. It celebrates the 150th anniversary of Victoria's Coronation. An inscription on the base also notes that 1987 marked the Centenary of the Golden Jubilee whilst for good measure the dates beneath Victoria's portrait are of her birth and death!

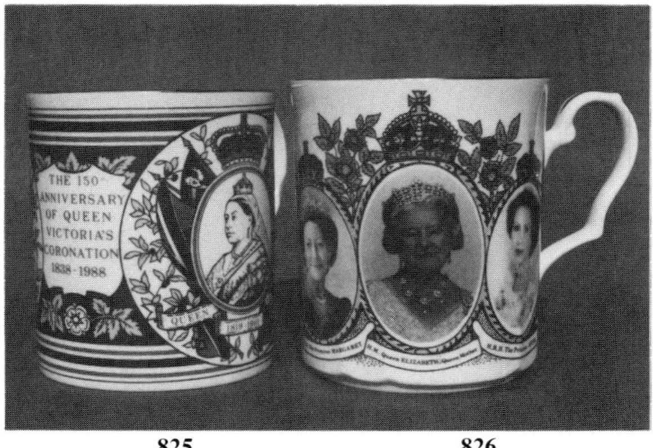

825 **826**

*826 *Coronet Pottery* took the opportunity of celebrating the 40th birthday of Princess Anne, the 60th of Princess Margaret and the 90th of The Queen Mother on this porcelain mug (9.5cm) suitably entitled "The Royal Ladies of August 1990". Colour portraits of the three Royal Ladies decorate the front whilst the reverse carries their respective ages and birthdays.

Bibliography

The following list of books, journals and exhibition catalogues may prove useful to the collector:
Commemorative Pottery 1780-1900 – John and Jennifer May – William Heineman 1972
Victoria Remembered – John May – William Heineman 1983
Fifty Years of Royal Commemorative China 1887-1937 – Davey and Mannion – Dayman Publications 1988
Royal Souvenirs – Geoffrey Warren – Orbus Publishing 1972
200 Commemoratives – Sussex Commemorative Ware Centre 1979
Commemorative Pottery and Porcelain – James Mackay – Garstone Press 1971
Royal Memorabilia – Peter Johnson – Dunestyle Publishing Ltd 1988
British Royal Commemoratives – Audrey B. Zeder – Wallace Homestead Book Co, Lombard, Illinois USA 1986
Fired for Royalty – Josephine Jackson – Henton Moor Printing Co, Stockport
Coronation Souvenirs and Commemoratives – David Rogers – Anchor Press Ltd

---

One Hundred Royal Years – Exhibition of Royal Crown Derby Commemorative Porcelain – Royal Crown Derby Museum 1990.
Here's a Health unto Their Majesties – Exhibition of Royal Commemoratives 1603-1953 – Wolverhampton Art Gallery and Museum 1973
Jubilation – Exhibition of Commemorative Pottery 1660 – 1935 from James Blewitt Collection at Bethnal Green Museum 1977
Jubilee Royal – Exhibition of commemoratives by Commemorative Collectors Society, Goldsmiths Hall 1977
A Princess for Wales – Royal Wedding Exhibition by Commemorative Collectors Society, the Guildhall, Windsor 1981
Sixty Years a Queen – Exhibition of commemoratives for Queen Victoria's reign – Society of the Friends of St George, Windsor Castle 1987
Long to reign over us – Exhibition of commemorative pottery made during Queen Victoria's reign – Newport Museum and Art Gallery, Gwent 1987
Journals of Commemorative Collectors Society – Secretary S. Jackson, 25 Farndale Close, Longeaton, Nottingham NG10 3PA

At the time of publication the museums listed below had royal commemorative china on show either as a separate collection or as part of their general exhibition of ceramics. Some exhibitions are modest in size and subject to change, so we advise would-be visitors to telephone the museum beforehand.

Arlington Court, Nr Barnstaple, Devon – Tel: 0271 850296
Brighton Museum and Art Gallery – Tel: 0273 603005
Castle Museum, York – Tel: 0904 653611
Dyson Perrins Museum, Worcester – Tel: 0905 23221
Minton Museum, London Road, Stoke-on-Trent – Tel: 0782 744766
Newport Museum and Art Gallery, Newport, Gwent – Tel: 0633 840064
Royal Crown Derby, Osmaston Road, Derby – Tel: 0332 47051
Sandringham House, Near King's Lynn, Norfolk – Tel: 0553 772675
Sir Henry Doulton Gallery, Burslem, Stoke-on-Trent – Tel: 0782 575454
Wedgwood Museum, Barlaston, Stoke-on-Trent – Tel: 0782 204141
Copeland Museum, Stoke-on-Trent – Tel: 0782 744011